LETTERS
TO THE
EDITOR
2008

LETTERS
TO THE
EDITOR
2008

Edited by Nigel Willmott
and Rory Foster

Additional research by Rosemary Hammond

guardianbooks

First published in 2008 by Guardian Books,
119 Farringdon Road, London EC1R 3ER
guardianbooks.co.uk

Guardian Books is an imprint of Guardian News and
Media Ltd

Guardian Books would like to thank all those letter-
writers who have given permission for their letters to
appear in this volume. Every effort has been made to
contact all individuals whose letters are contained within
this volume; if anyone has been overlooked, we would be
grateful if he or she would contact Guardian Books

A CIP record for this book is available from the British
Library

ISBN: 978-0-85265-115-5

Cover design: Two Associates

Text design: www.carrstudio.co.uk

Printed in Great Britain by TJ International, Padstow,
Cornwall

Introduction

"We send letters to newspapers because they get noticed. As long as newspapers are read, letters pages will be too, often by people who don't have time to scour the internet. The reaction I get to letters shows they are a valuable source of debate, and from my perspective they offer the chance to put across my organisation's view and to set the record straight."

Neil Bentley, director of business environment, CBI

A suitably brisk, businesslike reply from one Guardian correspondent to the question we asked a number of letter writers: why do you write letters to the press? How often, and what prompts you to write? And why write a letter for publication which will almost certainly be cut and edited, when you can write your views at length and unedited in one of the various forums on the internet?

We selected a cross-section of correspondents to ask — from the frequent to the one-off, from writers of pithy one-liners to authors of considered political positions. The replies often reflected the character of the respondent — from opinionated MPs to prolix local campaigners. But all gave an insight into why, every day, 200 to 300 or more readers still put pen to paper or fingers to keyboard in the hope that their letter will become one of the dozen and a half or so we print in each edition.

Many correspondents write in a professional capacity on behalf of their organisations, ranging from business groups such as the CBI to charities, NGOs and trade unions. For some, such as Amnesty International or ActionAid, it's targeting their core support. For the CBI's Neil Bentley, it's a chance to "set the record straight" with a more sceptical audience. In his letter that we published on June 9 he uses Polly Toynbee's support for polyclinics as a slightly cheeky peg to try to gain the odd adherent for the CBI's call for more private providers in the health service.

One professional body which ought to have considered views on the role of letters to the press is the Society of Editors. Its director, Bob Satchwell, wrote (April 4) to put the society's views on data protection. He gave three reasons for writing: "First, in this case, it was to enlarge on a point made in a Guardian report that did not fully explain the context in which the Society of Editors and other media organisations were mounting a campaign. Second, it was to widen debate on a subject the society believes deserves wide attention and coverage. Third, a letter to a major newspaper targeted at its main readership is a way of encouraging publicity about an issue in that the letter can become news itself."

Among the letters to the Guardian which caused a bigger splash last year are David Hockney's attack on New Labour for its censoring of images (June 4), Martin Amis's defence of his comments on Muslims (October 4), and the head of the Bar Council's attack on the TV series Criminal Justice (July 2). Our letter writers' (and bloggers') comments on the prospect of a state funeral for Margaret Thatcher (July 15 and 16) earned a full-page article in the Daily Mail under the heading "Why is the Left so full of hate?".

For others, from career politicians to grassroots activists, the aim is more directly political. Few people in political life have had as long and distinguished a career as Baroness Shirley Williams, who told us: "I write letters for print media for three reasons: persuasion, putting my position on public record and taking a stand." Her firm but considered letter (November 21) on the plight of the Palestinians after the Annapolis summit certainly did the latter two; whether anyone was persuaded or not in this intractable dispute is a moot point.

Letters can be an even more important platform for a fourth party trying to break into the political debate dominated by the three main parties. According to Caroline Lucas, newly designated leader of the Green party and a regular correspondent: "Writing to the letters pages of national newspapers remains a crucial way for people to communicate ideas and beliefs on the vital issues of our time. The Guardian letters page in particular presents a balanced and insightful view on the top stories in current affairs, which allows for both sides of a debate to flourish."

At the other end of the spectrum is Lindis Percy, a campaigner against US bases in Britain (February 14). "I often feel very strongly about things and so it is a way of sparking a debate and expressing my frustrations," she said. But that doesn't mean she writes just to get it out of her system: "I am very disappointed if the letter isn't published – but it's probably because it wasn't very good." Not necessarily so, but letter writers have to be prepared for the possibility – if not probability – that their treasured words will not appear in print.

Sheila Oliver has a more modest target than US imperialism, namely Stockport council. "I am the Keith Flett of the Stockport Express," she said. But her letters to the Guardian, even if less frequent, still hit the spot. "Most important of all, I said in a Guardian letter that I didn't know about Belarus, but Stockport council operated a repressive regime. You put it under the headline 'Sub-prime

Stockport', for which I will be eternally grateful. The council was furious." Who can doubt it?

For others the reason is even more personal. Lecturer Hillary Shaw, who bravely explained the logic of market forces as all others were abandoning ship (April 4), rather honestly said: "It must be partly about ego, to see one's views printed nationally." She added: "It also appeals to 'teachy' types like myself, as we like to 'correct' wrong views, set matters straight, fill in knowledge gaps etc. Then there is the practical angle — people have got back to me in response to a letter, sometimes becoming useful contacts."

For some it's a mixture of public and private communication. The Rev Geoff Reid, one of our many clerical correspondents, put it this way: "As a preacher, I often find myself uttering 1,800 words to less than 100 people. If the Guardian publishes a letter of mine, I can make a point in 100 words which reaches more than 1,800 people." And he added a sentiment expressed by several other writers: "It is perhaps also a way of saying 'Hello, I'm still alive and still reading the newspaper as I have done for nearly half a century'."

For Georgina Barnes the motivation is both personal and, well, familial, as she competes with her father, Peter Barnes, over the number of letters they get published. She listed her reasons succinctly as: "For the challenge and distraction of thinking up something erudite/satirical/facetious in an otherwise mundane working day; for the satisfaction of writing something that a letters editor thinks worthy of print in a national newspaper; so that my father has to concede I've beaten him in his Christmas round-robin letter."

Ron Hill's focus is even narrower: it's him and us. "I suppose I treat it as a game of wits between me and the letters editor," he said. "Sometimes an item in the day's paper just strikes a chord and I want to make some 'clever' or 'funny' comment on it. Normally I write very short letters, just a sentence or two, although they may have a serious political point behind them. When they then spawn a series of further comments over the next couple of weeks it gives me a great feeling of satisfaction." But sometimes we baffle him: "I have still not worked out why some letters that I think are certainties don't appear while others that I didn't have much faith in are there in print the next day. But that too is part of the joy of playing this 'game'."

Of course, it's not a game for us – heaven forbid! And even if it were, we wouldn't be giving away the rules. Ron, like many others, counts his "hit rate". "I have written to the Guardian on and off over the last 50 years ... 2006-07 was a good period, only a dozen letters sent and I think four were published, much above the normal success rate. Things have not been so good in 2007-08 but that makes me try even harder."

Chris Connolly (January 3) claims a rare 100% record. "I wrote three letters to the Guardian this year, all in the first few weeks of the year, and all were published, although not in their original form." That for him is an important point. "How do I feel when a letter is published? Pretty good, depending on how much has been cut out."

The need to cut letters because of the limited space available in print format, and the editing that goes with it, is a key distinguishing factor in comparison with newer, online forms of reader response. "User-generated content" on websites is not generally restricted in terms of space, although "moderation" – and increasingly pre-publication moderation – for defamation, racism and other forms of crude abuse means that a form of editing is being introduced into the process.

Not surprisingly, those who still write letters accept, even welcome, the editing process. As the Green party's Caroline Lucas put it: "The use of an editorial team for such pages maintains an element of quality control which is sometimes lacking in comment spaces on the internet."

Labour MP Denis MacShane, one of our most regular parliamentary correspondents, was rather more robust: "I can hardly bear to read the blog threads. If I start I feel I am in some virtual Guantánamo Bay cell, my head forced between my legs as people scream and screech at you without any self-control. Moreover, the blog threads break the first rule of discourse as developed since the Reformation and Enlightenment, which is that you take responsibility for what you say or write. I think papers should require publication of names and addresses of those who comment on blogs."

However, his indignation at some of the responses has not stopped him being an active blogger, with no fewer than 15 contributions to our online forum Comment is Free in the past 12 months.

Shirley Williams was more conscious of her preference for letters as a personal choice: "I am wary about writing for blogs, mainly because I am drawn to the semi-permanent nature of printed letters; perhaps because my generation are very conscious of history. The sheer number of blogs also appears to me to dilute their influence, even though there are some very good ones."

But she then perhaps points to the real issue, adding: "Looking at this from a generational perspective, my assistant's view is that blogs can be very useful and, because anyone can write one, are intrinsically democratic."

Janice Small, one of a gallant band of Conservative letter writers (even more gallant in trying to convert her party to proportional representation – see her letter of October 26), made a similar point about the age profile of letter writers more bluntly in giving her reasons for writing to the Guardian: "Because there is still an elderly audience who are voters and deserve our opinions who are not internet users; because the political audience still read letters and I would like to change opinion and get people voting Conservative."

She may be right in her implication that letter writers are a dying breed, but our correspondents range from five-and-a-half-year-old apple-core eater Ivor Nash to sprightly 80-year-olds such as Chris Birch. Somewhere in between is that modern doyen of letter writers, Keith Flett – who, despite some sceptics, does exist, and writes to us and many other publications very frequently indeed (and consequently has a very low hit rate – please note, those who occasionally moan that he gets too many letters printed).

Who better to make the point that people will use whatever means of communication are available to express themselves, and that online and print are not mutually exclusive, but complementary, each with their own strengths: "As the day job is as a trade union official in the telecoms industry, I am fully familiar with the interweb, email, texts, IM, blogs etc etc and use them all, except actually writing a blog, which I simply don't have time for.

"However, letters, it seems to me, selected and edited as they are, provide a more rational forum for democratic debate, where there is a certain sense of order and line of march. You can get so overwhelmed with views on the net that you forget the argument. Sharply written and short letters provide a focus that is still absent elsewhere."

So what, finally, of Gordon Brown's view – that's right, the Gordon Brown of Farnham, Surrey, whose letter we published on July 31. His timely comment on David Miliband's intervention in the frenzied speculation about a Labour leadership election in August turned out to be at the other extreme to the prodigious output of Keith Flett: "This was my one and only letter I've ever written."

But whether it's once a day or once in a lifetime, we hope we still consider every letter on its merits and that, the odd gripe apart, most letter writers trust us to edit them with care and respect.

This book would not have appeared without the efficient and tireless work of our desk administrator, Rosemary Hammond, who added even more hours of archive research for this year's book to all her other daily tasks. Nor could it have been possible without the input of our regular editing and subediting team over the past year: Yvonne Singh, Julia Cook, Mike Carter and Mike Power.

Guardian Books publisher Lisa Darnell came to us with the idea for the book and recommissioned it. Thanks also to Guardian Books managing editor Helen Brooks; to Rich Carr for design and layout work; and Amelia Hodsdon for proofreading. This year we have been able to include a couple of the wonderful illustrations by Gary Kempston and Gillian Blease that visually lift our page every day – and often add an extra perspective on the words.

Most of all, of course, our thanks go to our letter writers, who keep us in a job and continue to make the letters page an invaluable forum for debate.

Nigel Willmott, letters editor
Rory Foster, deputy letters editor

Illustration by Gillian Blease, first published on June 27 2008 with letters on the building of ecotowns and a planning bill that would make the expansion of airports harder to oppose.

"The criteria are clear that ecotowns can only happen if they achieve much higher standards than other developments, particularly to address climate change. The nimby assertion that they are already substandard before plans have been drawn up borders on the nutty."

October 2007

The theme of the year might well be captured by
the first letter in this collection: Go now, Gordon!
At the start of October 2007 it meant Gordon Brown
should call an election and go to the country. He
didn't, and his credibility and poll ratings never
recovered; not much later the call was for him
simply to go. Few weeks have been so pivotal in
politics. The situation of David Cameron's Tories
seemed desperate in the face of a resurgent Labour
under a new prime minister. Maybe the only hope
was for them to give everyone a puppy, one reader
suggested. Only four days later another wondered
if they had, for the positions of the parties had
switched after the shadow chancellor, George
Osborne, revealed his plan to lift the inheritance tax
ceiling, to be paid for by a new levy on non-doms,
and Cameron gave a confident conference speech
without notes. Brown's subsequent decision not
to call an election, and his denial that this was
influenced by the opinion polls, handed the Tories
a lead that grew ever larger as the year went on. In
the wake of all this, Labour supporters discussed the
direction and values of the party, and a wider debate
on political funding began, with a growing feeling
that MPs were more interested in themselves than
the public good. Amid this turmoil, the resignation
of Menzies Campbell as Lib Dem leader caused few
ripples. On a lighter note, a first edition of Oscar
Wilde's The Importance of Being Earnest was found
in an Oxfam shop – in a handbag.

October 1

Following the materialisation of the culture secretary in Manchester (Now you see him, now you don't, September 29), I would like to point out that the verb "to Photoshop" is the most irregular in the English language: I enhance; you alter; he she, it fabricates. We adjust; you interpret; they lie.

Alan Entwistle
Buckhurst Hill, Essex

October 2

Derek Draper (In defence of talk show 'bear-baiter', September 26) sounds as useful a psychotherapist as Jeremy Kyle. Both appear happy to peddle the fiction that the underclass are in need of "responsibility and restraint". What the poor actually need is money and dignity.

Tim Fredericks
Crewe, Cheshire

October 1

Go now, Gordon!

Gordon Brown should stop dallying, and call a general election (Brown to decide this weekend on snap election, September 28). I, for one, a former Tory member, would bite my tongue and vote for the Labour candidate in Kensington and Chelsea. David Cameron has nothing to offer the country or the Conservatives. Post-election, the Tory party – well-versed in ruthless disposal of unpopular or failed leaders – can be relied upon to do the necessary on Mr Cameron, should he fail to fall on his sword. For the health of democracy (and the Tories), Gordon Brown should call an election without delay.

Dominic Shelmerdine
London

October 1

The politics of greed

Well, maybe I expected no better from Peter Goldsmith (So, Lord Goldsmith, what attracted you to the £1m-a-year job?, September 27). But Alan Milburn, an ex-health secretary, advising Pepsi? Stephen Byers ditto a Greek-Lebanese construction firm? Not one of them needs the money; how despicable they are, these men and women who love power and money above all else. Ethics? Values? Forget them – if indeed they ever had them. I was always one of those people who thought voting should be compulsory, used to say people die to have a democratic vote etc etc. I'm going to stop saying that. I'm not even sure that I will be bothered to vote again. Why should we engage in the process and by so doing support this greed that masquerades as New Labour?

Christine Beels
Leeds

October 2
Sexuality and religion

I have usually had much respect for the writings of Giles Fraser, but his latest contribution (Comment, September 27) is a great disappointment, and reveals a superficial and insensitive understanding of the complexities faced by the Archbishop of Canterbury. In general I would support Fraser in upholding the rights of gay people, but he concentrates on the attitude of the US Episcopal church, and almost seems to ignore the different cultural and political situation in which a large section of the Anglican communion now finds itself. This section has to be listened to and not dismissed so arrogantly. As I read his article I could hear a voice from the past, of a white colonial telling his black servants what they ought to do and believe according to western understanding. Faced with our present disagreement, we need to show more humility and more patience.

Rt Rev Tony Dumper
Birmingham

October 3
Tories' tax plans stamped on

Even if we assume the 115,000 non-domiciled tax avoiders accrue only £500,000 a year, that creates a total annual income of £57bn. A derisory

October 2
The Tories are clearly desperate for a vote-winning election gimmick. How about giving everyone a puppy?

Bruce Paley
London

October 3
I see Richard Dawkins wants people to "take full advantage of the tiny slice of eternity they have been granted" (Atheists arise: Dawkins spreads the A-word among America's unbelievers, October 1). That would be granted by … er … whom?

Anthony French
Doncaster

October 3
Is it possible to have a snap election (Leaders, October 2) after we've all been talking about such a prospect for weeks?

Dr Alistair Clark
Queen's University Belfast

October 4

I note that Severiano Ballesteros's auto-biography is called Seve: The Official Autobiography (Interview, Sport, October 2). This does raise the rather surreal question as to what an unofficial autobiog-raphy would be.

Patrick Briggs
Teddington, Middlesex

October 4

In his article on the possible vanishing of the Norfolk Broads (October 3), David Adam says they are one of Britain's greatest natural treasures. They are not. They are one of our greatest man-made treasures, for peat's sake.

Neil Baldwin
Big Sur, California

October 5

I was just reaching the end of David McKie's characteristically entertaining column

£25,000 donation (Election battle lines drawn as Tories defend tax plans, October 2) would generate £2.87bn, or a tax take of just 5%. If, however, the non-dom rule were to be scrapped and these same people paid tax like the rest of us, a 40% tax take would generate £23bn. Even if 50% of them decided to leave the UK, that would still leave a tax take of £11bn. Many non-doms are in the UK because of its geographical location: London sits midway between the US and Asia — crucial when working in the global financial markets.

Alan Gent
Cheadle, Cheshire

October 5

Cameron and Dr Johnson's dog

Many commentators, remarking on David Cameron's notes-free speech at Blackpool (Report, October 4), make him sound like Dr Johnson's dog, walking on its hind legs: it is not done well, but you are surprised to find it done at all.

Mike Mitchell
Hove, East Sussex

October 6

A critical time for contemporary music

Until orchestras accept that they need to make contemporary music the core of their programme planning, audiences will continue to age and dwindle (The classical issue, Film & Music, October 5). Every other art form offers about 90% contemporary work. Go into a bookshop and almost everything on display is by a living author. With theatre it is similar and most films on release are new. Most art galleries, too, focus on new work. But look at the schedules of most symphony orchestras and nearly all of the music is by dead composers. Perhaps composers should shoulder some of the blame for working solely within the comfort zone of the contemporary music ghetto. That may not be their choice, as orchestras are notoriously timid about programming new work, but the result is that many classically trained composers, eager to avoid the safe path of teaching, are looking at other ways of subsidising their "serious" work, such as film music, working with pop musicians and forming their own ensembles to perform their music.

It's probably still true that many young people will come to classical music via a Beethoven symphony or a Tchaikovsky ballet, but audiences show there are fewer and fewer of them. I asked Roger Wright, head of Radio 3, a few years ago why the BBC didn't broadcast more new music. We get too many complaining letters was his reply. So, audiences will have to be educated and brought in with imaginative planning as well. There are contemporary composers writing music that the average music lover could embrace given the chance to hear it. No one wants to see our wonderful orchestras disappear, but they will unless these problems are addressed.

Geoffrey Burgon
Stroud, Gloucestershire

October 8

Mega-indies are behind lack of trust in TV

Your leader on the BBC (October 6) mistakes the symptom for the disease. The loss of trust

on last utterances (On the matter of final words, October 4), wondering if he'd be interested to hear that my granny's last words were "That was a nice cup of tea" (probably not), when I reached his shocking denouement, that this will be his last column. I'm bereft at the thought that there will be no more McElsewhere musings. His warmth, wit and endlessly curious humanity will be greatly missed.

Giles Oakley
London

October 5

I'm always surprised by how often the word legend, usually when applied to sportsmen, ends up hyphenated to legend (Harassment trial lifts lid on sex and sleaze at the New York Knicks, October 4). Is this a game played by subeditors to ensure the word is always split? If so, please arrange for this letter to be suitably edited so I can become a legend in my own lifetime as an occasional letter writer to the Guardian.

Ron Brewer
Old Buckenham, Norfolk

October 5
The only possible musical accompaniment for Marcel Marceau's funeral (Obituary, September 24) is John Cage's 4'33".

Hal Dunkelman
Bampton, Oxfordshire

October 6
As a reggae fan, I was at first horrified to see the Tories had co-opted Jimmy Cliff's You Can Get It If You Really Want from the film The Harder They Come (Report, October 4). But then I remembered that after the hero moves to Kingston in search of fame and fortune, he is ripped off by

in broadcasters is not just the consequence of unsupervised independent production. It is the result of the rise of a new and virtually unaccountable broadcasting sector – the mega-indies. Companies like RDF, which produced the offending documentary about the Queen, and Talkback Thames, where Peter Fincham, the departing BBC1 controller, was formerly a senior executive, are now larger and more powerful than many of the old ITV companies. They have squeezed many of their smaller independent cousins off the screen. BBC and Channel 4 commissioners have expressed in public their preference for dealing with a few big players in the independent sector. It is a convenient way of maintaining their statutory quotas and competing with rival digital channels. The rash of lifestyle and reality programmes which has dominated the past decade is only one consequence of this opportunistic policy. As long as our public service broadcasters hand over large slices of their output to such commercially driven operations, British television will continue to be dominated by such cynical and untrustworthy output.

Dennis Marks
Former head of music, BBC Television

October 11

Land grabs make Palestinians' lives a misery

What double-speak it is to say the road envisaged by the Israelis is to "improve the quality of life" of Palestinians, when it is choking them (Israeli army orders confiscation of Palestinian land, October 10). In the distant past, people in Abu Dis lived a normal life. And even after Israeli occupation in

1967, people used to work in Jerusalem to the west, visit the Dead Sea to the east, and go north and south to Ramallah and Bethlehem.

Now they are cut off by the Israeli separation wall and its fierce "terminals" – on the west they can't get to Jerusalem or jobs, hospitals, education and services; unemployment is around 65%. The wall curves round north and is being built on the east to cut the route to Jericho and Jordan and divide Abu Dis from the massive settlement of Maale Adumim, a no-go area for Palestinians. This new land grab means the road south from Abu Dis will be cut too. There will be a fenced "security corridor" from Bethlehem to Jericho, effectively making another wall for Abu Dis – Israeli settlers on one, separate road, then the wall, then a fenced-off Palestinian road where people are forbidden to stop.

Abu Dis people face many agonies – they are losing village land and they face the massive development of the racist and militarised settlements in their vicinity. Last year a sick man from Abu Dis was killed at an Israeli checkpoint and this year two women had babies at local checkpoints. Children have been beaten by Israeli soldiers inside their school, dozens of young boys are in prison.

And with this serious new land grab and another Israeli "fact on the ground" slotted into place, the first thought that is coming to people is that the prison is nearly complete – they will have nowhere at all they can go. Is Israel's view of "improving" Palestinian "quality of life" to make it so intolerable that people have to leave?

Nandita Dowson
Camden Abu Dis Friendship Association

Abdul Wahab Sabbah
Cadfa coordinator, Abu Dis, Palestine

his capitalist record company, betrayed by his girlfriend and eventually dies under a hail of police bullets. One love!

Steve Rigby
Manchester

October 6
Upsurge in the Tories' poll performance (Cameron bounces back, October 5)? Did they promise every household a puppy (Letters, October 2)?

Dr Keith Syrett
Bristol

October 6
Ron Brewer writes (Letters, October 5) about the hyphen-ation of legend to leg-end. Wouldn't this have been more appro-priate as a footnote?

Phil Marson
London

October 6
Ron Brewer shouldn't limit his comments to

sporting legends. Take Michael Foot — now that's what I call a legend.

Brian Fitzgerald
London

October 8

I wish to claim authorship of the original Michael Foot legend letter (Letters, October 6). I can't recall the long-ago date but it was in response to a suggestion that, were the great man ever to become defence secretary, the Guardian could proclaim "Foot heads arms body".

John Smith
Sheffield

October 8

No wonder people are disenchanted with politics when Brown treats the timing of an election as if he were deciding when to play the joker in It's a Knockout.

Glynn McDonald
London

October 12

Our national heritage is not a luxury

The government's comprehensive spending review guarantees an inflation-based increase of funding for the arts, museums and galleries (Arts world greets increase with round of applause, October 10). No such guarantee is offered for those who care for the nation's heritage.

Over the past 10 years the heritage sector has been treated as the Department for Culture, Media and Sport's Cinderella, with over £100m in funding lost from its budgets. Despite increased efficiency, this has meant a 13% fall in real terms.

Last year the History Matters campaign involved 1.2 million people and demonstrated the huge public commitment to our historic places. Heritage is the backbone of Britain's tourist industry and a powerful force for social cohesion. We now need relatively small sums to implement a new heritage protection bill and to support heroic, hard-pressed communities to maintain our ancient churches.

As historians, we appeal to the government to ensure that budgets for heritage are not once again treated as a dispensable luxury.

Antony Beevor, Raymond Carr, Linda Colley, Artemis Cooper, Niall Ferguson, Antonia Fraser, Max Hastings, Eric Hobsbawm, Bettany Hughes, Tristram Hunt, Philip Mansel, John Julius Norwich, Simon Schama, Dan Snow, Anne Somerset, David Starkey and Adam Zamoyski

October 12

I did not advocate harassing Muslims

Terry Eagleton inhabits a parallel universe of groaning and blundering factoids. His Comment piece of October 10 (Rebuking obnoxious views is not just a personality kink) begins: "In an essay called The Age of Horrorism ... the novelist Martin Amis advocated a deliberate programme of harassing the Muslim community in Britain."

The essay, which was published over a year ago, contains none of the sentences that Eagleton goes on to quote. The "vile views" he instances come from a newspaper interview I gave in the summer of 2006, a day or two after the exposure of the plot to blow up 10 transatlantic commercial jets. And my remarks were preceded by the following: "What can we do to raise the price of them doing this? There's a definite urge – don't you have it? – to say ... [etc, etc]."

I was not "advocating" anything. I was conversationally describing an urge – an urge that soon wore off. And I hereby declare that "harassing the Muslim community in Britain" would be neither moral nor efficacious. Professor Eagleton is making a habit of this kind of thing. A marooned ideologue, he has submitted to an unworthy combination of venom and sloth. Can I ask him, in a collegial spirit, to shut up about it?

Martin Amis
London

October 12

Medical procedures and disabled people's rights

My daughter also suffers from cerebral palsy and, like Katie, is unable to move or talk and has almost no understanding of the world around her (Mother defends hysterectomy for disabled daughter, October 8). My daughter is only two but the decision taken by Alison, clearly a caring

October 9
Could the fertility watchdog not have used a term other than "handful" to describe the number of UK sperm donors aged over 65 (Report, October 6)?

Richard Cooper
Rugby, Warwickshire

October 10
According to the polls, inheritance tax has overtaken health, welfare, education and security as the biggest concern of voters (Comment, October 9). To those of us working in the voluntary sector, the main worry of most families is keeping a roof over their heads, not having in excess of £300,000 to their name.

Val Hince
Leighton Buzzard,
Bedfordshire

October 11
Could the "organisers" and "male part-

ner" in your article (The art of seduction: sex through the ages, October 10) be legends?

Mic Porter
Monkseaton, Tyne & Wear

October 12
In Kent, protesters occupied E.ON's Kingsnorth power station and shut down its generators (Greenpeace protesters take over power plant, October 8). E.ON knows well that unpredictably intermittent wind needs constant backup from fossil-fuelled power or the lights will go out. We hope E.ON finds some money from its massive wind-power advertising budget to explain this to the people of Britain as we approach winter. Greenpeace's fairyland suggestions for locally distributed generation can neither supply the gigantic power demand of the UK, nor

mother to Katie, is one we will be thinking about in years to come. Decisions about the rights and wrongs of this procedure are definitely not black and white, and I am concerned that this is how the media — and indeed many of the charities that should be supporting Alison and Katie — have portrayed this story.

My daughter has undergone two operations — one to insert a feeding tube and one to prevent reflux. Neither operation was essential for her — she could be fed by naso-gastric tube and suffer from reflux for the rest of her life. But clearly her comfort levels were enhanced by these operations and no questions were asked about these (common) procedures being performed.

The operation proposed by Alison, a loving mother, is expected to improve Katie's comfort levels. The relative merits of this procedure should not be tried in the press, they should be addressed in court with a calm, rational debate involving the people who know and understand the situation. It is embarrassing for all concerned that charities like Scope have waded into this debate and chosen sides.

Name and address supplied

• It may not have come to the attention of the general population that Hitler undertook a Holocaust of disabled people known as Operation T4 prior to the Jewish extermination programme. One of the first steps in this systematic degradation was the sterilisation of disabled women. We do not want to countenance the possibility of another Operation T4.

Becky Butler (I have cerebral palsy)
London

October 15

Is it the end for social democracy?

Thank you to Polly Toynbee for articulating the dismay I felt last week (This was the week that Labour's leaders left social democracy for dead, October 12). The dismay was the greater for my having believed that while a Brown government might not go as far as I would want in reversing the tide of inequality, it would at least place the eradication of child poverty at the heart of its agenda. After all, ever since entering parliament Gordon Brown has inspired many with his visceral detestation of poverty. Instead, apart from an increase in benefit for 16- to 17-year-olds, this first real Brown milestone offered only crumbs alongside regressive tax handouts.

Toynbee ended on a note of hope and called on Brown to spell out the vision he talks so much about. That vision is likely to remain clouded so long as he is fixated on short-term tactical point-scoring. Moreover, a vision is more than a set of policies and values strung together in seemingly random fashion. It is time Brown made clear his vision of "the good society".

Ruth Lister
Professor of social policy, Loughborough University

October 17

Polar education

I was interested to read Admiral James Perowne's letter (October 11). He hopes that schools and colleges are teaching our youth about the polar heroes of the 20th century. The Fuchs Foundation, an educational charity, is sending science and

provide the necessary support for intermittent renewables.

Dr David Bellamy
Bishop Auckland,
Co Durham

Dr John Etherington
Llanhowell, Pembrokeshire

October 12

The leg-endary King David of Israel, when old, could not keep warm, if you know what I mean (Letters, October 11). They found him a gorgeous young maiden called Abishag, who gets very interestingly hyphenated in some editions of the Bible (see 1 Kings 1:3 ff).

Fr Alec Mitchell
Manchester

October 12

Has anyone noticed the similarities between David Cameron and Gromit (A bear baited by bottles, October 11).

Gerard Parker
Kendal, Cumbria

October 13
Was it coincidence
that Doris Lessing
appeared in the cryptic
crossword the day you
announced her Nobel
prize (October 12)?

Marjorie Brooks
Bridgnorth, Shropshire

October 13
Have you noticed
the likeness between
Brown and Nixon
(Letters, October 12)?

Bob Schweizer
London

October 13
So, in a study for the
French wine industry
of "1,000 regular
[British] male pub-
goers", a large majority
were said to regularly
move on to wine
after the first pint of
beer of the evening
(Report, October 12).
Even more hilariously,
68% were revealed as
"preferring to share a
bottle between friends
rather than taking it
in turns to buy rounds

geography teachers to the polar regions. The first
expedition leaves the UK on November 3 for
the Ellsworth mountains in Antarctica – four
teachers with two leaders to do significant science
projects from which the teachers will produce
teaching materials. These will be published on
www.fuchsfoundation.org. The next expedition
will be to Greenland in 2009.

This year is also the 50th anniversary of the
Commonwealth trans-Antarctic expedition of
1955-58, led by Vivian Fuchs, which completed
the first crossing of Antarctica. This anniversary
is celebrated at the Royal Geographical Society
next week with two lectures on the journey and
its scientific legacy.

Peter Fuchs
Chairman of trustees, Fuchs Foundation

October 23

Government rejects Iraq abuse claims

I do not for one moment accept Phil Shiner's
allegations of "a catalogue of abuse", or of "a
systematic policy" leading to "scores" of executions
and "the torture of countless more" by British
forces in Iraq (Comment, October 19). In the
case of the incident in Amara, no evidence was
found of any systematic or deliberate mutilation.
All the injuries were found to be consistent with
battlefield injuries.

Where service personnel are accused of
wrongdoing, the allegations are fully investigated
and, where appropriate, prosecutions are brought.
Mr Shiner chooses not to inform your readers that
I have invited his firm – Public Interest Lawyers
(PIL) – to make any representations they think

appropriate as to any further inquiry which might be required in relation to the death of Mr Baha Mousa, following the Payne court martial.

It has been agreed that certain documentation from the court martial will be provided to PIL to assist them in making representations. We have also agreed that we will need time to consider whatever representations they make before reaching a decision. Meanwhile, the independent review of the criminal proceedings relating to Mr Mousa is ongoing.

Des Browne MP
Secretary of state for defence

October 23

More mothers died in earlier times

Mothers not dying is quite a recent phenomenon ('We've had war, we've had plagues, but never this...', G2, October 22). That's why so many fairy stories have stepmothers in them.

My grandmother's mother died in childbirth at 30. Her stepsister died young and left a small son to be raised by my grandmother. My other great-grandmother was a second wife taking on six children after their mother died of breast cancer.

We've been a lucky generation who believed scientific advance would cure everything. Perhaps that's why we find it so painful when life suddenly seems so fragile.

Sioned-Mair Richards
Sheffield, South Yorkshire

of beer". Who was the most pissed – the blokes answering the questions, the researchers who wrote down the answers, or the French who apparently believed them? Cheers!

Ric Carey
Portsmouth, Hampshire

October 16
In his interview with Karen Darby (October 12), David Teather says "she sinks into a northern accent". So what might she rise to?

Jerome Hanratty
Tynemouth, Tyne and Wear

October 16
In January 1977 a group of women from all over the UK formed a correspondence magazine to which they would each contribute a hand-written letter to be circulated among the group. This month sees our 368th magazine – still going strong after

more than 30 years. So we would agree with John Harris that the art of letter-writing is enduring and will never be replaced by email (The last post, October 13).

Sarah Akhtar
Stoke on Trent

October 17

"Free today: Collectable poster-size blueprint of Arnos Grove tube station" (October 16). Can the front page of any national newspaper ever have offered so tempting an inducement?

Robert Lacey
London

October 18

The Arnos Grove tube station plan inspired me to buy the Guardian for the first time in months: different strokes for different folks (Letters, October 17)?

Tudor Eynon
London

October 23

Class rules are more complex

"Riven by class and no social mobility – Britain in 2007" said your headline (October 20). It may be so, but nothing of the kind is shown in the ICM study that you quoted. In answer to the question, "Which social class do you feel you belong to?", 55% said working class and 41% said middle class. However, it is well-established in social research that simple questions of this kind reveal nothing worthwhile. "Working class" is quite commonly taken by respondents to mean "people who work hard for a living"; it is not surprising that the responses in the ICM study bore little relationship to social class as defined in more objective terms – by occupation and level of earnings.

The statement that there is "no social mobility" in Britain is ridiculous. All sociologists and economists accept that there is a large amount of fluidity between the generations in contemporary Britain. The key research question is whether there is less today than for earlier generations.

Anthony Giddens
Lab, House of Lords

• My grandparents played musical instruments, listened to oratorios and wouldn't have recognised a "faux" armchair if it bit them on the arse. They would also have been rather surprised to be branded middle class, since every one of them either worked underground or in domestic service.

Objective definitions of class have gone out of fashion. But by stumbling into the morass of identity politics, Decca Aitkenhead (Class rules, October 20) finds herself arguing, rather absurdly, that social mobility is as much about self-perception as it is about occupation, education and income.

Beneath this sloppy analysis lies a sloppier relativism that argues not for equality, but for equal respect for fundamentally unequal things. In the real world, rather a lot of us work hard for fairly meagre wages, while a tiny number of obscenely rich people run the show. And the problem is not that some people do posh things; it is that the wrong people get to do them. My grandparents would have been appalled.

Glynne Williams
Cardiff

October 24

Getting to the roots of developing-world poverty

While understanding Alan Rusbridger's wish to find a metaphor to dramatise the gap between European and Ugandan village lives, the middle ages seems the wrong one (Katine: It starts with a village, October 20). Perhaps, in Rusbridger's style, an anecdote may illustrate why.

Thirty years ago, one of us was sitting in a Senegalese village talking to a farmer struggling to make a living against drought and inadequate land and resources. He asked where I was from. "England," I said. "Oh yes," he said, "I lived in Bournemouth for a while." He'd fought in France and been evacuated from the Dunkirk beaches.

An African villager's life is caught up in our wars, our droughts, our economic structure. We are all of the 21st century. It helps understanding to know that.

Maureen Mackintosh and Doreen Massey
Faculty of social sciences, Open University

October 18
I must protest about your Sport strapline (October 17). If your style guide cannot come up with a more acceptable phrase than "veteran hooker" to describe Mark Regan, might I propose "mature sports worker"?

Bob Jones
Worcester

October 18
When the Fuchs Foundation's expedition (Letters, October 17) sets off, will we be treated to the reappearance of the legendary Guardian headline – Fuchs off to the Antarctic – which (it is alleged) greeted Sir Vivian's first expedition?

Charles Miller
Standish, Wigan

October 20

About Deborah Kerr's films (Obituary, October 19), I find that they were: stodgy, miscast, lack-lustre, staid, botched, routine, chaotic, dated, lugubrious and over-wrought. Wouldn't it have been better to have an obituary written by someone who likes films?

Copland Smith
Manchester

October 22

The build-it-yourself Empire State Building (September 20) seems too ambitious for my craft skills. Can I exchange it for a build-it-yourself Arnos Grove tube station?

Cliff Challenger
Bradford

October 22

Is King Kong in next Saturday's paper?

Dave Hanson
Hull

October 24

Batons won't help in young offender institutions

There is a certain irony in the fact that while the government is to consider allowing staff at young offender institutions to use batons to control children as young as 15, the unacceptable behaviour of prison officers is also under the spotlight (Reports, October 22). Misconduct offences by 1,300 jail officers, including assault and racial harassment, suggest the prison service should put its house in order before deciding whether to arm officers with batons to control youngsters. Martin Narey, chief executive of the children's charity Barnardo's and former chief executive of the Prison Service, has stressed the importance of treating child prisoners firmly, but with dignity, and "not beating them with truncheons". Challenging behaviour by children in custody is never an excuse for abusive policies or bad behaviour by staff.

Pauline Campbell
Malpas, Cheshire

October 25

Grand visions of a privatised NHS

Professor Le Grand's attempt to dismiss Seumas Milne's commentary on the destruction of the NHS as a "rant" is an all-too-typical New Labour response (Letters, October 22). Perhaps his own direct responsibility for New Labour's reforms, as Tony Blair's senior health policy adviser, which he did not mention, has made him lose objectivity.

Milne's article was based on the clear evidence of the government's stated intention to dismember the NHS and create a healthcare market. Le

Grand's letter is the sort of spin one has come to expect from the CBI or a rightwing thinktank, not from an academic. All serious academic observers agree that far from being inefficient, as he declares, the pre-reform NHS was the most efficient — and also one of the most equitable — of all national healthcare systems.

The claim that independent sector treatment centres have significantly assisted the NHS to cut waiting times and increase choice is simply false. The Commons health select committee could find no evidence for this, and an in-depth study by Stewart Player and myself at the University of Edinburgh shows that, on the contrary, ISTCs are not innovative and have if anything reduced choice and NHS capacity. Their real purpose has been to establish a hugely expensive and ringfenced bridgehead for private providers in NHS secondary care, at the cost of NHS trusts having to close services and lay off staff because their patient income is being diverted to for-profit providers.

Colin Leys
Honorary professor, Centre for International
Public Health Policy, University of Edinburgh

October 26

PR would abolish marginal seats

Bill Rammell and Labour (Private funding of Tory contenders in marginal seats is insidious, October 25) cannot have it both ways — voting themselves £10,000pa "communications allowances" (opposed by most Conservative MPs) and taking money from the unions. There is a simple solution — voting reform. If the government had honoured its promise to publish the long-awaited review

October 23

Paul Oestreicher's moving piece (Face to Faith, October 20) about Franz Jäger-stätter, executed in 1943, had a very misleading headline. Jägerstätter was not a pacifist. He, a military reservist, was willing to defend his country were it attacked but he would not take the unconditional military oath and refused to serve in what he judged to be an unjust war. That is what makes him such a significant challenge to the military of our day.

Bruce Kent
London

October 24

Following his state-ment that black people are less intelligent than white people (Report, October 20), perhaps the geneticist Dr James Watson should be reminded of his earlier — and far more astute — comment about the limitations of scientists: "One could not be a successful scientist without realising that, in contrast to the popular conception supported by newspapers and mothers of scientists, a goodly number of scientists are not only narrow-minded and dull, but also just stupid."

Dr PD Smith
Winchester, Hampshire

October 24
Your Country Diary (October 20) informed us about the scurry of partridges and the hiccuping cock-pheasant, the dry-husked grasses and the daytime tawny, but I looked in vain for the doings of the questing vole and the other inhabitants of the plashy fen. Brilliant satire!

Will Atkinson
Culham, Oxfordshire

of Britain's voting systems, rather than just gerrymandering its own preferential systems in the union's devolved legislatures, then we may have been having a sensible discussion on how marginal seats could become a thing of the past. The single transferable voting system would stop money being poured into marginals, make MPs directly accountable to the electorate rather than the party hierarchy, and end tactical voting. But turkeys are not going to vote for Christmas unless there is a hung parliament.

Janice Small
Conservative Action for Electoral Reform

October 26

EU opt-outs and the Lisbon treaty

After the Lisbon summit there is a debate on the need to submit the reform treaty of the EU to a popular referendum in the UK. Gordon Brown should propose a referendum with the following question: Should the UK remain as a member of the EU, yes or no? A no would free the EU from opt-outs and unhelpful blockings. A yes would allow a more decent reform of the EU, a union in which Britain could play a much more prominent and positive role.

Robert Goebbels MEP
Former minister of the economy, Luxembourg

October 27

Why I donate to the Conservative cause

Bill Rammell denounces Conservative campaigning in marginal constituencies as a "distortion of democracy" (Response, October 25). In doing so, he himself demonstrates a shaky grasp of the concept. Responding to the argument of Robert Halfon, his Conservative opponent in Harlow, that parliamentary communications allowances give him an inbuilt electoral advantage (Letters, October 16), Mr Rammell says that such taxpayer-funded allowances assist him in "taking up constituents' concerns and responding to local issues". Indeed so; that is as it should be. Extraordinarily, Mr Rammell argues that his opponents should be prevented from doing the same, even with funds they have raised privately.

While it is true that parliamentary allowances cannot be used for party-political advertising, a letter from an MP detailing his work and record of success on behalf of his constituents will enhance his reputation and make it more likely that he will be re-elected – whether it says "vote Labour" or not. And while Conservative MPs are entitled to the same allowances as others, the combined effect will be to benefit the party with the most sitting MPs, thus disproportionately assisting the governing party of the day.

Mr Rammell's accusation that I am "hand-picking" which candidates receive financial support is simply wrong. Along with other donors I contribute to a central fund, administered by Conservative campaign headquarters, from which support is given to local constituency campaigns. I do this because I am a passionate Conservative and, along with millions of others, I want to see a change of government with David Cameron as prime minister. I do not give directly to local candidates or campaigns, and the claim that I am trying to "buy" seats is ludicrous and offensive.

Nobody could object to MPs communicating

October 24
I do not know who is responsible for moving the sudoku to the back of G2, but they are to be congratulated. There is now no longer a need to dismantle my newspaper each morning to allow my wife to start the puzzle before I have even read the headlines. You have probably saved our marriage.

Shaun Soper
Trevillick, Cornwall

October 25
Your report of the discovery of a first edition of The Importance of Being Earnest (Wilde gener-osity gives Oxfam shop a £650 boost, October 20) omits the highly relevant fact that it was found in a handbag.

Robert Hill
Leeds

October 25
So the Garda think
the 10 men, of the
15-strong gang, who
set about Paul Quinn
with iron bars and
wooden bats "had
probably not meant
to kill" him (Report,
October 23)? It's the
way they tell 'em.

Gary Williams
Weston-super-Mare

October 25
If all it takes to save
Mr Soper's marriage
(Letters, October 24)
is a slight rejig of his
newspaper, he should
think himself lucky.
We had to buy an
automatic car.

R Phillips
Bury St Edmunds, Suffolk

October 26
You reported (October
23) that the home
secretary asserted that
36% of the 1,228 people
held under the anti-
terror laws had been
charged. According
to the Home Office,

effectively with their constituents. But it is
cowardly for sitting MPs to seek to restrict the
campaigning capacity of their opponents while
protecting their own sources of support and
exploiting the advantages of incumbency.

Michael Ashcroft
Deputy chairman, Conservative party

October 29
Brick Lane's many narratives

As a mixed-race novelist (hell, just as a novelist),
I would like to say to your leader writer (The
trouble with Brick Lane, October 27) that I reserve
the right to imagine anyone and anything I
damn well please. If I want to write about Jewish
people, or paedophiles or Patagonians or witches
in 12th-century Finland, then I will do so, despite
being "authentically" none of these things. I also
give notice that if I choose, I intend to imagine
what your muddled writer quaintly terms "real
people" living in "real communities". My work
may convince or it may not. However, I will
not accept that I have any a priori responsibility
to anyone – white, black or brown, let alone
any "community" – to represent them in any
particular way.

If Monica Ali isn't brown enough or working-
class enough or Sylheti enough for you, then, well,
that's your weird little identity-political screw-up.
Presumably she's not white enough for someone
else. I'm sick of all this cant about cultural
authenticity, and sick of the duty (imposed only
on "minority" writers) to represent in some quasi-
political fashion. Art isn't about promoting social
cohesion, or cementing community relations. It's

about telling the truth as you see it, even if it annoys or offends some people. That's called freedom of expression, and last time I checked we all thought it was quite a good idea.

Hari Kunzru
London

October 29
Doris Lessing on 9/11

Although conceding that Doris Lessing might have been admirably brave to say the September 11 atrocity was "not that terrible" when compared with what the IRA did, Kathryn Hughes (Comment, October 27) supposes that many people will think this "plain wrong". Tony Blair has indeed said that he couldn't imagine the IRA committing murder on the scale of al-Qaida. If you take the respective populations of Northern Ireland and the US, and perform a simple equation, then the numbers of those killed by the IRA in the province would be the equivalent of around 300,000 Americans, as many Americans as who died in the second world war, not to say about 100 times as many as those killed in New York six years ago. Perhaps Mrs Lessing wasn't plain wrong, even in the simplest terms.

Geoffrey Wheatcroft
Bath, Somerset

October 30
Treading on Tread Lightly's dreams

Surely Ben Goldacre must be setting his Bad Science sights on your Tread Lightly campaign (October 27). I hope Ben will tell us exactly by how

only 13% were charged under terrorism acts and other criminal offences and just 3.3% convicted. Clearly the debate on the government seeking further counter-terrorism powers should not be misinformed about their effectiveness.

Saleh Mamon
Campaign Against
Criminalising Communities

October 27
A letter on Europe's future from Goebbels and a double-page photo spread of Katie Price (October 26), and you say the use of cannabis is down?

Bob Hargreaves
Bury, Lancashire

October 29
The Putney debates (A jewel of democracy, G2, October 26) of 1647 would make October 28 an excellent candidate for a new national holiday — "Democracy Day"

— and go some way to making my birthday even more memorable!

Fred Pickstone
Ulverston, Cumbria

October 30
Is it just me, or does anyone else agree that Pete Doherty is beginning to resemble a young John Prescott (G2, October 26)? It could explain a lot.

Paul Steeples
London

October 31
As elderly but committed environmentalists we dutifully turn our thermostat down every time we are told to (If we all Tread Lightly we can make a difference, October 27). We are currently shivering at seven degrees. Do you think it might be more helpful if someone could recommend a specific temperature?

Peter and Vera Hall
Allestree, Derby

much we will slow climate change if we "turn off a coal-fired power station for one day, one hour, 46 minutes and one second". And I'm sure he'll point out that the G-Wiz is only as carbon-free as the electricity that must be generated to power it.

The idea that readers can "save the planet" by offsetting air miles, changing a few light bulbs or turning down thermostats by a degree or two is attractive but, alas, misleading. The world's largest economies need to make a fundamental change in the technologies we use to generate electricity and to move around if we are to reach the 60-80% cut in global CO_2 emissions that scientists tell us is required to prevent dangerous climate change. As Professor Gwyn Prins and I recently pointed out in Nature (October 25), only massive new public investment in alternative energy technology can achieve this — and it simply is not happening on the scale needed.

Of course, efficient use of energy is desirable and reducing our carbon footprints may make us feel good. But there is no strong precedent to suppose that such acts of voluntary frugality will lead "politicians to see the profligate use of fossil fuels as unacceptable". Regrettably, it seems just as likely that Tread Lightly will act as a safety valve, helping to release the necessary pressure for the fundamental technological transformation that neither governments nor the media are willing to face up to.

Steve Rayner
James Martin professor of science and civilisation,
University of Oxford

November 2007

With the big electoral contest postponed, the focus turned to the smaller players in the increasingly fragmented politics of Britain. In Scotland the successful first six months of the minority SNP government reopened the West Lothian question; the Lib Dem leadership election became a two-horse race between moderniser Nick Clegg and former Guardian journalist Chris Huhne; and the anarcho-environmentalist faction in the Green party tried to fend off attempts by eco-realists to appoint a leader for the first time. The growing importance of cultural politics was reflected by debates over migration and the right to wear religious symbols and clothing — spilling over into a more toxic argument over whether comments about Muslims by Martin Amis were racist, with fellow writers Ronan Bennett and Ian McEwan leading the attack and defence. Abroad, an attack on the judiciary in Pakistan started a political crisis that would lead to both violence and the restoration of democracy; and yet another Middle East peace process was initiated in Annapolis, to little optimism outside the negotiators. The Princess Diana inquest ended, a year of floods continued, the Spice Girls returned, the iPhone became latest must-have gadget, and a 3-2 home defeat to Croatia meant England failed to quality for Euro 2008. But there was one British success: St Pancras station reopened as the Eurostar terminal to almost universal acclaim — not least for the longest champagne bar in the world.

November 1

I'm alarmed that armed people could fire guns so close to Prince Harry and his esteemed friend and yet not be noticed by bodyguards etc (Prince Harry quizzed by police about shooting of rare birds, October 31). Who is ensuring that our potential head of state is secure from terrorists?

Mike Woodcock
Olveston, Gloucestershire

November 2

I realise that Quick Crossword No 11,695 was a coded message to me (20 Across, great conqueror, nine letters, Alexander; 4 Down, type of hut, six letters, Nissen) but was not sure whether to meet you in Highgate (3 Down), Victoria (11 Down) or Soho (8 Across). Apologies for not showing up.

Alexander Nissen
London

November 1

Better answers to West Lothian

The Tories are about to propose an English grand committee in the House of Commons, a variant on their earlier idea of banning Scottish MPs from voting on English matters (Leaders, October 29). This is riddled with practical difficulties and fails either to provide England with an executive like that of the other three nations of the UK, or to address the underlying problem, just as the old Scottish grand committee failed. The Westminster parliament currently has two mutually incompatible roles, as a federal parliament for the whole of the UK on non-devolved subjects such as foreign affairs, and simultaneously as a parliament for England on everything. The UK government has the same contradictory double role. There is only one solution: a parliament and government for England, the only one of the UK's four nations still without either, and (eventually) full devolution of all domestic affairs to the four parliaments and governments, making Westminster a fully fledged federal parliament and government dealing with all non-devolved and shared subjects.

Here is Gordon Brown's golden opportunity to outflank the Tories, resolve the West Lothian question, make sense of the second chamber (a federal senate), satisfy Scottish aspirations for more devolution, rescue the union of the four nations by putting them in a durable democratic relationship, and push power further down to local people, as well as build a national consensus on a new long-term constitutional settlement for Britain.

Brian Barder
London

November 1

Rosbaud's risks

Paul Rosbaud was indeed Britain's most important spy during the second world war (Spy left out in the cold: how MI6 buried heroic exploits of agent 'Griffin', September 22). He got away with it for so long not only due to his charming personality but also to the fact that he was a commissioning editor for Springer Verlag. As such, he had easy access to some of the leading scientists in Germany and could glean information from them on a casual basis. He also became a member of the Nazi party and wore the Nazi uniform to cover his tracks. In this, he took enormous risks. Rosbaud was exfiltrated to Britain in late 1944.

Rosbaud never mentioned his wartime activities, which gave even some of his close associates reason to doubt that he was "the Griffin". It is only correct that he should now be given proper recognition for his contribution to the war effort. However, there may be a measure of self-interest in the refusal of MI6 to release Rosbaud's files to the public. When he reported on the development of the V2 rocket in Germany, for example, it wasn't believed in the British intelligence community. The war ended more than 60 years ago. Rosbaud's files need to be opened to find out what really happened.

Geoffrey P Glasby
Göttingen, Germany

November 2

Migration, prejudice and public services

It is sad to note that calls for an honest debate on migration are almost exclusively confined to

November 3

The result of your poll, "Do you want the 2018 World Cup to be hosted by England?" (Sport, November 2) was "Yes: 66%". Even those who vote in such polls just keep harking back to the past.

Toby Wood
Peterborough

November 5

I was amused to read that Christopher Foyle's favourite word is kakistocracy (Raconteur who wrestled to keep Foyles in the family, November 2), but confused by the fact that it apparently describes "a system of government where the rulers are the least competent, least qualified or most unprincipled citizens". Surely the word "government" already conveys this meaning on its own?

Chris Coates
Colchester, Essex

November 6

It was interesting last week to see Gordon Brown stating how he would "not tolerate" schools that failed to get 30% of pupils with five good GCSEs (PM gives failing schools five years to improve results, November 1). He wants to replace them with academies. But 13 out of the 14 academies open in 2003 failed to meet Gordon's target by 2006. The 2007 results are not out yet, but it is certain that most will still be failing. What does he propose to do with these incredibly expensive schools? His options will be constrained since they are all now in full private ownership.

Roger Titcombe
Ulverston, Cumbria

November 7

It is reassuring to note that accuracy in the Guardian hasn't deteriorated

commentators such as Jenni Russell (Comment, October 31) – politicians themselves shy away from it. Yet many aspects of migration offend traditional leftwing principles. Migration causes a massive increase in travel, which is detrimental to the environment. It drives down wages and working conditions. It deprives countries of much-needed skills, as well as disrupting families and communities. It leads to massive populations in already overtaxed areas, which worsens living conditions for immigrants and local residents alike.

Are these not issues that can and should at least be debated by the left? The logical conclusion does not have to mean draconian immigration controls. Infinitely more difficult is to address the issues which cause people to emigrate in the first place.

Walter Cairns
Manchester

• Yes, the inflow of migrants creates winners and losers in the host economy. But if, as you say, "for the country as a whole, the benefits outweigh the strains on housing and services" (Leader, October 31) then why need there be any losers? It's part of a government's job to capture from winners – manufacturing, service and agriculture companies – a chunk from their winnings sufficient to compensate the losers: people in areas facing extra pressure on housing, hospitals and schools. The lack of data, and the dilatory grant allocation to local authorities, demonstrate that the government hasn't even begun to set up mechanisms for compensatory transfers. That would be a better use of the Whitehall brains that are currently devising points systems for migrant workers.

David Chambers
London

November 3

Questions remain over De Menezes

The health and safety trial against the Metropolitan police may have been costly, but had the enormous virtue of exposing the details of events on July 22 2005 to a large audience (De Menezes verdict, November 2). Some important questions have been aired. Why, if the "shoot-to-kill" policy was not in operation that day, did an elite firearms officer pump seven bullets into Jean Charles de Menezes when he was pushed back in his seat, unable to move, let alone set off a bomb? When Commander Cressida Dick told her officers to "stop" De Menezes, why did she not specify exactly what she meant by the word, given its ambiguity? If she knew 15 minutes after De Menezes had been killed that he was neither carrying a bomb nor the man they had thought they were tracking, why was Ian Blair not informed of this straight away?

The Met had a very difficult task and were under huge pressure. It's not surprising that mistakes were made. But, tragically, an innocent man was killed in a ruthless and shocking way. For Ian Blair to say there was no systematic failure by the police is either a piece of sophistry (the failure was not due to the system but to individual error) or a blinkered denial of the errors revealed in the trial.

John Marzillier
Oxford

November 3

Muslim drama

Michael Billington says there have been no plays "telling us what it is like to be a Muslim living in

(Karl Marx, leading socialist thinker, dies in Paris, The Archive, November 5). He actually died in his armchair in London.

John Green
London

November 7

Do you need five good asbos to qualify for a neet (A taste for learning, November 6)? Round here we have a lot of neets, the favourites being "satdy neet" and "a gud neet aht". Didn't some politicians have "summat at neet abaht em"?

Dave Kiernan
Barnsley, South Yorkshire

November 7

First Worcester is flooded and now Tabasco (Report, November 5). Can we expect to see a thousand islands under water by the end of the year?

Steve Walker
London

41

November 8

Peter Viertel (Obituary November 7) "credited with introducing surfing into Europe" in 1956? In a 1943 novel, The Small Back Room by Nigel Balchin, two characters discuss the surfing potential of a beach while nerving themselves to defuse a particularly nasty bomb dropped by the Luftwaffe. Priorities, eh?

AJ Mullay
Edinburgh

November 9

If, as the president of the US and commander-in-chief of its armed forces proclaimed, you "cannot be the president and head of the military at the same time", the logic of his position is that Bush should resign forthwith (Bush puts pressure on Pakistani president, November 8).

Neil Henderson
Stornoway, Western Isles

Britain" (Lifting the curtain, G2, October 24). In the last four years we have commissioned five plays by female writers, including Manjinder Virk, the lead in Channel 4's Britz; Nasima Begum, the first Muslim British-born Bangladeshi playwright; and Amber Lone, whose Romeo in the City is currently on tour and highlights the relationship between a Muslim Pakistani girl and her Somali boyfriend. Most of our performances are in schools. When we do play in public venues, critics ignore our productions. This adds to the marginalisation of our work.

Natalie Wilson
Director, Theatre Centre

November 3

Remembering Dina

I burst into tears when I read that Dina Rabinovitch had died (Obituary, November 1). Although she'd hinted in last week's piece that the end was drawing near, I was fooled by her vigorous prose into thinking that she had more time left and that we'd soon be reading about a spontaneous remission brought about by her strength of character. Dina's initial story about her cancer diagnosis in September 2004 was the first item I read in the Guardian the day I moved here from the US. In following her instalments ever since, she became like a distant friend. I've never had cancer, but I could relate to her concerns as a mother and as someone who has lost several dear friends to cancer who left behind young children.

Donna Anton
Hayle, Cornwall

November 6

We Greens must not remain leaderless

As committed Greens we are delighted that more and more members of our party are being elected to public office. Given the dire threat of climate change, however, we are concerned that the Green party is not a much bigger player in British politics. Crucially, we believe the party's current set-up is failing to properly engage the electorate and hampering our ability to communicate the green message more effectively. Most people relate not to abstract ideas, but to the people who embody and espouse them.

For that reason we are calling on party members to support proposals for an accountable and easily identifiable leadership team composed of either a leader and deputy leader or two co-leaders. Every member of the party has the chance to vote on the issue in a referendum taking place this month and beginning this week.

We know that some traditionalists shy away from formal leadership structures. However, the biggest supporters of the Green party remaining leaderless are not these well-intentioned members, but the leaders of the other parties who know that a more visible and effective Green party poses far more of a threat than it does at present.

Now, more than ever before, the Green party needs to be providing clear political leadership on the green agenda. For this reason we urge all Greens to vote yes in the leadership referendum.

Jonathan Porritt Chair of the Sustainable Development Commission, **Mark Lynas** Author of Six Degrees and High Tide, **Caroline Lucas MEP, Darren Johnson** Member of the London assembly, **Sian Berry** Green candidate for London mayor, **Clive Lord** Founding Green party member **and 24 others including 12 councillors**

November 9

Kathryn Hughes is a little behind the times in announcing the arrival of the "knork" (Comment, November 8). My grandfather used a combination knife/fork for more than 40 years after he lost his right arm in a mining accident. So even in cutlery, fashion appears to be regularly reinvented.

Stuart Marshall-Clarke
Liverpool

November 9

The less comically named Splayd was invented in Australia in the 1940s. The single implement can function as knife, fork and spoon.

David Farrell
Oxford

November 10

Am I the only one to wonder how it's possible for Mr Piccolo to be Mr Big and at the same time be at large ('Boss of bosses' successor arrested at mafia summit, November 6)?

John Belshaw
Nottingham

November 10

I find that, when cutting bacon with a knork (Letters, November 9), it's easier if you hold the meat still with a second knork (or Splayd). A bit like a knife and fork, really.

Copland Smith
Manchester

November 12

Your article (Europe just got closer, Travel, November 10), only emphasises that the great 20-minute-faster Eurostar remains nothing much more than a branch line, its realistic destinations still restricted to Paris, Brussels and Lille. If St Pancras were a true European terminus, we would be looking

November 8

Green party doesn't need a leader

The Green party is as one in our determination to address climate change through radical and urgent political action. Yet we remain unconvinced by the seductive line pursued by some colleagues about the necessity of a party leader. In the past, the Greens have consistently rejected proposals such as this, not through adherence to "tradition", but because we recognise the imperative of grassroots participation. We cannot achieve our goals through political office alone. We need the wider society to mobilise too. Nor should we assume we would be immune to the flaws of the conventional leadership model. We and over 300 others have publicly reaffirmed our commitment to collective leadership ahead of a ballot on the issue (www.greenempowerment.org.uk). The Green party differs not for the sake of it, but because conventional politics has shown itself to be unfit for purpose.

Dr Shahrar Ali London policy coordinator, **Cllr Jenny Jones AM** Convenor, Green group, London assembly, **Cllr Alan Francis** Milton Keynes, **Cllr Romayne Phoenix** Lewisham

November 8

Parties block a fair deal on funding

Your leader on party funding (The spending game, November 6) was absolutely right. It is in no one's interest for the spending race to continue. Nor can it be right for individual donations to buy or appear to buy influence. That is why the talks chaired by Hayden Phillips, in which I participated, were so important, and why it is so regrettable that the Conservatives walked away from an agreement that we had so nearly reached. A broad consensus, with or without the Tories, is still possible, but only if Jack Straw can resist the temptation to retreat into party tribalism. Phillips's proposals form a very satisfactory basis for such an agreement. A one-sided attempt to deal with Michael Ashcroft and his millions in isolation, however understandable, does not. The focus should be on genuine reform, not crude political advantage.

David Heath MP
Lib Dem constitutional spokesman

November 9

Lack of faith in educational values

I do hope Simon Callow rises above this malodorous situation to support those of us who think it is important to proceed with the Oratory school's World Aids Day concert (Callow in threat to quit Oratory post, November 8). We will make our own donations to the Terrence Higgins Trust for those in our midst who suffer illness and adversity. As composer of the requiem to be performed at the concert, written at a time when friends and colleagues were dying of this hideous disease, I abhor the decision to change the beneficiaries from the original recipient, the Terrence Higgins Trust. The requiem must go ahead, though, because its intent stands above the paucity of love and exclusive care displayed by these moral pygmies. Unconditional love? Its polar opposite.

Gareth Valentine
London

at through-trains to Berlin, Barcelona and Brindisi, Munich, Milan, Moscow and Madrid – and a significant reduction in short-haul European flights with their massive carbon footprints. Who knows, the tunnel might even make a profit.

John Howlett
Rye, East Sussex

November 12
Deborah Hart (Letters, November 10) is unlikely to have her messages banned from American websites because they contain the word "socialist", but rather because they contain the word "Cialis", an anti-impotence drug. As an employee of the socialist magazine Tribune, spam filters blocking this word are the bane of my life.

Oli Usher
London

November 13

Much as I admire Stephen Fry and share his enthusiasm for shiny gadgets, I wonder whether the frenzy over Apple's latest object of desire, the iPhone, went a little too far (Not sensible, but oh, the joy of it!, November 10). If Apple feel that daily advertising in the Guardian is necessary, perhaps they should pay for it.

Sam Thomas
York

November 13

Your correspondents (Letters, November 10) must either lack the dexterity of my one-armed grandfather or have knorks of inferior design. His had a curved blade that terminated in four tines. By rocking the blade back and forth he could cut even the toughest meat.

Stuart Marshall-Clarke
Liverpool

November 9

Why east Germans still wish for the lives of others

Timothy Garton Ash, in his valediction to the Berlin Wall and the GDR (The path of the fallen wall is hard to find, but a powerful example lives on, November 8), has clearly not digested the results of the survey you report in the same issue (Germans hanker after barrier, November 8): 73% of ex-GDR citizens still think socialism is a good idea and a significant percentage would even like the wall back. I'm sure most of my former compatriots would not want a return to the claustrophobic and restrictive system of the past, but they would like a return to stability, secure jobs and housing, as well as a society where money and property were not the keys to social relations. The image of the GDR as a totally repressive regime, as portrayed in the film The Lives of Others and by Garton Ash, is as much a travesty as is the image of it as a socialist paradise.

John de la Motte
Aberystwyth, Powys

November 10

Minority report on Samina Malik

The conviction of Samina Malik recalls the Times's "breaking a butterfly on a wheel" judgment on an earlier act of youthful folly. It will also be read as an insult to her community and culture. Like other Walter Mitty Islamist fantasies, her story is just one of a million about late-teens/early-20s bedroom-fantasy scribblings – with the exception that her fantasies weren't those of the average heavy metal, goth or conehead fantasist, which this week were concretely linked to people being murdered in snowy, peaceful Finland.

She may have been misguided, but her possession of downloads of subversive material is probably no more than radical chic decor, or bricolage, like the copy of Towards a Citizens' Militia that I might still have buried somewhere. If I remember, it tells me how to disable tanks and airport runways, although I haven't felt moved to try either. Whimsicality aside, the judgment on this young woman is a farce, and one with an ugly racist undercurrent. A 23-year-old WH Smith employee reduced to tears in a court is not a hardened suicide bomber, just a kid with weird ideas.

John Gill
Ronda, Andalucia, Spain

November 10

Building on past glories

I am confused and disappointed by Simon Jenkins' response to the film I made for the opening of St Pancras station and the high-speed railway that serves it (Not just a building, but a joy to behold. Ken Livingstone must hate St Pancras, November 9). I don't mind him finding it "dreadful", but quite what I did to be "Blairite" baffles me. I also fail to see the "political correctness" of five white middle-aged men talking about infrastructure spending. True, some of the £10.5bn of investment that has been generated by the high-speed rail project will help the urban poor, but that hardly makes my film the gooey paean to softcore socialism that Jenkins implies.

Mostly, though, I am disappointed by the blinkered focus on the achievements of the

November 15
I am now aged 95 and was born without a left hand. There's no need to use any of these trick "gadget" fork-knife-spoons (Letters, November 13). I can cut anything (even a steak, along the grain) with the edge of any ordinary-sized fork. Gadgets are usually more nuisance than help.

Harry Overy
Welwyn Garden City,
Hertfordshire

November 15
Russell Brand (G2, ad nauseam, November 13) is clearly very excited about himself, and writes about it very well, but, I must say, I find my own narcissism infinitely more compelling.

Gil Elliot
London

November 16

The knork (Letters, November 15) sounds like what my Canadian family called a pie fork: we used them to eat dessert. Unencumbered by class anxieties they may be, but as a leftie I always found them difficult to use, as the blade was on the wrong side. Classism? What about handism?

Rev Jenny Welsh
London

November 16

I guess that Jonathan Aitken's problem (Conservatives bypass Aitken, November 13) is that he'll always have Paris.

Nigel Todd
Newcastle upon Tyne

November 17

In connection with the current debate on the time limit for the detention of terror suspects (UK terror detention limit is

Victorians. I take nothing away from William Barlow, but in his wildest dreams he could never have imagined the astounding engineering achievement of the new high-speed railway. The revival of St Pancras is just part of an epic construction project that is a real modern-day triumph. For once we have achieved something that our Victorian ancestors would have been genuinely proud of. I think it a great shame that Jenkins' list of "those who should have been thanked" didn't include any of the architects and engineers of a contemporary success story which proves it is possible to build on past glories, not just build over them.

Benjamin Blaine
Brookmans Park, Hertfordshire

November 13

Gems from the Guardian digital archive

Thank you for the fascinating supplements (The Archive, November 5-9). In the "cultural archive" (November 8), my brother Julian and I were delighted to discover the review dated August 18 1914 of a play put on by our grandfather Iden Payne, with his then wife, our grandmother Mona Limerick, praised for her performance in the lead role. We suspect this was one of the last times they worked together. He was already successful in his theatre work with the likes of Shaw, Galsworthy and Yeats, and went on in the 20s to direct on Broadway, returning to Stratford-on-Avon and the then Shakespeare Memorial Theatre as director during the late 30s, before continuing in the US into his 90s as a director and university drama teacher.

But our grandmother, although feted as a

passionately dramatic and unusually beautiful actress, never worked again after he left her in about 1916. It has been poignantly pleasing to read this Guardian review. I shall always prefer the printed page to a work-associated computer screen, but this digitisation project certainly turns up gems.

Orlaith Kelly
St Albans, Hertfordshire

November 13

March against St Pancras hotel

Simon Jenkins' unbound enthusiasm for the St Pancras hotel has not always been shared (Comment, November 9). In 1959, as part of the Anti-Ugly Movement, I marched with perhaps a hundred other architecture students against the St Pancras hotel. It was a Scottish baronial concoction designed originally for Whitehall that Palmerston had wisely rejected in favour of the classical.

Sandor Vaci
London

November 14

Putting a cap on executive pay

As a former £14-a-week Millwall footballer, I do not see the anomaly in footballers' wages compared with musicians and actors (Letters, November 10). Economists use the concept of "economic rent" — a surplus that accrues to a factor of production, including labour, as a result of limited supply. It follows that the combination of huge amounts of capital coming into football from TV, driven

longest of any democracy, November 12), I note that 28 is a perfect mathematical number. I sincerely hope that the government will not attempt to put forward a case for raising the limit to the next highest perfect number, 496. My own view is that the lowest perfect number, six, is much more appropriate.

Michael Howarth
Guildford, Surrey

November 19

So Prince Charles won't be visiting Israel because it might burnish that state's reputation (Clarence House steers clear of Jerusalem visit, November 16); no such worries over the Queen's recent meeting with King Abdullah, head of that beacon of democracy and tolerance, Saudi Arabia.

Andrew Lee-Hart
Wallasey, Cheshire

November 19

Ashley Seager must
take the biscuit for the
pig's breakfast of mixed
metaphors served
up in the report on
house prices (House
prices to stagnate,
says Nationwide,
November 17). We
had a stagnant market
buckling under the
effects of stretched
affordability, tighter
lending and a slowing
economy. Alas, we
may be set on a course
from which, as Alan
Bennett once said,
wild horses on bended
knees cannot divert us.

Peter Pool
Leeds

November 19

"Yangtze bears record
load of dumped
sewage", says your
headline (November
15). I am glad to hear
that Chinese animals
are not only aware
of environmental
pollution, but have
learned to keep a
scientific record of the

by advertising, and the limited supply of football
talent will result in inflated wages.

Pat Brady
Chislehurst, Kent

November 16

School uniform rules need clarifying

The Children's Legal Centre believes that the
case of a 14-year-old Sikh girl excluded from
school for refusing to remove a religious bangle
(Report, November 14) highlights the need for
the government to formulate clearer and more
detailed guidance to schools on their uniform
policies and how these should take account of
pupils' rights to freedom of religious expression.

In 2006 the Children's Legal Centre acted for
Shabina Begum in a case involving the exclusion
from school of a Muslim girl for refusing to
remove a jilbab. In reaching its decision, the
Lords commented that the government should
provide clearer guidance to schools to ensure all
uniform policies conform to the Human Rights
Act. The new Department for Children, Schools
and Families guidance includes some consideration
of a pupil's right to religious expression, but
this guidance is, unfortunately, not sufficiently
comprehensive or detailed to ensure that pupils
are not excluded in circumstances which may
violate their human rights to freedom of religion,
education and non-discrimination.

Without such guidance, pupils will continue to
be excluded from school and suffer disruptions
in their education in circumstances which
violate their rights. This also makes schools more
susceptible to legal challenges from such pupils

that have a negative effect on staff time and financial resources. School uniform policies should allow pupils to express their religion, where this expression is legitimate and proportionate, without fear of being excluded from school and having their education interrupted. The government needs to assist schools in ensuring the uncertainties are resolved.

Professor Carolyn Hamilton
Director, Children's Legal Centre

November 17
Leading the way to radical politics

Polly Toynbee (The Lib Dems face a clear choice, November 16) makes the bizarre and unfounded claim that I was "angry" with Liberal Democrats who went on the anti-Iraq war march in February 2003. At no point have I ever been anything less than an outspoken critic of the decision to go to war in Iraq. I remain enormously proud that the Lib Dems stood out from the crowd in opposing this illegal invasion. I was a Euro-MP for the East Midlands at the time and had to be out of the country on the day of the march. Is that now a hanging offence?

As for her equally bizarre suggestion that I am not zealous enough in my advocacy of electoral reform, let me be clear: I have repeatedly stated that coalition government will not occur unless it is preceded by a meaningful change in our political system. That is merely stating the obvious.

However, I do not believe the leadership contest should be used as a dress rehearsal for coalition negotiations which may never occur. The Liberal Democrats are in politics to make

amount. Do they do this in the woods?

Liz Tucker
London

November 19
The Spice Girls "donned 1940s military uniforms to perform one of the songs" (They're back. And just as good as before, November 18). Looking at the photo of them cavorting in high heels and clingy outfits revealing ample cleavage amid the satin and leather, I couldn't help wondering: which army was that?

Martin Brown
Coventry

November 21
Germaine Greer's assertion (G2, November 19) that no painter had convincingly represented Australian landscape and trees would have come as a surprise to Charles Conder, Tom Robert and Arthur

Streeton, who could claim to have made a pretty good fist of it in the 1880s. And the officer/s dubbed by Bernard Smith "the Port Jackson Painter" was/were, within his/ their technical limitations, accurately drawing gum trees immediately after the invasion in 1788. Plenty of other examples refute this hoary canard.

Michael Rosenthal
University of Warwick

November 21

Maggie Pearce tells us her mother-in-law called her combined knife/fork a "Nelson" (Letters, November 17). In the mid-1950s I played Nelson in a TV play, produced with the cooperation of the Greenwich Museum, which holds his relics. I used the real thing during the performance.

Barry Letts
Potters Bar, Hertfordshire

Britain more liberal – greener, fairer, freer from heavy-handed state intrusion, more decentralised, with a progressive foreign policy. We shouldn't let ourselves be characterised as a one-trick pony on electoral reform. I make no apology for a leadership campaign that is seeking to promote the widest possible vision for the Lib Dems in the years to come.

Nick Clegg MP
Lib Dem leadership candidate

November 19

Democracy and security in Pakistan

The judiciary and the entire legal profession of Pakistan are in the gravest danger. Thirteen judges of the supreme court of Pakistan are either under house arrest or in prison. Only four judges of the highest court under the constitution of Pakistan agreed to take the oath under President Musharraf's provisional emergency order. The lawyers imprisoned or under house detention, surrounded by police and soldiers, include Aitzaz Ahsan, president of the Supreme Court Bar Association, and Munir Malik, former president of the SCBA. There are many, many others.

The arrest and imprisonment of those whose lives have been committed to human rights and democracy is catastrophic as well as repugnant. The British government should authorise its representatives in Pakistan to visit these courageous people in their prisons, or houses surrounded by police and soldiers, to ensure their safety. The British government should also ask the president, military generals and officers to release these prisoners and immediately allow them to talk and write freely, and resume their constitutional and legal positions, and their human rights work.

The independence of the judiciary, its right in law to challenge a government, and the rights and freedoms of lawyers to challenge human rights abuses in the courts are not only corner-stones of a democratic state – they are also fundamental to maintaining the security of all peoples against extremists and terror in any shape or form.

Vanessa Redgrave, Nasreen Rehman, Richard Jolly
Institute of Development Studies, Sussex, **Massoud Shadjareh** Chair, Islamic Human Rights Commission, **Nicolas Rea, Helena Kennedy QC**

November 20

Death penalty ban

Ed Pilkington (Sentenced to death for crimes they did not commit: the men who lived to tell the tale, November 14) claims that "Venezuela became the first country to remove the death penalty in 1853". However, the first country to ban capital punishment (apart from China for a brief spell in the eighth century) was the Grand Duchy of Tuscany.

Eighteenth-century continental attitudes to crime and punishment had been crystallised by the Italian philosopher Cesare Beccaria (1738-94), and his writings strongly influenced Tuscany's leader, Grand Duke Leopold II of Habsburg (1747-92). Tuscany had not put anyone to death since 1769, and on November 30 1786 the penal code abolished capital punishment. This code remained in act until Tuscany became part of the unified Italy in 1860.

November 21
1000 Albums to Hear Before You Die (November 17)? Girls Aloud, Lily Allen, Cilla Black? Are you all on drugs? No? I suggest you start.

Terry Blacklock
Wellington, Somerset

November 23
Now the real reason for bidding for the World Cup in 2018 becomes apparent (Croatia 3, England Out: McClaren on the brink, November 22). England do not need to qualify if they are hosts.

David Hard
Kenilworth, Warwickshire

November 23
There's lots of coverage of firms like Umbro which are losing out with England's failure to qualify for Euro 2008, but almost none of those rubbing their hands with glee. I run a singles events

company and major sporting events, particularly football matches, are a disaster for us. The 2006 World Cup led to one of our worst months ever. If I bump into Steve McClaren I'll buy him a beer.

Ben Tisdall
Director, SpeedDater

November 24
The reason behind charging £4.99 and similar prices for an item (The missing millions, G2, November 20) is that the shop assistant is then forced to open the till to get the penny change. This reduces the chance of staff theft.

David Hebb
Grimsby, Lincolnshire

November 24
It is obvious where the missing child benefit data discs have gone (Report, November 23). Santa needs all the

Under the leadership of Riccardo Nencini, president of the regional council of Tuscany, November 30 has been, since 2000, the date of an annual Festa della Toscana — a regional holiday celebrating Tuscany's role in the movement against the death penalty. The Tuscan government is very active in protesting against the practice of capital punishment.

George Ferzoco
University of Bristol

November 21

Gaza must be the priority in Annapolis

The situation in Palestine is even more dire than Jonathan Steele suggests (Comment, November 16). The West Bank is ruled by Fatah with an iron fist; the scale of settlements already built by Israel — together with the scores of checkpoints making movement very difficult — has effectively reduced it to a string of little Bantustans.

In Gaza, a humanitarian disaster looms. The closing of the Rafah crossing by Egypt, and now the Sufa crossing by Israel, will reduce humanitarian aid by 70% — and this to what Israel calls a "hostile entity", 50% of whose people are unemployed, 84% of whom live below the poverty line, and where the World Bank estimates that 46% of its public service workers (half those with jobs) have insufficient food.

The impending collapse of Gaza could be a recruiting ground for terrorism greater than anything we have seen yet. Urgent representations by the UK government and the EU must be made to put the Gaza disaster at the top of the Annapolis agenda.

I have no time for Hamas, but if that means talks with Hamas on this one issue, so be it. We cannot let 1.4 million people starve.

How can we still talk of a viable Palestinian state living side by side in peace with Israel? The prospect of this, the best hope for a secure and peaceful Israel, fades by the day.

Shirley Williams
Former Lib Dem leader, House of Lords

November 21

Martin Amis is not a racist

A religion is above all else a thought system. Since Islam, like Christianity, has many adherents and makes highly specific, extravagant and supernatural claims about the world, it should expect, in an open society, to be challenged. Ronan Bennett (Shame on us, G2, November 19) insists that because religion is "also about identity, background and culture, and Muslims are overwhelmingly non-white", to criticise this thought system is "Islamophobic", and therefore racist. This is an old ploy, familiar to the extremes of the political left and right, of attempting to close down debate. Seventy years ago, a critic of the Soviet Union could expect to be called a fascist. Something of the same spirit prevails today in relation to Islam, especially in the pages of the Guardian.

Much of what passes for moral guidance in the Bible, especially, but not only, in the Old Testament, appears to me to be morally repugnant. I like to feel free to say so. Similarly, there are firmly held beliefs in "mainstream" Islam that are questionable. One instance is apostasy. The orthodox view appears

children's addresses for December 24 ...

Celia Weber
Reading, Berkshire

November 26

Last week you included a magazine (November 23) devoted to promoting "discovery moto tours ... Luxury Guided 4x4 Adventures". It describes an "unforget-table adventure into Burma, giving us the chance to experience this country annexed from the world for so long. Enjoy a massage and delicious food on the terrace back at our hotel." Indeed, while enjoying that massage and the delicious food, the adventurous tourist can reflect on the fact that much of Burma's tourism was built with forced labour, including child slaves, whom I filmed. I also filmed the elected leader of Burma, Aung San Suu Kyi, now imprisoned in her home by a murderous military regime, appealing to tourists not to come to Burma until its people were free. Guardian readers, and the Burmese people, deserve better than lousy, immoral advertising.

John Pilger
London

November 26

Now that Neil Diamond has declared his inspiration for penning his hit song Sweet Caroline (Report, November 21), will he also reveal who Cracklin' Rosie was? She sounds a lot more fun!

Ian Joyce
Milton Keynes,
Buckinghamshire

November 27

In 1988 a letter in the Guardian led to the formation of a pressure group called Abbey Members

to be that men and women who turn away from their religion are guilty of a serious thought crime. Recommended punishments range from ostracism to death. There are numerous websites now on which courageous ex-Muslims across the Middle East, Pakistan and Bangladesh correspond with each other in secret. The dominant emotion is fear of being discovered. Such a dispensation appears to me to be an offence to rational inquiry and free thinking. To say so, Mr Bennett, is not to be a racist, but to exercise the gift of consciousness and the privilege of liberty.

I've known Martin Amis for almost 35 years, and he's no racist. When you ask a novelist or a poet his or her view of the world, you do not get a politician's or a sociologist's answer. You may not like what you hear, but reasoned debate is the appropriate response, not vilification by means of overheated writing, an ugly defamatory graphic, and inflated, hysterical pull-quotes. I wonder whether Ronan Bennett would care to expend so much of his rhetorical might excoriating at similar length the thugs who murdered – in the name of their religion – their fellow citizens in London in 2005.

Ian McEwan
London

November 22

Amis & McEwan: speaking truth or stereotyping?

Ian McEwan's defence of his friend Martin Amis (Letters, November 21) rests on two arguments, which are conflated. The first is the freedom of speech argument. But just because one has the right to express an opinion does not mean it is right to express it. In any case, Ronan Bennett's article (Shame on us, G2, November 19) did not argue that one should not criticise Islam or Muslims per se; rather, it was the manner of the criticism — sweeping generalisations and stereotypes, holding all Muslims responsible for the opinions and actions of just some — that he found objectionable, and rightly so.

To excuse those generalisations, McEwan cites views on apostasy which he says are both "morally repugnant" and "mainstream". But just because something is "in" a religion doesn't mean it is mainstream. Christians and Jews are not assumed to be selling their daughters into slavery, even though that is in the Old Testament, and neither are mainstream Muslims necessarily baying for the blood of coreligionists who turn away from their faith. There are indeed some Muslims — perhaps even many — who agree with the "repugnant" views on apostasy, but there are also many Muslims who are not particularly religious, or have lost their faith, living quite happily within Muslim communities and societies.

McEwan's logic would have us believe that a non-religious or secularised Muslim is an impossibility for fear of the repercussions — an Orwellian vision of a totalitarian Islam that is itself a stereotype. In defending his friend, he merely confirms that both of them do not really know what they are talking about.

Dr Anshuman Mondal
Brunel University

• Despite his strong words, Amis did what every writer is honour bound to do — speak the truth as one sees it. Immigrants like myself who have come to the west to escape the often violent

Against Flotation. Our purpose was to argue against building societies becoming banks. We said that, if they did, at best they would be taken over by foreign banks (the Abbey is now Spanish-owned) or at worst, they would collapse (Revealed: massive hole in Northern Rock's assets, November 23). We were generally derided as being naive.

Andy Lewis
Brentford, Middlesex

November 27
As well as carp, Poles eat and fish for perch (Report, November 26). And if you don't find the idea of Poles using rods to catch perch funny then you've been using the metric system for too long.

Chris Parkins
Stanmore, Middlesex

November 27
Neil Diamond's
Cracklin' Rosie is not
a woman, it is a wine
(Letters, November
26). It is the story
of life on a Native
American reservation
where there were not
enough women to go
round, so the unlucky
men had to make do
with booze — "a store-
bought woman".

Sandy Guthrie
Amberley, West Sussex

November 28
Any chance of free
wrapping paper this
year? Our tree goes up
next weekend.

Teresa Hewitt
Cheltenham,
Gloucestershire

November 29
Your splendid tribute
to the retiring French
ambassador (In praise
of… Gérard Errera,
November 28) might
have added a sentence
in praise of Mme
Virginie Errera. Her

homophobia and misogyny — often backed by
the state — will never stop speaking out. As a gay
Indian man, I face threats where I live every day —
largely from religious immigrant groups. To speak
out against these cultures and religions is not a
test of "racism" or painting "broad brush strokes",
as Ronan Bennett suggests, but a test of our truly
liberal society — something millions of people like
me have not been able to do in our native lands.
The reason why Burmese, Zimbabweans, secular
Muslims and gay Indians make Britain our home
is because it lets us be ourselves and speak out — as
Amis has — about the wrongness of illogical belief
sponsoring violence.

Sorab Shroff
London

November 28

Setting the boundaries on freedom of speech

It was astonishing to see Max Hastings describe
David Irving as "an energetic and original researcher,
whose findings are not always perverted", not
least because he goes on to call Irving, correctly,
"a spokesperson for the Nazi regime" (Students
need to know what sort of dangerous people are
out there, November 26). The judgment against
Irving in his libel case against Deborah Lipstadt in
2000 set out proof that it was precisely Irving's self-
appointed role as Nazi propagandist that led to the
systematic distortion of history and rendered his
version of the past utterly unreliable.

All the Oxford Union has done is give Irving
more publicity and assisted his phoney campaign
to become a martyr to free speech. For, apart from
defending the reputation of a totalitarian regime

and its murderous Führer, Irving has himself tried to suppress criticism of his views. That was the purpose of his self-destructive libel case against Lipstadt. A few weeks ago he threatened the Jewish Chronicle with legal action if it described him as a Holocaust denier. Thanks to the internet there is no need for prestige institutions like the Oxford Union to give platforms for hate-mongers to prove that free speech is alive and well. As for the "nuggets" of history unearthed by Irving, which Hastings so values, they are turned into false gold by the sludge of toxic lies in which he buries them.

David Cesarani
Royal Holloway, University of London

November 29

A bear called Muhammad is no blasphemy

As an alumnus of Unity high school in Khartoum, I am saddened by the shameful treatment of Gillian Gibbons ('My name is Muhammad'—school project leaves British teacher facing 40 lashes, November 27). Unity is the best school in the city, and has stayed true to its founding principles of academic scholarship and a deep respect for other cultures and religions — important in a country as divided as Sudan. This incident exemplifies the degeneration of the country into one in which tolerance and the pursuit of knowledge have no place, and where religious zealotry, corruption and greed are the only currency. Central to the charges against Gibbons are accusations of blasphemy on the grounds of idolatry. In the time of early Islam, the restrictions on religious idolatry were seen as a key part of the prophet's crusade against the *jahiliyya*

beauty, charm and intelligence have contributed much to his mission. In this respect M Errera has surely been one up on Talleyrand in whose footsteps, as you point out, he has followed.

Antonia Fraser
London

November 30
It is a sad loss to the smirking franco-phobe in us all that French tourists no longer disembark the Eurostar at Waterloo. If only the archi-tects of St Pancras International had installed, rather than a champagne bar, a gin court.

Alice Claire
Norwich

November 30
Did Teresa Hewitt (Letters, November 28) throw away the Great Modern Buildings series? There's enough

paper there to wrap a
sleigh.

Michelle Gibson
Balsham, Cambridgeshire

November 30
We have been saving
your Eyewitness centre
spreads all year and
have no need to buy
any wrapping paper
this year.

Tony Gregson
Little Somerford, Wiltshire

November 24
I was disappointed to
see Poland omitted
from your list of
"who to support next
summer". With over
1 million of us from
various waves of immi-
gration living happily
here, it's quite clear
that the only team to
follow are the initia-
tors of the now great
tradition of knocking
England out of major
tournaments.

Jan Wiczkowski
Manchester

(forces of ignorance). With the coming to power
of the military dictatorship, widely acknowledged
to be a front for Islamic fundamentalists, Sudan
entered its own *jahiliyya*, and the repercussions
have been the detention, torture and harassment
of its citizens, the prolongation of the war in the
south, and the ethnic genocide in Darfur.

Dr Halima Izzeldin Ali Amer
London

November 30
Diana inquest

Jon Henley scoffs that little has come out of the
Diana inquests that isn't already known (Shortcuts,
G2, November 28). I wonder if he's bothered
to listen to the evidence. For it's now emerged
that those connected with the security services
were in fact reporting on Diana's movements
in 1997, despite denials over the last 10 years.
Diana suspected this and frequently changed her
phone number. The jury's heard how shocking the
paparazzi's behaviour was on the night. We know
how celebrities like Kate Middleton and Prince
William are pursued, and the inquests provide a
valuable chance to address this issue. And it took
the coroner's own expert to debunk the myth
that the French did all they could to save Diana. A
"window of opportunity" was missed where Diana
could have been taken to hospital. What of the
British police's multimillion-pound investigation
involving "12 experts" now?

Katharine Witty
Director of press and public affairs, Mohamed Al Fayed

December 2007

Two former prime ministers were at the centre of the news. In Pakistan, the grudging retreat to a full restoration of democracy by President Musharraf was marred by tragedy as Benazir Bhutto was killed in a bomb attack during an election campaign that would almost certainly have restored her to power. At home, Tony Blair's long-expected conversion to Catholicism was not received well by all his new coreligionists. One letter writer compared him with Thomas More, who rejected the wishes of his secular king (read Bush) to obey the Pope, while Blair ignored the present Pope's opposition to the war in Iraq; Bruce Kent's invoking of the penalties imposed after the battle of Soissons in AD923 also showed that memories can be as long in religion as in politics. The already beleaguered Brown government came under attack on civil liberties and reform (aka privatisation) in the health service. But the writer Harold Pinter's letters were saved for the nation at the British Library, prompting another prolific epistolarian, Keith Flett, to call for a permanent display of historic and notable correspondence. The modernist composer Stockhausen died just as his stock was rising again, while football fans hoped that Tommy Cooper lookalike Fabio Capello would be more on song than his unlamented predecessor as England manager, Steve McClaren. As Christmas loomed, readers discussed the storage possibilities of the tubes in which malt whiskies are sold.

December 1

Paul Simons may be
right to cite the hallu-
cinogenic effects of fly
agaric as the cause of
shamans seeing flying
reindeer (Plantwatch,
November 28). But
its colouration is
not responsible for
Santa Claus's mytho-
logical red suit. Santa's
apparel was originally
green; Coca-Cola
changed it to red in
the 1930s to match its
corporate colours for
an ad campaign.

Martyn Smith
Aberdare, Mid Glamorgan

December 3

The myth that Father
Christmas is a fly agaric
mushroom in disguise
(Letters, December 1)
is an urban one, most
probably started by the
poet Robert Graves
in the 1970s. It is true,
however, that the
mushroom's psycho-
active ingredients are
excreted unmetabo-
lised. Consequently, in
Siberia, the less wealthy

December 1

Labour hobbled by Brown's lack of vision

I agree with every word Polly Toynbee says,
including her top two priorities for important
themes the government should push hard (Labour
must go on the offensive to get out of this vortex of
failure, November 30). Unfortunately, I'm almost
certain it won't happen.

I've been going through my pile of old Guardians
recently, ready for recycling, and what stands out
is a plea made over and over, by Toynbee, Jackie
Ashley and others, for Gordon Brown to show
some leadership and vision, to show us what he
passionately believes in. But he hasn't; the best
we've had is a few fine speeches (like the one on
climate change), which are contradicted within
days by other announcements (in this case plans
to expand Heathrow).

There's no vision, no attempt to work out how
policies fit together, no recognition that hard choices
have to be made. Toynbee correctly identifies the
causes of this craven timidity, including "endless
appeasement of Murdoch and the Daily Mail". This
has become such an ingrained habit that I doubt
Brown is capable of changing. It's a tragedy; we
could have had a great government.

Richard Barnes
Windermere, Cumbria

December 1

Democracy in action in Venezuela

We believe that the lives of millions of Venezuelans
have been transformed by the progressive social and
democratic policies of Hugo Chávez's government.

Extreme poverty has been halved, illiteracy nearly eliminated, participation in education has more than doubled and free basic healthcare extended to nearly 20 million people. Unemployment has fallen to a historic low.

The constitution introduced by President Chávez, approved by Venezuelans in a referendum, is one of the most democratic in the world and enshrines rights of previously excluded and minority groups. An emphasis on social inclusion has improved the position of women and Venezuela's black, mixed-race and indigenous majority.

Venezuela's government has directly promoted participatory democracy through community councils, urban land committees and other local bodies. President Chávez's sweeping social, political and economic agenda has been endorsed by Venezuelans in 11 democratic elections that have been consistently judged free and fair by international observers. Tomorrow the Venezuelan people will once again be called on to vote on a series of reforms to the 1999 constitution proposed by President Chávez (Chávez forced to battle for long-term future, November 29).

Venezuela is one of the few countries in the world where both the constitution and any revisions to it must be approved by a majority of citizens in a national referendum. We call on the international community to respect the outcome of the coming referendum and support the sovereign and democratic right of the Venezuelan people to self-determination.

Ken Livingstone, Colin Burgon MP Chair, Labour Friends of Venezuela, **Jon Cruddas MP** Treasurer, Labour Friends of Venezuela, **Harold Pinter, Tony Benn, Ken Loach, Diane Abbott MP, Lembit Opik MP, Caroline Lucas MEP, Billy Hayes** General secretary, CWU, **Lee Jasper and 43 others**

would drink the urine of the wealthy, a rare example of a trickle-down effect that works.

Dr Andy Letcher
Author, Shroom: A Cultural History of the Magic Mushroom

December 3
We always greet the Osborne bulls with cries of "toro!" when driving through Spain, but are even more delighted when we spot the Tio Pepe bottle (Bulls mark 50 years of roadside ads, November 26) – apparently there are only seven left in Spain.

Lynne Armstrong
Brixham, Devon

December 3
First baking every day, now Christmas recipes and handicrafts (Make your own presents, December 1). What is this, Woman's Weekly?

Ann Caldwell
Edinburgh

December 4

Chris Mullin is entitled to assert that Lord Bridge of Harwich (Obituaries, November 28), when presiding over the trial of the Birmingham Six in 1975, overbore in displaying hostility towards the defence. But what Mullin overlooks is the fact that there were seven defendants on trial for the two bombings of the public houses in Birmingham. The jury acquitted the seventh defendant, which might suggest that the jurors exhibited a degree of independence of mind from that of the judge.

Louis Blom-Cooper QC
London

December 4

A red-suited Santa (Letters, December 1) was first sighted on a Christmas card in 1885, and the New York Times reported on November 27 1927

December 3

Broader studies of GM's effects needed

GM is invasive and, if allowed to develop freely, will deny alternative choices for ever to those who wish to avoid it (Brown must embrace GM crops to head off food crisis — chief scientist, November 28). I remain doubtful that such a fundamental step should ever be taken, and it certainly should not be without thorough empirical evidence of safety to human and animal health and to the environment. Such evidence needs to be painstakingly accumulated over a long period. It cannot be rushed. The suggestion by some, who should know better, that the absence of legal challenge in the US over a 10-year period is evidence of GM's safety to humans is puerile. How can members of the public be expected to challenge the biotech companies in the absence of sound epidemiological evidence on the effect of GM in humans? Such research does not exist because neither the US government nor the biotech companies have wanted it.

Dino Adriano
Former chief executive, J Sainsbury plc

December 3

Cross-fertilisation in music is not so revolutionary

Trumpeter Hugh Masekela and conductor Gustavo Dudamel are indeed brilliant performers. Simon Jenkins, though, seems to believe that such experiences began with concerts like Dudamel's during the summer or Masekela's this week, and that they are somehow new phenomena (These nights of exhilarating live performance are reinventing music, December 1). In fact that's what live music has always has been like; it can disappoint, frustrate, bore — but can also uplift and inspire. There's an element of unpredictability that any concertgoer has to accept. The idea that thrilling, mind-expanding experiences are only to be had from recent "crossover" enterprises is way off-beam too; throughout history music has always been cross-fertilising and reinventing itself. That's one of its essential features, whether seen, to take two examples, in the Middle Eastern influences that swept through Europe in the wake of the crusades, or in the discovery of jazz by musicians everywhere in the 1920s and 30s. Celebrate special occasions, Simon, by all means, but don't assume that all the concerts you didn't get to were boring, meaningless rituals.

Gwyn Parry-Jones
Stratfield Mortimer, Berkshire

December 4

Loneliness and care for older people

I have to smile when I see in John Carvel's article that "the ICM poll found 40% of Britons fear being lonely in their old age" (Prospect of moving to a care home frightens two thirds of Britons, December 3). You see, at the age of 81, I am the sole carer for my 54-year-old autistic, insulin-dependent diabetic, asthmatic, learning-difficulties son, who lives with me. I love him to bits, but the continuous years of strain and the fact that more and more cutbacks means that there is even less help available than ever makes me wish I could have the opportunity at times to be lonely!

Barbara MacArthur
Cardiff

that "A standardized Santa Claus appears to New York children. Height, weight, stature are almost exactly standardized, as are the red garments, the hood and the white whiskers."

Mark Williams
Oxford

December 4

So "Taxpayers' support for Northern Rock soars to £30bn" (November 30). I think we ought to start queueing to get our money back.

Rev Ron Forster
Morpeth, Northumberland

December 5

Thank you for the gift wrap with the name Jesus Christ all over it (December 3). We buy the Guardian for its liberal content, not to have religion rammed down our throats.

Fr Ed Hone and
Fr Michael Henesy
St Patrick's, Edinburgh

December 5

So Mark Wallinger
has been awarded
the Turner prize for
"his meticulous re-
creation of Brian Haw's
anti-war protest"
(Report, December
4). Why doesn't Brian
Haw get the prize?

Peter Johnson
Ilkley, West Yorkshire

December 6

Sarah Churchwell
(High noon for Belle
Starr, December 4) is
wrong to condemn
The Outlaw Josey
Wales because it seems
"as if the female popu-
lation of the old west
consisted entirely of
prostitutes". Its leading
female characters are
a sturdy Christian
pioneer grandmother,
her shy granddaughter
and a feisty Native
American rape victim.
Other Clint Eastwood
westerns also have
strong, complex female
characters; while
Unforgiven was about
prostitutes, it is in a

December 5

The value of fifth columnists

If Mark Thomas's friend was a spy for BAE (G2,
December 4), it would seem his work for the
Campaign Against Arms Trade far outweighed
the value of what he did for his paymasters. It was
ever thus. MI5's spies in the Communist party
generally sold more Daily Workers and distributed
more leaflets than your average party member.

Chris Birch
London

December 8

Return on parental investment

As any prudent would-be parent would do, I carried
out 10 years ago the in-depth financial appraisal
that the proposed child-creation project warranted
(Lifetime cost of bringing up child £186,000 – and
rising, December 7). My spreadsheet forecast a
massive household cash inflow in the early years
of the investment. No more long-haul holidays,
theatre tickets, restaurant bills and other singleton
expenses; clothes bills plummet. And in 2027, the
year I have a 25% chance of incipient dementia,
the investment begins to pay off in a serious way.
Without a child, taxi services, shopping, defrosting
the fridge and tax returns are all chargeable at full
labour cost. With the investment, the grown-up
child will do it all for free. Over a five-decade span,
the investment is profitable. And by the way, you
get the conversation, the company and the sheer
fun of it thrown in for free.

Adam Somerset
Aberaeron, Dyfed

December 8

How Coca-Cola saw red over Santa

Mark Williams is not right to say "a red-suited Santa was first sighted on a Christmas card in 1885" (Letters, December 4). I have a number of earlier cards in my collection showing a red-suited Santa. One printed in London by Goodalls was sent in 1866. However, Martyn Smith (Letters, December 1) is right to draw attention to Coca-Cola's use of Santa Claus in its ad campaigns of the 1930s. Their depiction of a jolly rotund figure has now become the accepted standard, but he is wrong that the apparel was originally green.

Up to the 1920s Santa Claus was sometimes shown wearing green, but also white, blue and brown, but most frequently, throughout the late Victorian period, it was red. Coca-Cola banished the other colours for ever, together with the birching rod tucked into his belt that sometimes appears on Victorian scraps. This bound bundle of birch twigs was reserved for those who could not answer truthfully his question "Have you been a good child this past year?" We have forgotten that his presents are only reward for good behaviour and his rod was for naughty children.

David Groen
Enfield, Middlesex

December 8

Dora's V2 survivors

Your article on the V2 (Nazi rocket scientist's secret papers up for sale, December 4) omitted to mention that production was moved from Peenemünde to the concentration camp of

context of self-help and collective action.

John Post
Castletownbere, Cork

December 6
If Arthur Duckett (Eyewitness, December 5) really is an animal technician rather than a cowman, what has he got in that portable equipment carrier that looks like a bucket?

Dudley Ward
Lewes, East Sussex

December 7
Simon Hoggart's obsession with what I wear is beginning to display disturbingly fetishistic tendencies. His latest description of my clothes (Sketch, December 5) worryingly demonstrates that he requires urgent assistance not only from a psychiatrist but from an optometrist. He writes that my suit was puce and my socks lavender. Both in fact were brown. My shirt

was not gingham, as he says, but cotton. As for Hoggart's own clothes, it really is time that you hiked his pay so that he can afford something other than his present Oxfam rejects. Or are his outfits what the stylists call retro?

Gerald Kaufman MP
Lab, Manchester Gorton

December 7

So dogs can distinguish photos of other dogs from landscapes, prodding with their noses to correctly choose the dogs 72% to 80% of the time. If the experiment had used a photo of a certain part of the dog's anatomy – the part that looks like a pencil sharpener – I'm sure the score would have been 100%.

Jim Parry
Crosby, Merseyside

December 8

Joe Cohen, CEO of secondary ticketing site

Dora, a satellite of Buchenwald, in 1943, after British bombers destroyed the research base at Peenemünde. V2s were made by slave prisoners in appalling conditions in Dora, a unique camp created to served the Nazi war machine; 20,000 died between 1943 and 1945. Dora's survivors are angry that little is said about the camp because of the association with US space exploration. Von Braun and other Nazi engineers should never have been allowed to go to the US. They should have remained in Germany to be tried. Contrary to what Catherine Williamson of Bonham's might think, there is nothing great about Von Braun's career – it is based on the deaths of thousands of prisoners.

Françoise Dupré
London

December 10

Car companies support Bali talks

As CEOs of auto companies and board members of the European Automobile Manufacturers' Association, we write to support the talks on climate change in Bali this week (We would be fools to banish global business from the great climate battle, December 5). Governments must embrace sound measures to follow Kyoto. Any such package will shape the framework in which our industry will make its contribution to carbon reduction. We are proud of our achievements in reducing greenhouse gas emissions from our vehicles. We shall be all the more successful if we can develop a partnership with policymakers based on a common vision of what our industry can achieve, how this could be enhanced by other policies and in what timeframe. Coherent public policies would, for example, encourage consumers to choose vehicles with carbon-lowering technologies.

Much of the €20bn we spend every year on research and development is dedicated to vehicles that emit less CO_2 and will ultimately function wholly or largely without fossil fuels. We do this without losing sight of other important needs, such as increasing road safety, improving air quality and continued employment for the millions of workers in the automotive industry. In a framework that will enable us to sustain and increase research and development, we can say with confidence that our industry will meet the expectations of our customers and the societies in which we operate.

Norbert Reithofer BMW Group, **Wendelin Wiedeking** Porsche, **Aad L Goudriaan** Daf Trucks, **Christian Streiff** PSA Peugeot Citroen, **Dieter Zetsche** Daimler, **Carlos Ghosn** Renault, **Sergio Marchionne** Fiat Group, **Leif Oestling** Scania, **Lewis Booth** Ford, **Martin Winterkorn** Volkswagen, **Carl Peter Forster** General Motors, **Leif Johansson** Volvo, **Hakan Samuelsson** Man

December 10

Keeping Khartoum under pressure

Robert Booth's excellent report from Darfur (No money, not enough food, rampant sickness, night-time raids. Darfur today, December 7) should perhaps have explained that the delegation he accompanied, "led" by me and Michael Howard, was in fact arranged by the Anglo-Arab Organisation, which invited the parliamentarians. It was both a fact-finding and a goodwill visit. We were much relieved that Gillian Gibbons was

Seatwave, claims the 400 artists and 50,000 songwriters behind the Resale Rights Society fighting for the rights of consumers and performers are a "bunch of pigs at the trough" (Bands want slice of profit from resold gig tickets, December 5). The real "pigs at the trough" are the venture capitalist-backed operators like Cohen, trying to make a fast buck out of musicians without giving anything back to the people who invest in and create concerts in the first place.

Jazz Summers
Chairman,
Music Managers Forum

December 8
Ellen MacArthur sails round the world and is made a dame. John Darwin, in his late 50s, spends five years canoeing to Panama and back and gets arrested (Report,

December 5). Where's the justice?

Daniel Tarpey
Manchester

December 8
Darwin's story disbelieved? Haven't we been here before?

Murray Gray
Harleston, Norfolk

December 10
I fear that Jim Parry may be looking at the wrong part of the dog (Letters, December 7). As a practising vet, I suggest that the part that looks like a pencil sharpener would probably be less interesting to a dog than the bit that looks like a sharpened pencil.

Christopher Chesney
Tiverton, Devon

December 11
Ivan Hewett suggests that Karlheinz Stockhausen (Obituary, December 8) became a marginal figure in

released the day we arrived, thus clearing that matter out of the way.

We were disturbed at the lack of progress in establishing the stronger UN/AU peacekeeping force agreed for Darfur and questioned President Omar al-Bashir on three points: on the objections to Norwegian and Swedish units participating we found his arguments groundless and tried to persuade him and the parliamentarians we met that they should lift their objections. On the 6pm flights curfew the president maintained this was a matter for local governors in Darfur but agreed to relay our concerns that this was limiting the AU forces in maintaining security; and on the delays in releasing equipment from Port Sudan he put this down to bureaucracy and agreed to try to improve this.

A further matter that we learned from the aid agencies was the time-consuming bureaucracy in dealing with repeated short-term visa applications. On these issues the Sudanese government will be judged, but we would not all agree with Michael's assertion to your reporter that they are deliberately hampering the efforts of the peacekeepers. We must certainly keep up the pressure on the government to assist security and a return to normality in the Darfur region.

David Steel
Lib Dem, House of Lords

December 12
Coming out – or not

Justine Hankins should mind her own business and leave Jodie Foster to mind hers (Congratulations on coming out, Jodie. Why did it take so long?,

Shortcuts, G2, December 11). A statement of thanks to a person one considers beautiful hardly amounts to a coming-out statement. Jodie Foster did not have to come out at all, and non-celebrity lesbians and gay men do not have to do it every time they meet someone new. They always have the option to remain silent about deeply personal matters and in so doing maintain their privacy.

If gays need a role model, they had one in Jodie Foster, who was "famously protective of her privacy". Why should we wish to raise lesbian visibility? Most people have no interest in anyone else's sexuality. Straight people do not assume that everyone else is heterosexual; they assume that it is none of their business. I dare say that that is true for lesbians and homosexuals too.

Ron Warner
Uttoxeter, Staffordshire

December 13
DNA, liberty and justice

In her libertarian cri de coeur, Natasha Walter condemns the power of the government to keep a permanent DNA database of everyone who has ever been arrested (The liberties stripped from the weak today could be lost to us all tomorrow, December 10).

On the contrary, I believe our liberties would be enhanced by a universal DNA database of all citizens, but one which is administered by an authority entirely independent of government.

DNA has been proved to reduce the risks of miscarriages of justice that have been a blot on our criminal-justice scene. One need look no further than the case of Lesley Molseed, for whose

the last 25 years of his life. This may have been true within the death-wish milieu of classical music, but in more dynamic regions the opposite was the case. The sustained diffusion of his ideas, initially through key artists such as Miles Davis, the Beatles and Kraftwerk, means that the Stockhausen influence is evident in our contemporary sound world. Whether we are listening to Wu-Tang Clan, Sparklehorse or Kylie Minogue, we hear significant traces of Stockhausen's innovative genius.

David Toop
London

December 12
Conrad Black "once counted Lady Thatcher, Henry Kissinger and Princess Michael of Kent among his friends" (Relief and defiance: disgraced press baron smiles but a long

reality check awaits, December 11). Says it all, really.

Henry Cleere
Wadhurst, East Sussex

December 13
I've often been stung by a booking fee (Letters, December 12)!

Doug Meredith
Manchester

December 14
This week: a Led Zeppelin concert; "Legs" Larry Smith and Maddy Prior on Radio 4; a Kremlin clampdown on the British Council. Have I woken up in 1973? Am I mad, in a coma, or back in time?

David Hall
London

December 15
Our football managers are crap, our footballers are crap, our politicians, civil servants and bankers are crap. But when the

murder in 1976 Stefan Kiszko, an innocent man, was convicted and served 14 years in prison, dying two years after his release. It was only a month ago that DNA evidence resulted in the conviction of the true offender.

Benedict Birnberg
London

December 14

How Spies for Peace burgled RSG-6

Richard Kirkwood (Letters, December 13) says that "Spies for Peace did not break in to a nuclear bunker" and that "the nearest thing to a break-in came when a few hundred of us staged a sit-down outside the RSG near Wargrave". He is wrong. In February 1963 a group of peace campaigners broke into the regional government secret headquarters (RSG-6) that lay at the east end of Warren Row, a village near Reading. We did so on two occasions: the first time we found the doors that led through a boiler room to the underground office complex unlocked, the second time we picked the lock.

The second time, we took photographs and traced maps and copied documents, which formed the basis of the pamphlet to which Kirkwood refers. These documents included the telephone numbers of RSG staff, which may be why Kirkwood prefers to believe that the information was given to us by telephone staff. The pamphlet was typed and duplicated in secret and then sent out to press, MPs and protesters on Wednesday April 10 1963.

After the huge success of that original break-in, which became front-page news and which started the gradual process of the dismantling of the civil defence system for nuclear war, Spies for Peace and others did go on to break into other government buildings, but without so much success.

All of the Spies for Peace who are still alive keep our identities secret. At the time, the Sunday Telegraph speculated that "It would not be surprising if investigation does not bring to light a shrewd political mind directing this brilliant subversive operation." But Nicolas Walter told the real story straightforwardly in an anonymous article in the anarchist periodical The Raven in 1988, which formed the basis of an essay by Natasha Walter in the New Statesman in May 2002, for which she also interviewed some of the spies. The facts are available for those who wish to seek them.

Name and address supplied

December 15

Why it was right for Jodie to come out

Ron Warner (Letters, December 12) is deluded when he says that straight people "do not assume everyone is heterosexual". Whenever I meet new people — students, work colleagues or in social situations — I am regularly asked: "What does your husband do?" And these are not, on the whole, bigots. Once they are told of my partner and can fit me into a box, they are fine, although woefully ignorant; the most common reaction when my partner and I had a civil partnership after 30 years was: "What made you wait so long?" Ron Warner's letter shows why we need lesbians like Jodie Foster to come out.

Jane E Shutt
Scarborough, East Yorkshire

immensely successful Fabio Capello offers to manage one of our national sides (Sport, December 14), some of us turn our noses up because he's Italian. I'm for more of them. If we had a Swede for prime minister we wouldn't do idiotic invasions. German civil servants wouldn't be as likely to lose our personal data, Dutch bankers might not offer 125% mortgages to people who can't afford the payments, French footballers might win occasion- ally. I could go on.

Peter Nicklin
Newcastle upon Tyne

December 15
While the purchase by the British Library of Harold Pinter's letters is welcome (Report, December 12), it may be hoped this will be the spur to get the library to provide permanent exhibition space for a selection of

letters from the great, the good and not so good that it has stored away in its basements.

Keith Flett
London

December 17
Although never having been stung by a booking fee (Letters, December 12), I did have a friend who called her daughter's kitten (are you there, Blue Peter?) Cookie — short for cooking fat.

Carole Underwood
Kendal, Cumbria

December 18
I was surprised to read of the size of the new England manager's back-up team (Sport, December 15), as I thought a Capello would have been unaccompanied.

Ian Kinley
Kendal, Cumbria

December 18
I'm sure he can put

December 15
Cadbury job losses

Your article (Cadbury Schweppes beats targets as sales of chocolates recover, December 12) made only passing reference to the decision to close the Keynsham plant with a loss of 500 jobs and move production to Poland. In the not too distant past, the loss of so many jobs in one small community would have been front-page news. The communitarian-minded Quakers who founded Cadbury's provided not only employment but also housing, as in the model village at Bournville. About 97% of the chocolate made at Keynsham — where the world's first chocolate bar was made — is consumed in the UK. Moving production to Poland will add 1,500 food miles to every bar sold. Shame on the directors for straying so far from the founding fathers' vision and on you for not picking up on the human aspect to this "business success".

Christopher Orlik
Bristol

December 17
Our Big Brother on wheels

I have been following Anita Sethi's articles with interest (End of the road for the OzBus after 84 days of mishaps and mayhem, December 10), as I too was on OzBus 1 (my blog is at www.travelblog. org). I am on a world tour and my reason for travelling overland was because as well as wanting to visit the major sites, which anyone can see by plane-hopping, I wanted to see the terrain gradually change over the miles, and see ordinary people in villages and remote areas in between the tourist spots.

Before I joined OzBus, I thought it would be like Big Brother on wheels — and to an extent it was, in that we quickly became institutionalised and felt like a family. Unlike Big Brother, we worked as a team, sharing experiences, equipment, clothes and shampoo, and this is where my experience differs radically from Anita's. For me, and many others, being part of the group was one of the important aspects, and we feel friendships have been formed that will last; common experiences — either enjoyable or frustrating — bind us, and the disparities in ages and backgrounds are sunk in the community of OzBus 1 — the pathfinders.

There were minor frictions and some venting of frustrations (not surprising with 39 people cloistered in a bus for 12 weeks), but on the whole the group dealt with these by a quick outburst followed by calm discussion, which meant that relationships improved and tolerance increased. On this type of trip it's important to be open-minded, tolerant and a team player. For the 20 or so still in Sydney now, our friendship grows and we are planning our "orphans' Christmas" with cooperation and glee.

Jennie Hawley
Sydney

December 18

Business journalism is not for nerds

Peter Wilby is an observant commentator but his dismissal of business editors who become editors as "nerds" isn't very fair (How journalism's nerds became masters of the universe, Media, December

some magic back into the beautiful game, as Fabio Capello is clearly the offspring of the late Tommy Cooper. I'm expecting all England's woes to be fixed just like that.

Ian Hall
Chipping Norton,
Oxfordshire

December 19
Potential strike action by the police (Report, December 12) presents both political and practical difficulties. How could lawful picketing be ensured without the police present to enforce it? Using the army may present the most practical option, but might we ask the miners to help out?

Sid Hilton
Lewes, East Sussex

December 20
How many remember ice on bedroom windows (Letters, December 18)? Last Wednesday morning,

since you ask. Who
heats their bedrooms
in this age of climate
change?

Peter Reason
Bath

December 22

Stuart Jeffries conveys
truly that I lost my
rag in talking to him
about an old adver-
sary and about the
question of what it is
for you to be conscious
of the room you're in
(Enemies of thought,
G2, December 21).
Really wish I hadn't.
Elsewhere I didn't.
For the substan-
tive argument about
consciousness, see
www.homepages.ucl.
ac.uk/~uctytho/

Ted Honderich
London

December 22

This seems a good time
of year to ask how
other Guardian readers
recycle cardboard
or metal tubes from
bottles of malt whisky.

17). All the business journalists turned editors who
he lists — Robert Thomson, James Harding, Will
Lewis, Patience Wheatcroft, Will Hutton, Andreas
Whittam Smith and myself — all served time in
many other roles as well as business.

Peter writes about "business" as if it exists
separate from the rest of modern life in its
own space or section. It does not. Like the arts,
science and politics, business is interwoven into
our civilisation, and an understanding of the
capital markets is a huge advantage for any editor.
Moreover, the two biggest recent deals in global
media — Thomson's acquisition of Reuters and
News Corp's purchase of Dow Jones — have been in
the area of financial journalism. Indeed the future
of business journalism is booming.

And what's all this about some of those listed
being bad editors? I'm sure everybody on his list
stands by their editing record and is proud of it. I
certainly am of mine.

David Yelland
London

December 20

Labour and the debate about our liberties

A small point about John Pilger's admirable article
(Left for dead by New Labour, liberal Britain must
urgently fight back, December 18). When he wrote
that in 1995 I celebrated Blair as an almost mystical
politician he is being a little unfair. What I was
saying in the quotation he has dug up is that
Blair presented himself as a harmoniser for all the
opposing interests in British life. Obviously this is a
very different thing from stating that he was that
harmoniser. But Pilger is right in his final message

– we do all need to wake up to what has gone on under New Labour. There have been few more urgent cases for a cross-party protest movement.

Henry Porter
London

December 21

Money is not the motivation for GPs

John Carvel (GPs offered £150m for longer opening times, December 20) describes doctors as "a well-paid profession that works too little and grumbles too much". If one believes that the British Medical Association is the face of British medicine then that view is fair. But many doctors find the BMA's greedy, selfish, petulant, arrogant, pompous, elitist and out-of-touch attitudes increasingly damaging and repellent. The BMA's view is not representative of most doctors. Its leaders are part of an inward-looking club that prefers the self-aggrandising entertainment of medical politics to the serious business of creating a better health service.

Over Christmas and the New Year thousands of health workers will put the welfare of the public before time with their families because they believe in the ideals of the NHS. The commitment they show is not dependent on money, contrary to the impression the BMA conveys. Doctors don't want or need to be offered more money to do a better job. What they want is a government that backs an ethos of science and solidarity among health workers with one guiding purpose – to build a fair, responsive and high-quality health service dedicated to a healthier and more equal society.

Dr Richard Horton
Editor, The Lancet

My father kept his long painting brushes in one. As they are very airtight, we use them for pasta, bombay mix and porridge.

Keith Seacroft
Durham

December 24

I was sorry to see a suggestion (Leaders, December 22) that the possible cancellation of the loans to the Royal Academy's Russian exhibition was politically motivated. In weeks of negotiation with the authorities in Moscow and St Petersburg, there has been no evidence of this. Their concerns have been legal, concerning the robustness of the 1978 State Immunity Act. Now that the government has promised to bring forward new legislation we are confident that these anxieties can be allayed.

Charles Saumarez Smith
Royal Academy

December 24
How times change
when it comes to full
communion with
the Catholic church.
After the battle of
Hastings substan-
tial penances were
imposed on William
the Conqueror's
soldiers by the bishops
at the Council of
Westminster. Even the
archers who fought
at long range and did
not know whether
they had killed anyone
had to do penance
for three successive
Lents. They got off
lightly. After the battle
of Soissons (923) all
those who took part
had a year of excom-
munication, and then
bread and water only,
for three days a week.
Tony Blair has had it
easy.

**Bruce Kent and
Valerie Flessati**
London

December 24
Three days before
Christmas, and our

December 24
Why we need control orders

Gareth Peirce's article (Britain's own Guantánamo, December 21) seriously exaggerates both the use of, and conditions for individuals on, control orders.

The UK faces an unprecedented threat from terrorism and the government's top priority is to protect the public. There are certain individuals who we have strong suspicion are involved in terrorist activity but who we cannot prosecute or, if they are foreign nationals, deport.

Peirce's claim that considerable numbers of people don't know the case against them is simply wrong. We use control orders only in a limited number of carefully selected cases. Fourteen people are currently subject to a control order and none of them is under house arrest. Control order obligations are tailored to the risk posed by the individual concerned.

There are also strong safeguards to protect their rights. For example, where a controlled person cannot see the evidence against them for security reasons, an independent legal representative is appointed who can see the evidence and make representations on their behalf. And each control order is subject to mandatory review by the high court.

The House of Lords recently endorsed the principles of the control order regime, and the independent reviewer of counter-terrorism legislation, Lord Carlile, concluded in his last annual report that control orders remained a necessary and proportionate response to the current threat.

I wish we did not need control orders. Sadly,

given the threat we face and the activities certain individuals are undertaking to harm us, we do.

Tony McNulty MP
Minister for security, counter-terrorism, crime and policing

first snowdrops are already out.

Pete Dorey
Bath, Somerset

December 24

More Christmas myths debunked

How I agree with Polly Toynbee (Sorry to disappoint, but it's nonsense to suggest we want to ban Christmas, December 21). This week I've been to the nativity play at the school that my granddaughter attends. The cast were of many nationalities, as was the audience: a grandad or two in Muslim dress; some mothers in hijabs; one mum veiled; and all joining in. They were not "offended" by witnessing their children taking part. A good time was had by all.

Barbara Bennett
Lancaster

December 27
Congratulations on the very succinct job you did of illustrating your front-page plug for "Everything you need to know about Christmas TV and radio" with a picture of Ken Dodd and Penelope Keith (December 24).

Patrick Dodds
Richmond, Surrey

December 28

The reality of prostitution

Harriet Harman's proposal is just a lingering example of Blairism: eye-catching, ill-defined and its consequences not thought out (Harman calls for prostitution ban, December 21). There are many types of sexual relations where money, goods or services pass from one party to another — marriage for a start — not all of which are surely intended to come under a ban. The law might make an exception for married couples, but that would have to extend to unmarried couples who live together, and then those who do not live together, and then

December 28
David Starkey ought to get his quotation right, if he uses it to criticise the Queen (Report, December 22). Firstly, the remark about culture is attributed to Goering — who may indeed have used it — and not Goebbels, and secondly the originator of it was Hanns Johst in his play Schlageter: "When I hear of

culture, I release the safety catch of my Browning."

Professor Lewis Elton
University of Manchester

December 29

So the new Miss France was photographed "eating yoghurt in a suggestive manner" (Call for Miss France to quit over photos, December 24). Can those of us ignorant of such niceties be fully informed of the consequences via a full-colour spread in your Weekend section?

Sean Gallagher
Ardara, Co Donegal

December 29

Keith Seacroft may have the luxury of recycling the tubes from bottles of malt whisky (Letters, December 22), but poorer mortals have to make do with Pringles crisp containers.

Harry Hawkins
Penrith, Cumbria

those who go out on a date without splitting the costs equally and end up in bed.

All these cases might be excluded on the grounds that the payment to the sexual partner was not specifically for sex, so where one party happens to employ the other as a secretary or a gardener, or hires the other as a yoga teacher or a childminder, there would be no offence. Yet the law would presumably try to include cases where the sexual partner was hired as a masseur or an escort, regarding these as merely covers for sex — a hard line to draw clearly.

Ministers should first decide what the purpose of prohibition is. Sex is not a bad thing, nor is earning one's living, nor is it obvious why the former should not be a means to the latter. The ill effects of prostitution are not intrinsic, but associated with it, and include violence, forms of slavery, illegal immigration and exploitation. However, these are against the law already, except for exploitation — when the prostitute is miserably paid for his or her services. Yet the proposed law would provide legal backing to the customer who leaves without paying.

Anthony Matthew
Leicester

December 29

Catholics are joining the police service

The suggestion that Catholic recruitment to the Police Service of Northern Ireland "remains weak" is not correct (Chuckle Brothers head for White House, December 4). Since 2001, out of 80,460 applicants to the PSNI, 29,571 (36.75%) came from the Catholic community. In the most recent recruitment campaign, in June, 3,294 out of 7,419 applicants were from the Catholic community. And up to the last intake on November 25, out of 2,898 posts, 1,458 members of the Catholic community have been appointed (50.31%).

The Independent Commission on Policing recommended that 50% of recruits appointed to the PSNI should be Catholic and 50% from Protestant and other community backgrounds. This was viewed as a means of making the police service more representative of the community it serves and was subsequently legislated for in the Police (Northern Ireland) Act 2000. It is clear that the PSNI is a positive career choice irrespective of community background. The PSNI is attracting applicants from right across the community and particularly from within the Catholic community.

Professor Sir Desmond Rea
Chairman, Northern Ireland Policing Board

December 29

Pakistan's future after Bhutto

Benazir Bhutto's assassination represents another tragic episode for Pakistan (A tragedy born of military despotism and anarchy, December 28). It is tragic not because she was considered the answer to the country's prayers, but because she was merely the product of another corrupt cause that gave not just her people but indeed the world a false hope.

Bhutto's alleged commitment to the return of democracy in Pakistan was inconsistent with not just her own but her father Zulfiqar Ali Bhutto's record on human rights while they enjoyed power. It is important to remember that her father introduced legislation that to this day

December 29
Any self-respecting homme du monde knows that malt whisky tubes are for storing one's linguine.

Jeff Instone
Eastleigh, Hampshire

December 29
My father bought me your Letters to the Editor 2007 book for Christmas — I suspect primarily to gloat that two of his letters, but none of mine, made the cut.

Georgina Barnes
London

December 31
The world's first cookbook was not by Bartolomeo Scappi (Last night's TV, G2, December 28). The earliest in Europe is that of Apicius, written in the first century, and edited in the fourth. It contains recipes from an earlier Greek work.

Brian Bishop
Leigh-on-Sea, Essex

December 31

On Christmas Day
I opened one more
bottle of wine than was
required. A 35mm film
canister over the neck
resulted in a perfect
bottle two days later.

Brian Clapham
Cobham, Surrey

December 31

My Scottish wife
informs me that the
East Lothian way to
recycle whisky tubes
is to hold knitting
needles (Letters,
December 29).

Graeme Hutton
Sawtry, Cambridgeshire

December 31

My year 10s at Bingley
grammar turn
Pringles tubes (Letters,
December 29) into
pinhole cameras.

Anne Taylor
Otley, West Yorkshire

discriminates against certain religious minorities, bowing to the demands of fanatical clerics that led to the blasphemy laws affecting particularly Christian and Ahmadiyya Muslim communities. Persecution of these groups intensified in the 1970s and killing sprees of their members ever since have mostly gone unpunished. The same occurred during Nawaz Sharif's tenure as prime minister.

Whether or not the elections go ahead, if the PPP or PML ever did return to power, there is little expectation that either party would implement democracy. It is a far cry indeed from Muhammad Ali Jinnah's vision of a tolerant and progressive nation in which peace and prosperity could flourish. For as long as Pakistan remains in the grip of those committed to injustice and oppression, it will continue to be plagued by discord and misery.

Waqar Ahmedi
Birmingham

December 31

Life after politics could be hell for Blair

When Thomas More was forced to choose between his temporal and spiritual ruler, between his king and the pope, he chose the latter – and was martyred. He has become one of the most revered of English saints. When faced with a choice between his temporal and spiritual ruler, between George Bush and a pope who condemned the proposed invasion of Iraq, Tony Blair chose the former. The decision by the Catholic church to admit Blair without a full, public repentance for his acts over Iraq is a case of low standards in high places.

Eoin Dillon
Dublin

January 2008

The US presidential primaries took centre stage, with a battle royal set up between the Democratic favourite Hillary Clinton and her charismatic challenger Barack Obama. The emergence of Obama as frontrunner, and possibly the first African-American president, filled many liberals with new hope after eight years of despair under the Bush presidency. The determination of Clinton supporters to carry on the fight promised a long and potentially divisive campaign. Another election, in Kenya, led to widespread violence after a disputed ballot saw the president re-elected despite a clear parliamentary victory for the opposition. In Afghanistan British troop levels and casualties both increased. One former British official in Iraq called for the policy to be reversed. At home the political funding issue was highlighted as Peter Hain admitted more expenses than originally disclosed in his deputy leadership campaign, while the Tory MP Derek Conway was revealed to have employed his family on his parliamentary expenses. In the growing climate of public dissatisfaction, Peter Mandelson wrote to clarify his famous quote about being relaxed about the "filthy rich". Arthur Scargill turned 70 and the maverick chess genius Bobby Fischer died (and the two were strangely linked on the letters page); Hollywood actor Heath Ledger died of a prescription drug overdose. Readers were enlightened by correspondence about the rights and wrongs of making badger stew.

January 2

My new year resolution is to write letters to the Guardian until I have one published. Could you print this so I might return to the inactivity I enjoyed so much in 2007?

Jonathan Bryant
London

January 3

I offer this recipe for making a pigeon feeder from a Pringles tube (Letters, passim) and a sardine can: people.brunel.ac.uk/~eesridr/feeder.html

Ivan Reid
Uxbridge, Middlesex

January 3

Pringles cans are ideally suited as aerials for wireless computer networks — already legend in geek circles.

Gordon Joly
London

January 4

It may well be tasty,

January 1

Burning issue of what men really want

Tanya Gold's article on speed dating (Men want us lobotomised, December 29), while pointing out the unarguable fact that independent, intelligent women tend to find it difficult to find a date, also clearly highlights that intelligence/educational achievement may not have been the deciding factor in her rejections.

As a gay best friend to a number of highly intelligent, well-educated and beautiful women, I would be reluctant to hang out with someone who introduces the topic of abortion or her 60-hour week, or whose opening lines referred to her PhD in economics. Would Ms Gold have wanted to date a man who made such a potentially alienating first impression? He would sound like a bore, or someone with a chip on his shoulder, or low self-esteem. If she had found a common interest to talk about, maybe shown some interest in his work as an engineer, or shared a good joke with him, he would probably have found her attractive — and then been interested in learning more.

It's not just a question of what you have achieved in your career or your educational attainment that matters — it's simply how you treat other people that will either get you a date or leave you single.

Olly Mead
Bristol

January 3

Winning equal pay in the public sector

Your articles (Councils face £2.8bn bill for equal pay; Fight for equality that could put jobs at risk; A deal under siege, January 3) seem to have missed the point. Globally, capitalism thrives very well on the chronic underpayment of women and children, and yet to assert that we do not have enough resources to pay people equally is absurd. As a species we are excellent at providing for ourselves, but hopeless at doing this in an equitable manner.

Women are yet again being fobbed off and threatened with cuts to other vulnerable people if we assert our rights. This is merely a bullying tactic to preserve the systems of patriarchy. I personally feel that the unions have contributed nothing to furthering equal pay and that they should be challenged. Certain systems will have to crumble and fall for the new to evolve.

Genevieve Smyth
Wallington, Surrey

January 3

1970s reality check

I don't recognise Britain in the 1970s from Jonathan Freedland's description of a country whose infrastructure was shabby, if not falling down (2008 will be a year of decision, January 2). We may indeed have had hospital treatment in old workhouse buildings rather than PFI structures with their magnificent works of modern art, but these old hospitals were at least accessible, being in town centres rather than at the side of ring roads; nursing mothers were not expected to provide their own nappies and towels; and if an ambulance was needed, there was a better than even chance of it turning up within a few minutes. If, like me, you needed a bus to get you to work for 5am, there would be one available, British Rail ran a

but badger casserole is illegal (How to make a perfect casserole, January 2). Under the Protection of Badgers Act 1992 it is an offence to possess a dead badger or any part of a badger. That would seem to include a stew.

Ray Knagg
Bristol

January 4

For the first time in my 12-year experience, we had to arrange the early return home of two children from Germany on the annual school one-week exchange (The helicopter parents have landed, January 3). The mobile phone played a large part in conveying their intolerable homesickness to their parents; it seems to act as an extended umbilical cord and so, to some extent, prevents total participation.

Victoria Paleit
Southmoor, Oxfordshire

January 5

Whisky tubes (Letters, passim) are great for bottles of cooking and olive oils, which always get oily on the outside. Especially good are the wider, squatter tubes of Bunnahabhain.

Mike Sheppard
Ware, Hertfordshire

January 7

I have two kids in secondary education and I get phone calls at work if they misbehave in class (Letters, January 4). If they fail to complete homework on time, I get letters home. If they have even the most minor illness or accident at school, I am contacted and expected to drop everything to pick them up. If they were to truant, I could end up in court or even prison. Do these teachers perhaps get the helicopter parents they deserve?

Chris Rotheram
Cleveleys, Lancashire

system where a single ticket could take a passenger all the way from Penzance to Thurso, and local authorities provided affordable accommodation for people and families in need. Every street corner had a shop on it, so someone running out of bread had no need to use the car.

The 1970s were, it's true, a time of bad fashions and heavy rock. There was no internet or text messaging and there were only three TV stations. But then again, ITV showed World in Action whereas today they have I'm a Celebrity ... Get Me Out of Here! More significantly, in those years a working-class person could afford to do most or all of the following: buy a home, go to university, catch a train, consult a dentist or afford a medical prescription.

For those of us who did go to university in the 70s, it was a time of radical politics, when radical had the opposite meaning to the one it has today – idealism rather than cynicism, and hope for better things in the future. The contrast with the prevailing mood at the beginning of 2008 could hardly be more stark.

Chris Connolly
Chesterfield, Derbyshire

January 4

Stealing wealth and democracy

The horrific massacre of people sheltering in a church in Eldoret (Kenya at breaking point, January 2) is a form of ethnic cleansing brought about by tribal rivalries, but its roots lie in the grotesque and desperate social conditions which make some people commit the most heinous of crimes. A class of kleptocrats, bureaucrats and businessmen have been stealing the wealth of the nation for the last six decades, leaving the vast mass of people to face "nasty, short and brutish" lives.

The rigging of the election was part of the ongoing theft by this class and the Kenyan constitution has been desecrated. In such a situation, the brutal mob displays its insane and obscene behaviour. The causes of the mob's behaviour lie in extreme socio-economic inequalities rather than in tribalism. Kenya is one more example of countries that have wholeheartedly adopted the neoliberal policies of global capitalism, but are wrecked by social disharmony and unhappiness of the majority of the people.

Burjor Avari
Manchester

January 5

Theatre drama becoming a crisis

Last month I wrote an article expressing concern about the Arts Council's decision to downgrade new playwriting in its new theatre review (Theatre audiences deserve the next Ravenhill and Kane, December 13) in favour of "experimental practice", circus and street arts.

There could be no more chilling portent of what this change of policy will mean than the Arts Council's proposal to cut its grant to the Bush Theatre by 40%. From its tiny theatre on Shepherd's Bush Green, the Bush not only presents, tours and transfers new plays by upcoming and established writers (as it has done for over 30 years), but its unique skills and experience enable it regularly to risk putting on playwrights' first plays.

Its literary department reads 1,000 scripts a year

January 7
Catherine Page wonders (Letters, January 5) why the BBC has so many people in the US covering the first skirmishes of their presidential election. I wonder whether the Guardian really needs items on pages 1, 2, 6, 7, 8, 9, 33, 34, 37 and a leader on page 38 on the same subject.

Ron Brewer
Old Buckenham, Norfolk

January 7
The Backstory to the interesting report from Angelique Chrisafis (Academic tug-of-love over De Beauvoir legacy, January 4) was wrong in one respect. In the quoted examination, De Beauvoir came first – Sartre came second.

Geoffrey Robinson MP
Lab, Coventry North West

January 7
Whisky tubes filled

with pebbles make great doorstops (Letters, passim).

Judith Kent
Barnet, Hertfordshire

January 7
Anyone know a way to convert whisky tubes into free weights for the army fitness programme?

Jeff Scott
Brighton, East Sussex

January 8
I was surprised that your list (50 people who could save the planet, Weekend, January 5) didn't include José Mourinho. Saving the planet would be no more than a morning's work for the Special One.

Gary Dickson
Holywood, Co Down

January 8
If Rob Froud (Letters, January 4) needs a whisky tube to store broken wine and

and reports on them to their authors, distributes bursaries, mounts workshops, commissions playwrights. This winter, two Bush plays by unknown writers (Jack Thorne and Abbie Spallen) play off-Broadway. It is this work – the seedcorn of British playwriting in the future – which would be threatened if this proposed cut is implemented.

David Edgar
President, Writers' Guild of Great Britain

January 7

We have no choice – the future must be nuclear

It is unfortunate indeed that a group of academics should seem to be seeking further delay in government actions concerning nuclear energy designed to protect the environment and to deal with forthcoming issues of security and costs of electricity supply (Scientists take on Brown over nuclear plans, January 4).

While we have no brief in defending the present government per se, the urgency of climate change and the projected gap in baseload electricity generation capacity is undoubted, and we applaud attempts to address them. Last year's consultation over the decision to allow companies to build nuclear stations, providing they are prepared to take on the economic and other risks associated with such investment, did seem thorough to those of us who responded. Any consultation must put forward a proposal while allowing opposite views to be put, and in our view the government has fulfilled this.

For baseload power – the irreducible minimum electricity use, which runs to more than 20,000MW in the UK – intermittent sources of power, including most of the renewables, are ineffective. The practical choice is between coal and gas – major producers of greenhouse gases in the absence of carbon capture and storage – or carbon-free nuclear as energy sources. Last week we saw planning permission granted for a new coal-fired power station. A second "dash for gas" is already under way, despite concerns over growing reliance on imports. If new nuclear stations are to be built to replace the second-generation AGR stations expected to come offline from perhaps 2018 onwards then a start to the technology choice, planning and licensing procedures is needed now. The UK's record of rising carbon dioxide emissions over the past decade has been unimpressive; this can only get worse if a major tranche of practically zero-carbon energy is replaced by fossil generation.

Governments are elected to take decisions. In this case the only decision on which consultation has been held is to remove an artificial barrier to one technology – the only technology, alongside large-scale hydropower, with a proven track record in reducing greenhouse gas emissions – and allow companies to choose. If more attractive alternatives really are available then nothing in this consultation will prevent companies from choosing them. There have been two energy white papers in the last five years looking at the wider issues – now it is time to do something about them.

Malcolm Grimston Associate fellow, Chatham House, **Simon Franklin** Director, Imperial College Reactor Centre, **Professor Robin Grimes** Materials dept, Imperial College, **Professor Malcolm Joyce** Engineering dept, Lancaster University, **Dr Gareth Neighbour** Chair, British Carbon Group, **Professor Paul Nolan** Physics dept, Liverpool University, **Dr Paul Norman** Head of physics and technology of nuclear reactors, Birmingham University, **Professor Keith Ross** Institute of Materials Research, Salford

whisky glasses in, is it possible he might be collecting a few more tubes than is strictly good for him?

Jon Collins
Manchester

January 9

We sympathise with Denis Beaumont's discomfort about the Guardian supplying an army fitness programme (Letters, January 7). Perhaps, however, we should be reassured by the booklet's even-handed approach. Many of the exercises finish with the instruction "Swap sides".

Pam Laurance & Ian Saville
London

January 9

Unable to partici-pate in army fitness programme. Still too busy constructing Empire State Building (October 20 2007).

Charlotte Hofton
Ryde, Isle of Wight

January 10

I see that the cover of G2 (January 9) claims that "Britain rules the world in hairdressing". All we need now is the telephone sanitisers to get up to speed and we Brits will be assured of our rightful places on the first starships to explore the galaxy. If only Douglas Adams could have lived to see how prophetic The Hitchhiker's Guide to the Galaxy truly is.

Jim Parry
Crosby, Merseyside

January 10

I suggest a Portaloo for the empty plinth in Trafalgar Square (Report, November 9). It would be useful to the tourists as well as working as a piece of art, in the spirit of Duchamp.

Dave Barrett
Bath

January 8

Defining moment in US politics

The news from America truly is "Good news in bad times", as the headline on Jonathan Raban's article put it (January 5). Obama's win is something the progressives of my generation never expected to see. I grew up in the same south side of Chicago where Obama lives today. Working for black Democratic candidates for Congress and mayor in the 1970s and 80s was no joke. My mother, a few friends and I, among the few white supporters of the late, great mayor Harold Washington in our part of the city, were routinely sent to the all-white neighbourhoods to the west of us, where doors would be slammed in our face, and where one white election official directly confronted me with the words: "Why are you working for a black candidate?"

I hope that Obama's win in Iowa reflects a potential "defining moment" as he calls it. The years of Republican misrule may have been so extreme that this impossible event – the mass support of a progressive black presidential candidate – has become possible.

Rebecca Gumbrell-McCormick
St Albans, Hertfordshire

• Barack Obama may base much of his rhetoric on his local pastor, Jeremiah Wright, but his victory speech in Iowa clearly owes more to sources further afield: "But on this January night, at this defining moment in history ... " and "Years from now, you'll look back and say this was the moment, this was the place where America remembered ... " Ring any bells? "From this day to the ending of the world, but we in it shall be remembered … and gentlemen in England now a-bed shall think themselves accurs'd they were not here … " (Shakespeare, Henry V) and "men will say this was their finest hour" (Churchill) both come to mind. These were also the favourite sources of John F Kennedy – with whom Obama is frequently compared.

Richard Aldwinckle
London

January 10
On New Year's Eve I planted my whisky tube (Letters, passim) in the back garden and set off fireworks from it at midnight.

Roelie Collins
Swansea

January 9
Clear and reasoned case for setting aside nuclear

Our report directly addresses in some detail the spurious argument that there is "no alternative" to nuclear. In fact, the urgent challenge of responding to climate change is actually one of choice. In making these choices, the government has a duty to be open and accountable. Neither it nor nuclear proponents (Letters, January 7) should seek to cloak the issues in alarmist rhetoric about there being "no alternative".

It was suggested that our fears about radioactive wastes presenting a risk in perpetuity are scaremongering and that other countries, notably France, "seem to manage" their wastes quite nicely. The fact is that there is nowhere in the world – not even France – which has yet developed a proven or accepted method for the long-term management of these wastes. New-build would add an undefined and continuing burden of wastes, imposing incalculable risks on specific communities and future generations.

As to whether radiation pollution from nuclear plant is relatively safe or unacceptably risky: a reliable epidemiological study of 41 districts in the

January 11
Could I wish one of Yorkshire's greatest union leaders a happy 70th birthday today? A man who never deserted his principles or his workers, a man voted back by his members as an honorary president of the once-mighty NUM, unlike his adversary, Thatcher, who was stabbed in the back by her so-called loyal disciples. A man ridiculed in 1980 when he told us that the Tories were intent on destroying the coal-fields. Five years later it became a fact and gas and electricity hikes since have proven that it is folly to sit

on billions of tons of unextracted fuel, thus allowing the power barons to charge us whatever they like without so much as a whimper from government. Happy birthday, Arthur.

Terry Palmer
Barnsley

January 12
You quote my comments to California computer executives in 1998 that "we are intensely relaxed about people getting filthy rich" (Leaders, January 11). I do not object to being quoted, as long as I am quoted accurately and in full. What I in fact said on that particular occasion was "as long as they pay their taxes".

Peter Mandelson
EU trade commissioner

January 12
Will police on the pay protest march (Diary, January 10) undercount

vicinity of 16 nuclear power plants in Germany between 1980 and 2003 has established that the risk of tumour or leukaemia in children under five years of age significantly increases the closer they live to a nuclear power plant.

These and other issues — such as problems associated with nuclear fuel supply and manufacture, vulnerability to attack, security and nuclear weapons proliferation, reactor decommissioning, reactor design and siting, energy distribution models and true renewable and energy-efficiency modelling — are addressed in our report.

Taken together, we believe they make a clear and reasoned case for setting aside nuclear responses to climate change in favour of the abundant potential from safer, more secure and more environmentally sustainable alternatives.

Prof Frank Barnaby, Duncan Bayliss, Prof Andy Blowers, Paul Brown, Dr Paul Dorfman, Prof Dave Elliott, Prof Frank Fischer, Dr Jerome Ravetz, Hugh Richards, Prof Harry Rothman, Prof Andy Stirling, Prof Stephen Thomas, Dr Tom Wakeford, Prof Gordon Walker, Prof Stuart Weir, Dr Ian Welsh, Pete Wilkinson, Prof Brian Wynne
Nuclear Consultation Working Group

January 9

Why I fell out with Edward Bond

Could I respond to Edward Bond's latest attempt to rewrite history ('If you're going to despair, stop writing', January 3)? Of course I never returned the script of Restoration to him with notes in the margin. To do so to one of the Royal Court's iconic writers would indeed have been handing a hostage to fortune. To my certain recollection I have never responded to any writer thus. The only thing that is "uncanny" is how Edward's recollection of events always ends with him in a position of impregnable moral rectitude.

My recollection is that the disagreements I had with Edward over Restoration were mainly economic. The play was predicted to be and indeed was the most expensive production thus far in the Royal Court's history. But any attempt to moderate expenditure was regarded as wooden-headed and philistine. His own proposed solution was to raise the budgeted box office income from 40% to 70%. In the event, Restoration played to 37% of box-office capacity.

But in fact my rupture with Edward came a few years later, after the Royal Court had revived The Pope's Wedding and Saved. I recall that during the interval of the first preview of Danny Boyle's fine production of Saved, I observed Edward and Danny in conversation about the production. Afterwards Danny seemed stunned and disconsolate.

I concluded shortly after this that collaboration was impossible for Edward. This was reinforced by a production of The War Plays which Edward undertook himself at the Barbican and which reduced a talented cast into a stumbling and incoherent shambles of walking wounded.

Edward Bond is simply the most difficult person I have worked with in 40 years. I believe this may go some way to explaining why his work is so infrequently seen in this country.

Max Stafford-Clark
Out of Joint theatre company

their own numbers, I wonder?

Mark Henzel
Merseyside Stop the War
Coalition

January 14

Ray Knagg (Letters, January 4) claims "badger casserole is illegal. Under the Protection of Badgers Act 1992 it is an offence to possess a dead badger or any part of a badger." But badgers accidentally killed on the road do not come under the provisions of the act by reason of the following clause: "A person is not guilty of an offence ... if he shows that ... the badger had not been killed, or had been killed otherwise than in contravention of the provisions of this act or of the Badgers Act 1973." This makes it quite clear that it is not against the law to remove a dead badger from the highway or the verge to dispose of the body, and if that disposal involves casseroling and eating it, the act is no impediment to such an action.

Arthur Boyt
Davidstow, Cornwall

January 15
Surely the contribution of Peter Bazalgette to modern popular culture (Changing Rooms, Big Brother) is some kind of memorial to his grandfather Joseph Bazalgette (Letters, January 12), if only to remind us that away from people's homes is not the only direction in which crap can be transported.

Mike Hine
Kingston, Surrey

January 16
Free weights from whisky tubes (Letters, January 7)? No no no – time spent in the army taught me that perfectly serviceable free weights can be made from several

January 11

The irrelevance of titles in a modern world

Marcel Berlins asks "What is the point of the Mr, Mrs, Lord and Lady?" and is right that very few people appreciate these niceties (Writ large: Time for judges to drop absurd forms of address, January 7). Along with many people who believe in real equality, I see titles as divisive as well as pointless, and object to being forced to use one.

Many commercial organisations insist on using a title. When forced to choose I just pick one at random, and it seemingly makes no difference which I choose – they then process my order. I get mail addressed to Lord, Sir, Dr, Mr, None, Other and Plain in front of my name – and many more enlightened organisations just use my name.

How much computer storage and ink are wasted maintaining and printing something that went out of relevance with the feudal ages?

Roy Prockter
Thorpe-le-Soken, Essex

January 12

Dismay at British Council art cuts

We are dismayed to learn that the British Council intends to disband its individual art departments. We are specially concerned at the demise of its internationally acclaimed visual arts department. Although best known here for its participation in the Venice Biennale, the department's programme of over 60 exhibitions a year, shown everywhere from national museums to local galleries worldwide, would be an inexplicable and indeed tragic loss. These exhibitions, whether in Moscow or Beijing, Tehran or Maputo, represent Britain in the best possible light. The links and collaborations involved are surely the very essence of cultural relations.

Our trust in the department's professionalism and expertise has been built up over many years. It is partly the result of their work that contemporary British art is held in higher regard internationally than ever before. Why, without any consultation, does the British Council seem intent on abandoning the best proven means of conducting cultural relations through the arts?

Frank Auerbach, Lewis Biggs Liverpool Biennial, **Peter Blake, Quentin Blake, Iwona Blazwick** Whitechapel Gallery, **Melvyn Bragg, Richard Calvocoressi** Henry Moore Foundation, **Anthony Caro, Jake and Dinos Chapman, Professor Michael Craig-Martin, Dr Stephen Deuchar** Tate Britain, **Caroline Douglas** Arts Council Collection, **Tracey Emin, Lucian Freud, Gilbert & George, Antony Gormley, Richard Hamilton, Damien Hirst, David Hockney, Howard Hodgkin, Gary Hume, Jay Jopling, Anish Kapoor, Leon Kossoff, Joanna Lumley, Sandy Nairne** National Portrait Gallery, **Professor Magdalene Odundo** University College of the Creative Arts, **Grayson Perry, Julia Peyton-Jones** Serpentine Gallery, **Marc Quinn, Bridget Riley, Norman Rosenthal, Ralph Rugoff** Hayward Gallery, **Charles Saumarez Smith** Royal Academy, **Nicholas Serota** Tate, **Posy Simmonds, Sam Taylor-Wood, Gavin Turk, Mark Wallinger, Richard Wentworth, Rachel Whiteread and 74 others**

January 12

100% for Hillary

Congratulations on proving the old cliche — that the main obstacle to women's advancement is other women. By giving space to two harpies

empty plastic 1 litre water bottles, sand to fill, a six-foot tent pole, and miles of army "fixes everything" gaffer tape. Worked fine for us in the Gulf in 2003.

Simon Turner
Halifax

January 18
Joseph Bazalgette (Letters, January 15) is interred in a family mausoleum in the graveyard of Wimbledon parish church. This is in a near-ruinous condition, to the disgrace of the wider London community as well as his immediate descendants.

Russ Russell
Weston-super-Mare,
Somerset

January 18
Marcel Berlins (G2, January 9) takes the BBC to task for presenters mispronouncing Barack

Obama's name, and refusing, in the past, to accept how Berlins pronounces his own surname. Our policy for names of people from English-speaking countries is to consult, if possible, the individual. In Obama's case we found a video clip of him saying his name and based our recommendation on his own pronunciation: buh-RAAK oh-BAA-muh. If Berlins would like to supply us with his preferred pronunciation for his surname we will happily add it to our database.

Martha Figueroa-Clark
BBC Pronunciation Unit

January 18

A surprise and delight to read that Alexander Chancellor (G2, January 11) has "lived, on and off, in the capital for most of my life". Please hire more London-based columnists so we can learn more about this

— Germaine Greer and Lionel Shriver — in one issue (G2, January 10), you've demonstrated that men simply need to stand on the sidelines. It's just possible that Hillary Clinton is her own woman, with her own policies on welfare — which her husband failed to implement — and, as a 70-year-old woman who has seen many charismatic men get the world in the current mess, I'm rooting for her 100%.

June Brown
London

January 14
Security and our citizens' freedoms

Shami Chakrabarti is right to identify the importance of moral authority in addressing the threats Britain faces from terrorism (Comment, January 8). My first responsibility is to protect the security of our citizens and the freedoms they enjoy, and it is a duty I take very seriously.

We cannot wish away the threat of terrorism. Faced with a clear trend towards an increasing number of plots, of increasing scale and complexity, the responsible course for government is to take action.

The home affairs select committee concluded last month that we have to consider how to deal with the possibility that there may be circumstances in the future when terrorist suspects would have to be released without charge because there is insufficient time for investigators to charge them.

By commending the use of Civil Contingencies Act (CCA) powers in such circumstances, Liberty seems to accept that we may need to go beyond the current 28-day maximum period of pre-charge detention under certain circumstances.

Having listened carefully to these views, we have incorporated many of the key principles of the CCA in our proposals. Any extension of pre-charge detention would be temporary, with strict time limits in place, and it could only be triggered in exceptional circumstances. Crucially, it could only come into force subject to strict legal and operational thresholds being met by the police and the director of public prosecutions, and under close parliamentary scrutiny.

Rather than sitting on our hands and hoping for the best, it is right that we ask now what more can be done to protect the public from future threats.

Jacqui Smith MP
Home secretary

January 18

We need to reduce forces in Afghanistan

Why do you believe that Afghanistan needs more foreign troops (Leaders, January 17)? Britain has increased the troop presence in Helmand province from 200 to 7,000 in the last two years. This increase has led to no improvement in governance or legal economic development, and no sustainable improvement in security. Nor will future increases.

Afghanistan needs a decent police force; a clean, credible and popular government; and a convincing narrative of national identity. Britain and its allies lack the knowledge, the power, the will and the legitimacy to create such things. Our aim should be to contain a difficult situation and provide assistance without overextending or

fascinating part of the country.

Roger Osborne
Scarborough,
North Yorkshire

January 18
First the BBC sends Jonah Fisher to cover Japanese whaling, then you carry a piece on EMI Records by Decca Aitkenhead (Comment, January 17). Keep it up!

Graham Larkbey
London

January 19
Is the Northern Rock that has a half-page advert for a savings account offering 6.9% interest (January 17) related to the Northern Rock that Seumas Milne describes as a "failed bank" (Comment, January 17)? How does that work then? Is it anything to do with Kevin Keegan?

Fr Alec Mitchell
Manchester

January 21
Ken Livingstone says
that the Shard would
be to London what
the Empire State
Building is to New
York (High anxiety,
January 19). The
Empire State Building
was completed in 1931
at the height of the
Depression. It didn't
show a profit until
1950 and was one of
the worst real estate
investments ever
made.

Professor Philip Steadman
University College London

January 24
Maybe you'd have had
to spend time in the
closet to be as moved
as I was by Heath
Ledger's acting in
Brokeback Mountain
(Heath Ledger 1979-
2008, January 23). But
I like to think anyone
with an open mind
can see his portrayal
of a man trapped by
fear of being himself is
one of cinema's truly
great performances. I

being sucked into an unwinnable foreign military
occupation.

There are greater strategic priorities elsewhere.
Pakistan, for example, is more of a haven for
terrorism, Egypt more important for regional
stability, Africa for poverty and conflict. A rational
global strategy for Britain and Nato would reduce
our troop presence in Afghanistan over the coming
years, not increase it.

Rory Stewart
Kabul, Afghanistan

January 19
Creativity in music and television is alive and well

As someone who has been working in the music
business since I left university in 1972, I despair at
the claims made by Decca Aitkenhead (Cost cuts
at EMI could finally usher in some quality control,
January 17). It is obvious that the music industry
is facing huge challenges because of piracy and
the transition in the way we deliver music to the
consumer, from physical to digital. Nevertheless,
the central issue for record companies has been –
and always will be – the signing and development
of artists.

For Aitkenhead to claim that such companies
in the past five years "have more or less stopped
trying" in artist development flies in the face of
the evidence. Amy Winehouse, Arctic Monkeys,
Scissor Sisters, James Blunt, Keane, Katie Melua,
Mika, Snow Patrol, Leona Lewis and the Hoosiers,
to name only a few, have sold millions of CDs and
digital tracks in that time.

EMI used to be good at this. It has recently lost
its way, and that's at the heart of its problems. But

that is no reason to make sweeping generalisations, bereft of logic, about the business. It is about great artists and great songs, and there are still a number of record companies developing them very successfully.

Max Hole
Universal Music

January 21

Bold approach of Fischer's mother

Your reporter Stephen Moss (Death of a madman driven sane by chess, January 19) mentions that Bobby Fischer's mother was "an immensely strong-willed woman". In 1977, standing on the Grunwick picket line in north-west London, I recognised Regina Fischer and introduced myself.

"Ah yes," she said grimly, "you're the one who writes all those horrible things about Bobby." I explained that I would be delighted to learn that Bobby's alleged views on the inferiority of women, the evils of socialism and the duplicity of the Jews had been totally misrepresented, and I would be sure to get published whatever she told me.

She considered this offer carefully. After some thought, she handed me a slice of the orange she was eating and said: "I forgive you." She added some words on the significance of vegetarianism and the meaningfulness of giving fruit. "But now," she said with absolute conviction, "I will stop this bus."

For months, hundreds of pickets, including Arthur Scargill and the Yorkshire miners, had tried to stop the strike-breaking Grunwick bus from crossing the picket line, but without success,

thank him for leaving us that.

John Warburton
Edinburgh

January 24
I'm so pleased Martin Wainwright (Shortcuts, G2, January 23) can save a tenner on his £100 family shop. Don't suppose it's got anything to do with Morrisons' "winning formula", which includes "a tight grip on staff wages"?

Gordon Vassell
Hull

January 26
Picture caption: "Vicar Tom Ambrose: accused of bringing parish to its knees" (Report, January 25). I thought that was what vicars were supposed to do.

Andy Moorhouse
Barnard Castle, Co Durham

January 26
According to Joe Queenan: "When an

actor dies young, it is almost as if one's own child had passed away." Has Mr Queenan lost a child? He has no idea what he is talking about. Let that gut-wrenching emotion be left to Ledger's parents, not cinemagoers. And Ledger's perform-ance in Brokeback Mountain was "liter-ally heartbreaking". Literally? I wouldn't let that pass in a year 10 essay.

Su Coates
Frome, Somerset

January 28
So David Cameron thinks it is morally acceptable for middle-class parents to lie to get their children into faith schools (The question, G2, January 24). Would he also find it acceptable for poorer families to lie about their personal circumstances in order to receive benefits? After all, they are only trying to improve the

for massed police lines held back the pickets as the bus drove through the factory gates at speed. Some time later the bus appeared, as it did every day, cleaving its way through the enraged crowd. As it reached the gate, Regina threw herself in front of its wheels. Braking sharply, it ground to a halt. This was the only time during the historic Grunwick strike that the infamous bus was stopped by a demonstrator.

Graham Taylor
London

January 22
Black Shangri-la

US-based writer Lola Adesioye (Comment, January 21) seriously misunderstands the situation of black people in the US. The "affluence" she lauds is a result of the black community's decision to build its own institutions, its own wealth in the face of exclusion at every level.

Dr King came from a wealthy, all-black background. He didn't think living in his lovely house in a black neighbourhood because he effectively couldn't live anywhere else was what America was about. He didn't march and die so "sundown" segregation could flourish.

Many black Brits go to the States and think they've landed in a black Shangri-la, and they have by comparison. But we black Americans are still not equal people and, until that happens, even a gilded cage is a cage.

Bonnie Greer
London

January 23

Nato first-strike doctrine exploded

The Nato strategists endorsing a pre-emptive nuclear policy (Pre-emptive nuclear strike a key option, Nato told, January 22) are making a deadly but fearfully common mistake: they are forgetting the provocative effect of their own actions. In order to ward off an extremely remote contingency they are doing immediate and serious harm to international relations now. Such declarations may seem to their authors defensive, but they always strike outsiders as threats. Thus the news of President Reagan's Star Wars programme — which he doubtless thought was purely defensive — so terrified the Russians that their paranoia increased to the point of nearly producing a war. It is important to remember that "defence" or "deterrence" can sometimes be something surprisingly toxic.

Mary Midgley
Newcastle upon Tyne

January 26

Westminster 'village' must be cleaned up

One aspect of the Hain affair which has not received sufficient focus is the involvement of lobbyists in funding his campaign (Trail of cash for a failed campaign led to downfall, January 25). For many years, hard-working party members campaigned to make Labour electable. Clearly many saw this as an opportunity to turn the business of government into a business by becoming lobbyists.

Quite what skills they bring to the political process is hard to discern, but I find it informative

quality of life for their families.

P Machin
Gunnislake, Cornwall

January 28

Rupert Brooke warned us about such behaviour in that parish in 1912 (Vicar accused of spitting at church-warden faces sack, January 25). In The Old Vicarage, Grantchester he wrote: "At Over they fling oaths at one / And worse than oaths at Trumpington."

Robert Tee
Pudsey, West Yorkshire

January 28

Stuart Rose's defence of M&S underwear "a bit pants" (Letters, January 26)? Not at all — really well briefed, I thought.

Mark Ainsbury
Hertford

January 30

So Derek Conway is suspended from

parliament for 10 days after being found to have misused public money in supposedly employing his son (Report, January 29). For such an "administrative error" any employee in either the public or private sector would be dismissed and the matter referred to the police for further investigation. And politicians wonder why there is so much cynicism about so-called standards in public life.

David Benson
Shrewsbury

January 31
Laura Barton (Shortcuts, G2, January 29) tells us that hippos "kill more humans in Africa than any other animal". A cursory glance at other sections of your paper would suggest they come a poor second.

Phil McShane
Leeds

that the required skills appear to change with the political makeup of the government and amount to no more than having political connections. Look at the number of advisers who jump ship to the private sector.

So now we have a group of individuals who have enriched themselves from influence-peddling seeking to gain further influence by making significant personal donations to posts which hold ministerial office, which no doubt can then be "traded" to clients. We need to clean up not only the funding of political parties to restore public confidence but the Westminster "village" too.

Colin Adkins
Wrexham

January 30
Judgments on diversity

It was a little unfair on your readers to put my photograph (with the other nine recent high court judges) on the front page of Monday's paper (First 10 high court judges under new diversity rules: Independent committee under fire for white male appointments, January 28). I shudder to think how many breakfasts I ruined. As for diversity, I am the first Keele University graduate to be appointed to the high court and, as your summaries showed, only five out of the 10 of us went to Oxbridge. Diversity is happening; sometimes you just need to look for it.

Peter Coulson
London

February 2008

Continuing conflicts in Kenya and Afghanistan prompted new debate about intervention in the affairs of sovereign countries. An edge was given to the discussion by western recognition of Kosovo: in perhaps one of the most prescient letters of the year, the exiled "prime minister of the Chechen Republic of Ichkeria", Akhmed Zakaev, warned that Russia might "retaliate … by recognising the right of … Abkhazia and South Ossetia … to self-determination. That is, it will effectively annex them." Labour continued to upset many of its supporters by proposing to deny council housing to those on benefits who fail to look for work and holding out against a union-supported bill to enhance the employment rights of agency workers. But the government did carry out one old Labour policy, finally accepting that it had to nationalise Northern Rock. The first electoral test of David Cameron's new Tories got under way as Boris Johnson challenged London mayor Ken Livingstone. Peter Hain defended himself over election expenses that led to his exit from the cabinet; an arts world colleague accused the media of homophobia over "flamboyant" Henry Conway, son of the disgraced Tory MP Derek; and film director Mike Leigh pointed out "the difference between tetchiness and good old-fashioned Mancunian frankness". One reader revealed his use for the plastic bag that the Guardian's Saturday supplements come in, while others tried to find the G spot.

February 1

Is Derek Conway stepping down so he can spend more time with his staff (Tories plan ban on Commons jobs for MPs' children as Conway quits, January 31)?

Julian Harber
Hebden Bridge,
West Yorkshire

February 2

Admittedly hallucinogenic drugs were in plentiful supply, Country Joe and the Fish did their stuff and we were knee-deep in mud, but to describe the Bickershaw festival in 1972 as Britain's Woodstock ('I think he'd rather not have been a clown', G2, yesterday) is laughable. We are talking about a wet weekend in Wigan where the only comfort was a hot meat pie.

Mark Seacombe
Pucklechurch, South
Gloucestershire

February 6

The talented Henry Conway

I am horrified by the gross slurs on the very talented and creative Henry Conway because of the row over his father's accounting methods. Henry has been the subject of some extraordinary press comment, using aspects of his presumed lifestyle to make very personal and nasty attacks.

After a brilliant academic career at the Courtauld, Henry has proved himself to be a learned and entertaining writer — not least in Knit Couture, his recent book on the history of knitwear (Shortcuts, G2, January 31). I would see him as the natural successor to the fashion historian Quentin Bell, and predict that — like Quentin — he will end up as a teacher and academic. Certainly Henry is more Bloomsbury than Sloane, and his self-description "Queen Sloane", like his "Fuck Off I'm Rich" theme night, is deeply ironic.

No surprise that the likes of the Daily Mail centres on his openly gay lifestyle, using words like "flamboyant". But there was a tinge of homophobia in the Guardian too, plus a pop at his genuinely flamboyant fashion sense.

I have always found Henry a fount of knowledge, while he has been a great help to the Julia Margaret Cameron Trust. He did some great PR for us at the latest Isle of Wight Festival, where he fitted like a glove and curated a show for Dimbola Lodge Photographic Museum of classic Rolling Stones photographs, as that band of dandys and posh tramps were headliners.

Dr Brian Hinton
Chairman, Julia Margaret Cameron Trust

February 8

Judges in control of sentencing

In your leader (Judgment day, February 2) there is an implication that politicians legislate in haste and inevitably therefore get the design of the legislation wrong. This commentary was in relation to indeterminate sentences, in which there is an assertion that judges "warned" against the particular operation of the new sentencing policy.

In fact, judges required the legislature — which eventually agreed — to put the operation of the scheme to the new Sentencing Guidelines Council, chaired by the lord chief justice. The thinking — expressed very strongly in both houses of parliament — was precisely that judges should be "left" to design and operate the new sentencing programme. It was not prescribed, as you suggest, by parliament itself.

Parliament presumed such sentences would apply to heinous crimes. They were intended to deal with the perverse situation where judges were uncertain about the wisdom of allowing a prisoner out before they had demonstrated that they were safe on the streets — following some horrific examples, for instance, of repeat rapes.

On this occasion blame did not lie, I would suggest, with those who produced the original proposition, but with those who implemented it. No one, contrary to the assertion made, forced judges to provide indeterminate sentences for those crimes for which a very short sentence would otherwise have applied.

This would have been perverse because indeterminate was supposed to be exactly what it says — not an alternative to laying down a

February 2

If the Hayward Gallery had wanted to put on a proper show about humour and art (Laugh? You must be joking, G2, January 29), they should have organised an exhibition of cartoons. The Saatchi Gallery did this in 2003. Although the Hirsts, Emins and Ofilis were out in force, the "Artoons" section was, said the organisers, the most popular room in the gallery.

Kipper Williams
London

February 2

Don't forget malaria-carrying mosquitoes. They probably relegate hippos to third place in a league table of human-killers in Africa (Letters, January 31).

Nick Pepper
Kielder, Northumberland

February 4

In his article on a supposed filmic

renaissance (A new golden age in cinema, February 1), Mark Lawson never once cites a non-American film. Even Barry Norman forced himself to pay lip service to the existence of what used to be called "the rest of the world".

Gilbert Adair
London

February 4

Even the plastic sleeve containing Guardian Saturday supplements has its use. I take it with me when the dog has his Saturday walk.

David Moseley
Seaton, Devon

February 5

I and my two colleagues in Instant Sunshine would like to correct your obituary of Miles Kington (February 1). Yes, he did play double bass with us, but we aren't a jazz group. We're a humorous singing

substantive fixed sentence. Judges determine the sentence, not politicians.

David Blunkett MP
Lab, Sheffield Brightside

February 8

School choice has entrenched class divide

Even if Peter Preston's idea (Latte and lotteries, February 4) of distributing the "best" teachers around the state system were practical, it would have little effect. In spite of more than 10 years of conventional wisdom to the contrary, the quality of teaching is not the most important feature of a school. What really matters is the prior attainment of the pupils, their motivation to succeed, and the extra resources available outside school. These, in turn, are a function of socioeconomic circumstances.

The best chance for a child from a deprived background is to attend a school in which the peer-group culture is positive towards education. A proper system of comprehensive schools would make this a possibility for nearly all such children, but Labour's idiotic "choice and diversity" agenda has ensured that the children with the fewest resources are likely to be concentrated in the least "successful" schools. Labour's educational policies have actually entrenched social class division. Preston's contention that good teachers "transform lives, poor ones ruin them" is largely a myth derived from old plays and sentimental films. It suits government to foster this nonsense because it is easier to blame teachers than to face the truth, which is that Labour is now the party of wealth and privilege.

Michael Pyke
Campaign for State Education

February 8

Hain: party funding reform is long overdue

George Monbiot (Comment, February 5) raises the issue of the funding of political parties and especially the funding of progressive politics. I am not in a position to respond to his vitriol against me because of inquiries prompted partly by the very media he represents, though as someone who has risked my freedom and my life in 40 years of political activism I am used to rants from pundits. Nor do I recall him commenting on the 35,000-word pamphlet I wrote for my deputy leader campaign advocating progressive internationalism, a red-green agenda, more equality, democratic reform and party renewal – the only candidate to do this.

I have long argued that the regulation of the funding of politics needs new arrangements which both satisfy public opinion and are workable. It is for others to judge whether such regulation should be rushed in to satisfy an unaccountable and increasingly anti-Labour media – but reform is long overdue.

Monbiot more constructively calls for getting big money out of politics. I think both Labour party and Electoral Commission procedures should change so that what happened to me never happens to any other internal party leadership candidate. More broadly, I have consistently argued for extending existing public funding of political parties which, in a non-election year, is already over £10m. This should be drawn down for regulated purposes: local organisers, political research, education, training and so on. But not for campaigning or propaganda, which should be financed by donations.

The Tory proposal for a cap on donations is aimed

group, and Miles's special contribution was not so much his bass playing as his wonderfully acerbic quips and whimsical chats between songs. Many of his ideas live on in our current performances, and we hope our audiences will remember Miles and have a good laugh.

Alan Maryon Davis
Salisbury, Wiltshire

February 6

I wish Fabio Capello all the best in his first game as England boss. However, if it all goes pear-shaped, the Italian for turnip is *rapa*.

Steve Little
St Annes, Lancashire

February 7

My daughter has got a job. Can she have her council house now please (Labour: if you want a council house, find a job, February 5)?

Jan Trewin
Bromyard, Herefordshire

February 7

The research in your article (Rhythm of life is quicker up north, February 5) mirrors what has been often observed historically, most famously by Keats 200 years ago. He went to a dance in Ireby in Cumberland, and said the local dancing compared to London as did beating up batter to stirring a cup of tea. This pattern applies to folk music to this day, just as much as to dance music in clubs. I find the fusion band Shooglenifty at full pelt in Scotland a bit overexciting, whereas if I go to Brighton and hear Dan Quinn and Will Duke play I often fall asleep while waiting for them to play the next note.

Greg Stephens
Stoke-on-Trent

February 8

You report that The Sea at the Theatre Royal Haymarket

at destroying collective trade union donations, paid for by millions of individual members who democratically agree to do so. Meanwhile Lord Ashcroft is buying up marginal seats by financing local Tory campaigns. The real crisis for Labour and progressive politics in general is that the right is now outspending the rest of us massively — nicely in time for the next general election.

Peter Hain MP
Lab, Neath

February 9

Religious authorities should have less power

As a gay man, my civil liberties have been created and protected by the state, not the church (Uproar as archbishop says sharia law inevitable in UK, February 8). The civil powers exist to protect minorities like mine from minorities like religious fundamentalists — Christian or Muslim. Although I am an ordained priest, I'd like to see religious authorities having less power, not more. They are unaccountable, capricious and usually wrong. No Christian preference, no Muslim preference. Justice is justice.

Rev Richard Haggis
Oxford

February 11

US primaries: overhyped, overlong and over here

Before all your commentators, such as Simon Schama (Messy — and brilliant, February 9) get completely carried away with the hoopla of the US primaries, they might reflect on some of its shortcomings. It is grotesquely expensive: the total spent on White House campaigns will probably exceed $1bn. It is conducted in a policy vacuum: position papers are prepared, but candidates are rarely challenged on the costings of their vague aspirations. Relevant experience appears to be a handicap: candidates who can put the greatest distance between themselves and "Washington" make the running.

And the process is not merely tortuous, but absurd. The key momentum is established at small meetings in Iowa and New Hampshire. It's as if we subcontracted out our elections to coffee mornings in Norfolk and Cumbria.

Of course it's more fun than our electoral process, but is it really a fair basis for a reasoned assessment of the political options facing the world's remaining superpower, and of the abilities of the candidates for its leadership?

Julian Priestley
Waterloo, Belgium

February 13

Why litigants get kebabbed in court

Your article (The art of self-defence, G2, February 11) demonstrates the unfairness of the supposedly public legal system being so complex that only lawyers can participate in it effectively. Being unable to afford lawyers should be no bar to getting justice. However, many laws are themselves unjust and oppressive. Up against such laws, it can be very empowering to defend yourself and to speak up for the public interest directly.

In the McLibel case we were advised that the laws are so stacked in favour of the rich and

opened to "some mixed reviews and meagre houses" (The Guardian profile: Jonathan Kent, February 1). This is inaccurate. The front of the theatre boasts quotes from eight national newspapers that have given at least four-star reviews. We were always aware that presenting Edward Bond was a risk, but business has been very brisk.

Nigel Everett
Director, Theatre Royal
Haymarket

February 9
Steve Rose's article on the misleading nature of film trailers (G2, February 5) is perfectly true. Studios target as big an audience as possible, even though that audience is not right for a particular film. Our cinema is currently showing As You Like It, but the trailer hypes it as a martial-arts actioner,

thereby totally missing our demographic. My favourite trailer was for the French farce Les Visiteurs, in which the sonorous voice promised: "Starring people you have never heard of, speaking a language you don't understand." So refreshing.

Dougal Dixon
Rex Cinema,
Wareham, Dorset

February 12

I recall a train journey I made during national service wearing my army uniform (Military personnel should wear uniforms off-duty, says study, February 11). A woman opened the compartment door, shouted "Yuk! Soldiers!" and moved on. That I was reading the Manchester Guardian did not apparently count in my favour.

Gordon Peacock
York

powerful that we were unlikely to even get to trial. This only made us more determined to represent ourselves. We gained strength from the political-legal struggles of the recent past – for example around the poll tax and miners' strike, and for the right to protest.

Lawyers generally advise their clients to "keep your head down". But with political battles it's the opposite – it is vital to form defence campaigns and to fight the issues in the court of public opinion.

While we were slugging it out in the high court, the campaign was ensuring mass leafleting and publicity all over the world, contributing to increased public debate and opposition to McWorld and capitalism in general. Although it was exhausting for us, it was one more step in the age-old fight for a better society for all. We send our solidarity to all those who defend themselves against injustice.

Helen Steel and Dave Morris
(McLibel Two), London

February 14
Personal justice

I was in the high court last week in front of Lord Justice Moses, mentioned in your article (The art of self-defence, G2, February 11), and Mr Justice Sullivan at a judicial review hearing, where I represented myself (Letters, February 13). The litigant in person needs a computer, probably access to a law library, funds, and access to the protocol of bringing a case and getting the dreaded "bundles" together. Law firms have secretaries and stockrooms of files to hand. The law is incredibly inaccessible to the citizen. I was successful as it was a cast-iron case. Corby magistrates were heavily criticised by the judges for failing to issue summonses against a US military personnel (assault) and two Ministry of Defence police officers (watching but not intervening) at the US base at Croughton. This is just the start of a long haul to bring these three to court. It is a struggle, but essential if we believe that everyone is subject to the law.

Lindis Percy
Coordinator, Campaign for the Accountability of American Bases

February 14

Democracy is a dangerous export

David Miliband says the UK has a moral imperative to intervene, even sometimes militarily, to help spread democracy (Report, February 12). He should be aware that Tony Blair's supposed mentor, the philosopher John Macmurray, said the exact opposite: that there is no moral imperative to impose a way of life on others by force. To do so is to deprive them of their most precious possession, their freedom. Force may be justified to stop aggression or genocide, but never to impose an ideal.

Jeanne Warren
Garsington, Oxford

February 15

An idea for our time

Two hundred years ago an illegal war was launched by Britain on the basis of an idea (Letters, February 14). It lasted for 60 years. Legal action was initiated against Britain here and overseas. Opponents of the idea were trying to force a change

February 13
Terry Eagleton's done well to hold on to his job till 65 (Marxist critic Eagleton faces axe at debt-hit university, February 8). Where I work nobody retires, ever. Every two or three years a "restructure" carries out a cull of high-maintenance employees, starting with those in their mid-50s. Perhaps Eagleton could start a new Marxist magazine. Failing that, he should join the rest of us on the tills down the supermarket.

Trevor Stevens
Oxford

February 13
Had Peter Preston (Wrong man for the job, February 11) been at the World Economic Forum annual meeting in Davos as I was, he would have witnessed the acknowledged popularity of Tony Blair, who remains the biggest leader

Europe has produced for almost 20 years. The task of finding someone to fill this position – to be the EU's first president – is not easy, but Tony Blair is still young, fluent in French and listened to by the Americans, and has the stature to gain world respect for an EU with him at its head, should he want the job.

Sigmund Sternberg
London

February 13

Your article (Beatles to be beamed across the universe, February 2) claims "this is the first time any music has been transmitted deep into the cosmos". In fact the first musical interstellar radio message was The 1st Theremin Concert for Aliens, transmitted in 2001 from Evpatoria deep space station to six sun-like stars.

Alexander Zaitsev
Fryazino, Russia

in British policy. The idea was the abolition of the transatlantic slave trade. There were many innocent victims in this war, not least when chained slaves were thrown overboard when a Royal Navy ship was sighted. Others were killed when the navy entered harbours in foreign countries and burnt the slave boats. It seems that many of the Guardian's correspondents today would also have opposed the policy. Today democracy, the rule of law and human rights is an idea that might, when applied everywhere, give this world a proven mechanism for reducing armed conflict and liberating many people from tyranny. There is an idea of freedom and David Miliband is right to promote it.

Clive Soley
Lab, House of Lords

February 15

Temporary work can be just the job

We understand the potential for abuse in temporary work (Brown offers pay commission for 1m agency workers, February 14), especially of "vulnerable" workers. But there is little evidence to support the notion that exploitation of vulnerable workers has increased: on Office for National Statistics data, temporary work is stable. Indeed it has even fallen slightly since the mid-90s. Most new jobs created in the last 10 years are permanent and full-time.

The last decade has been a period of modest but significant extensions of employment rights – across issues ranging from older workers to low pay, and overwhelmingly to the benefit of working people. Yet improvements to the quality of working life do not always require legislation. Legislators have to balance the need to redress genuine grievance with the reality that some temporary workers value the flexibility of the arrangement as much as employers and earn more than they would if holding full-time jobs. There are plainly worries and some of the business groups are self-interested in their lobbying against any intervention; however, any initiative should not try to solve problems that do not exist.

Will Hutton
Chief executive, Work Foundation

February 16

Bush prepares his legacy

Chris McGreal is right that Pepfar has positive effects in Africa (George Bush: a good man in Africa, February 15); he is wrong, however, to claim it to be George Bush's primary contribution to the continent. That honour should go to his militarisation of US policy towards Africa: even before 9/11 Bush established the US navy base of Camp Lemonier in Djibouti, and last year he created the new US Africa Command (Africom) to guide American defence policy in Africa.

Africom was supposed to be based in an African country, but the proposal was so unpopular that its headquarters is now in Germany and will probably be spread across Africa when it becomes fully operational this year.

Indeed the 15-member Southern African Development Community, which contains the countries most afflicted by HIV/Aids and thus most likely to benefit from Bush's Aids policies, agreed that no member countries would host Africom. Concerns that Bush's policies have had less to do with humanitarian impulses and more

February 13
A terrible Essex joke
(Letters, February 12):
Nurse, in casualty,
to injured patient,
"Where are you
bleeding from?"
Patient: "I'm from
bleedin' Romford."

Philip Crowe
Oswestry, Shropshire

February 15
I was described in your
report on Happy-Go-
Lucky (Chin up. Gritty
director Mike Leigh at
last finds a reason to
be cheerful, February
13) as being tetchy at
my press conference
in Berlin. I was not
the least bit tetchy,
but good-humoured
and honest. Given
the noble ancestry of
your newspaper, your
reporter surely ought
to know the difference
between tetchiness and
good old-fashioned
Mancunian frankness!

Mike Leigh
London

February 15
It is a bit much for BAE Systems' ad (February 12) to claim a first in innovating radar. The first radar transmitters were designed and engineered at Metropolitan-Vickers in Manchester, under the supervision of my late father-in-law, Dr JM (Jock) Dodds, for the early-warning system that was crucial in the Battle of Britain.

Dr Norman Swindells
Prenton, Wirral

February 16
Your clarification (February 15) of the contrasting attitudes of the Communist Party of Great Britain and the Communist Party of Britain on the political opportunities afforded by a recession was appreciated. But what does the People's Front of Judea think? (Or haven't you asked her?)

Andy Cook
Holmfirth, West Yorkshire

to do with African oil and countering Chinese influence have driven much of this suspicion.

Dr Elliott Green
London School of Economics

February 18

Rolling over before Saudi threats

To read that the government rolled over to the demands and threats of Prince Bandar (Britain powerless in face of Saudi threats, February 16) is shameful but hardly surprising, for it has made a habit of prostrating itself before the decadent al-Saud family. When we sought the government's assistance in seeking legal redress after enduring 32 months of false imprisonment and torture in Saudi Arabia, the Saudis warned the Foreign Office minister Liz Symonds to back off and told her it would be counterproductive for the British government to get involved.

But the Foreign Office didn't just back off, it obstructed justice. When our lawyer, Geoffrey Bindman, won us the right to sue our Saudi torturers, the government granted them immunity. Our government looked the other way when we were sentenced to death and while we were being tortured, and then actually helped Saudi officials evade justice after the court of appeal ruled that there could be no blanket immunity in cases of torture.

I would have thought that the obstruction of justice is a crime in this country, but apparently not when it involves Saudi Arabia, which under this government appears to be above the law. The government has cheapened our moral values, flouted the rule of law and violated our human rights in the hope of winning favour and pleasing the corrupt princes of the house of Saud.

Sandy Mitchell
Sowerby, West Yorkshire

February 18

The Pandora's box that is Kosovo

Kosovan independence (World briefing: A great leap in the dark, February 15) will have profound repercussions in all of those areas previously suffocated within the embrace of the Soviet Union. No doubt Belgrade will declare the move invalid. But what of Russia? Vladimir Putin has said it would be "illegal, ill-conceived and immoral" and Sergei Ivanov, first deputy prime minister, warned that recognition of an independent Kosovo by European governments would open a Pandora's box. But this is a threat wrapped in a dilemma. Ivanov can only mean that Russia might retaliate against the perceived threat to its western traditional sphere of influence by recognising the right of the peoples of two republics in the Caucasus — Abkhazia and South Ossetia in Georgia — and Transnistria in Moldova to self-determination. That is, it will effectively annex them.

Yet such a move would of course confirm a precedent for the republic of Chechnya, held back from independence solely by the wars masterminded from Moscow, to have the same right of self-determination. Surely the international community must be responsible for justice in these matters and ensure that principles established are applied fairly and equally to all.

Akhmed Zakaev
(Prime minister of the Chechen Republic of Ichkeria), London

February 18

The US and Israel have expressed satisfaction at the car bomb explosion in Damascus which killed Imad Mughniyeh last week (Report, February 14). Could these two governments perhaps now clarify their position on the phenomenon of planting bombs in major capital cities so that we can be a little more clear on what constitutes a terrorist outrage?

Lawrence Glover
Bootle, Merseyside

February 19

It's a pity the seventh Marquess of Salisbury does not seem to have a sense of his own family history in putting forward the arguments of "former senior military and intelligence officers" in warning that Britain is becoming a soft touch for terrorism (Deference to multi-

culturalism under-
mines those fighting
extremism, generals
warn, February 15).
As the third marquess
and prime minister
in the 1890s said: "If I
listened to my military
advisers, they would
ask me to defend
the moon against a
possible attack from
Mars."

John Phillips
Liverpool

February 19
Looking again at the
St Pancras Lovers
(Arts, G2, February
18), I am reminded
of John Betjeman's
comment in London's
Historic Railway
Stations on one of
the nearby Victorian
capitals depicting a
man holding a model
engine: "Trousers have
been ever the bane of
sculptors."

Adam Sowan
Reading, Berkshire

February 19

Agency workers do need protection

I was surprised to see Will Hutton's take on
agency workers (Letters, February 15). He says
they are not facing growing exploitation and he
therefore opposes further legal protection. Of
course it is impossible to measure the precise level
of abuse. But any effort would not start with the
government's labour force survey, whose figures
are normally quoted to show that there has been
no growth in agency working – though even this
shows that agency workers are taking a bigger
share of temporary working. But the LFS is a
sample telephone household survey and probably
not good at finding migrant and other vulnerable
workers at home and ready for a chat. And by
design it excludes all workers who live at their
place of employment.

Indeed the 260,000 figure for agency workers
reported in official statistics should ring alarms.
The industry regularly claims more than 1 million
agency workers. This means there are around
800,000 invisible agency workers missing from
official statistics, and these will inevitably include
the most vulnerable.

But any exploitation or abuse is wrong; it
should not be necessary to prove that it is on the
increase to make it illegal. If unions are wrong,
and the employment-agency lobby is right, then
it is even harder to accept the employer argument
that modest measures to provide a basic level of
employment rights for agency workers will cause
massive disruption.

Unions are not against employment agencies.
Providing employers who have short-term needs
with staff who have short-term availability is a

perfectly respectable and useful business. But the whole sector is being tarnished by the actions of the disreputable. MPs on Friday have the chance to vote for Andrew Miller's bill and protect some of our most vulnerable workers.

Brendan Barber
General secretary, TUC

February 19

The Financial Times and non-doms

I had to pinch myself after reading Polly Toynbee's description of the Financial Times' reporting of the controversy over non-doms (The Tories and their allies in the rightwing media are gloating at the cabinet's inability to handle public politics, February 15). Our coverage was not polemical, spurious, unsourced, unchecked and disreputable, as she claims. We spoke to dozens of people in and outside the financial services industry in London and other cities, including Athens and Zurich. We did not parrot a press release from Greek shipowners, we talked to their lawyers and representatives. Our Athens correspondent spent days on the story.

Polly writes that the FT has rolled the government. If she had read our editorial line more carefully, she would have noticed that we favour reform of the tax treatment of non-doms. We merely object to the rushed and botched Treasury handling of the matter. The FT will continue to report the news, without fear and without favour.

Lionel Barber
Editor, Financial Times

February 19

Such multiple-seat privies (Three-seat privy listed, February 18) are common in rural areas of Norway. On a north Norway farm I visited some years ago the privy was a two-seater within a delightful miniature log cabin with a turf roof, and on a campsite in the south there was a three-seater like the one in Benenden. It is significant that the multiple-seaters all appear to have apertures of different sizes. An opportunity for a family get-together?

Terence Hall
Manchester

February 20

Alistair Darling's rescue of Northern Rock and Grace Darling's rescue of shipwrecked sailors from northern rocks – any family connection?

Steve Kirby
Fylingthorpe,
North Yorkshire

February 22

Many thanks for the Spotter's guide to climate change (February 16), but where's the tick-box for reading a letter in the Guardian remarking on an earlier than normal occurrence of one of the events?

Ian Joyce
Milton Keynes,
Buckinghamshire

February 22

Women will be pleased the G spot has been located (The elusive G spot really does exist, say researchers, February 21). Men can be consoled that it took a dedicated team of researchers and ultrasonic technology to find it.

George Leigh
London

February 23

Surely there must be somebody in the Labour party who

February 20

Saudi justice

I note with interest the comments of Sandy Mitchell (Letters, February 18) when he says that the British government "looked the other way" while he and his fellow expats were wrongly accused of the murder of my stepfather Christopher Rodway in Riyadh. I feel it necessary to point out that not only have their human rights been violated, but also those of Christopher and his family. Surely any murder victim is entitled to a thorough investigation leading to the capture of the culprit(s).

However, while the Saudi Arabian authorities have failed to identify the real perpetrators of this atrocious crime, the British government has failed to coerce them into making any effort to do so. Indeed at one point it was even alleged that the perpetrators may have been carrying out the orders of British officials in the kingdom. No doubt the Saudis feel they have such control over this government that they can even accuse it of perpetrating such crimes with no recriminations. After over seven years, Christopher's family are still awaiting justice.

Dave Taylor
Orpington, Kent

February 22

Grannies just grand

Do not belittle ordinary "low-flying" grannies – or should that be nans (Women, G2, February 20)? There's an army of us out here who fulfil the traditional role. OK, so we don't run companies or jet around, but we can read cracking stories and play fun games. Biscuit-making — yes, in a kitchen — is a big favourite too. We can also provide days at the seaside, with barbecues on the beach, exploring rockpools and beachcombing. Collected rocks need classifying and plants must be identified after a walk in the woods. Expensive treats? Are they more fun than what an ordinary grey-haired granny in a cardie can provide?

Elin Gibbon
Church Stretton, Shropshire

February 23

Why society is still failing prostitutes

In your front-page article ('He was one of the regulars. We didn't suspect him. But he was the killer', February 22) you refer to the five women murdered by Steve Wright as "sex workers", a term coined by those who claim that this is like any other job, and that women involved have choice about what they do.

Yet, as the reports inside the paper show, Tania Nicol, Gemma Adams, Anneli Alderton, Annette Nicholls and Paula Clennell had not made a career choice to be "sex workers". They, like 95% of street prostitutes, were driven to it by their drug addiction. And like prostituted women in any setting, they faced a daily risk of violence from punters.

It is time to stop romanticising the life of a prostitute and deal with the violence, degradation and trafficking which it involves. The House of Lords next week should vote to back MPs' decision to end fines for prostitutes and substitute meetings where women can get access to drug treatment, housing advice and the support which will give

can remember how to get a nationalisation right (Northern Rock nationalisation in turmoil over offshore trust, February 21).

Rev Geoff Reid
Bradford

February 23
So we can now intercept a satellite with a missile (Report, February 22). It's not rocket science, is it?

George McLean
Manchester

February 25
Re the G spot (Letters, February 23): my husband was wondering whether his satnav would help.

Hilary Drapper
Broadstairs, Kent

February 26
The amount of information it is proposed we should give when we travel (Government wants personal details

of every traveller, February 23), even on domestic flights, is poking into our private lives in a way unrivalled since the 1086 Domesday Book, which listed the ownership of every ox, cow and pig. New Labour has come a long way from the vision of Ernie Bevin, who wrote "my policy is to take a ticket at Victoria Station and go anywhere I damn well please".

Julian Phillips
Middlesbrough

February 26

I see Condoleezza Rice calls for change in Cuba, "releasing all political prisoners, respecting human rights" (Report, February 20). Would that be the Guantánamo bit?

Colin Baker
Hermanus, South Africa

them a chance to leave this life before it is ended – prostitutes are 40 times as likely to die violently as other women.

Politicians have been ducking this issue for too long. This should be a first step. I hope the next will be to follow the Swedish example and make the men who use prostitutes criminals.

Fiona Mactaggart MP
Lab, Slough

February 23

Cinéma vérité

Re Anita Sethi's covert attempts to chomp on smuggled-in chocolates at the cinema (Shortcuts, G2, February 20), I for one would prefer it if next time she did wait for the DVD. Just this Sunday I had to endure There Will Be Blood in a Worcester cinema with people slurping on pints of Coke, munching through buckets of popcorn, the subsequent coughing, seemingly endless visits to the toilet and general chit-chat. Is it really so difficult to go for a couple of hours without having to mindlessly stuff your face? By the end of the film I was in much the same frame of mind as Daniel Plainview. Unfortunately this kind of aural disturbance is not only restricted to the rude youth – the rustling of sweet wrappers and the resulting cavernous echoing of boiled sweets rolling around clanking dentures is often a feature of a nearby local "art house" cinema.

Charlie Hurcombe
Worcester

February 25

Unequal opportunities in journalism

David Kynaston cites Sutton Trust research on how
the UK's education system reinforces privilege (The
road to meritocracy is blocked by private schools,
February 22). But just as worrying is the lack of
opportunity in the major professions. Two years ago
the trust published a report revealing that over half
of leading news journalists were privately educated.
It also highlighted concerns that the national news
media are becoming even less representative of wider
society. Young (and equally talented) journalists
from less privileged backgrounds and from outside
the south-east are much less likely to survive the
low pay and high job insecurity at junior levels, and
to benefit from connections within the industry. On
this particular roadblock to meritocracy, there has
been a deafening silence from the media.

Lee Elliot Major
Director of research, Sutton Trust

February 27

Saviour of the left

The letter from Ruth Lister et al (February 25)
arguing Ken Livingstone's case is precisely the sort
of sycophantic nonsense which gives the left a
bad name. Typically, the letter fails to mention
the New Statesman's case against Livingstone, and
one presumes their "better" vision of political life
includes the vicious and pointless smearing of critics,
the misappropriation and waste of public funds, the
undermining and corruption of standards within
the ethnic minority communities, open contempt
for the electorate and its representatives, and the

February 26
My satnav locates
the Gräfenberg spot
(Letters, February 25)
at N 49.6449, E 11.2495,
in the centre of a small
Bavarian town north-
east of Nuremberg.

Martin Campbell
Bury St Edmunds, Suffolk

February 27
Like many "marriage
phobic" couples (For
whom the bells toll,
G2, February 25), we
only decided to marry
when advised that
we, on the premature
death of one of us,
would pay far more
tax — to Margaret
Thatcher's govern-
ment — than we
would if married. That
decided us: after 17
years and two children
we "did the deed". We
"vowed", however,
that when we had a
Labour government
we would divorce,
because we wouldn't
mind paying more tax
for a decent govern-
ment with better

public services. We're still married.

Lucy Craig & Gordon Best
London

February 27

Perhaps those fish are more savvy than we think (Researchers find that fish can count up to four, February 26) in not counting up to five and so avoiding being caught alive.

Andy Gunn
Thame, Oxfordshire

February 28

So police can get a warrant to enter your house if they suspect you are fertilising human eggs (The question: Who is allowed to break in to your house?, G2, February 26). Beats a headache as an excuse any day.

Tom Trainer
London

unflagging defence of a police hierarchy which was responsible for the slaughter of an innocent (and dark-skinned) man. Instead of automatically joining the mayor's denunciation of any inquiry into the behaviour of his own attack dogs as politically motivated, these doyens of the left should take a little time to reflect seriously on the implications of the allegations, both for London and the nation.

Dr Mike Phillips
London

February 28

Options for Kenya

Mark Malloch Brown's assertion that the Kenyan military is now "by far the best option" to stop violence is dangerous and premature. It is this kind of rhetoric that spreads panic when, right now, there is cause for concern, but not for panic. Having read your article (As talks break down, army is Kenya's best hope, February 27), I feel like packing my bags and running for the airport. Yet I know that thousands of Kenyans all around me are working for peace. Would it not be more helpful to suggest that these positive forces for change be engaged? I have been working for five years with Kenyan institutions of all sorts. They have risen to the challenges of conflict before, and in the lull between the January violence and now have also been at work. Remember, it was Kenya's civil society that brought government change five years ago. Let us support Kenyans to do this again, and keep military opinions quiet for the moment.

Stuart Worsley
Director, Kenya and Sudan, SNV – The
Netherlands Development Organisation

March 2008

Journalism itself came under fire after the breaking of a media embargo on the presence of Prince Harry in Afghanistan; those who had agreed to delay reports of the prince's tour of duty — including the Guardian — took most of the flak. "News should be reported when it happens, not when it's convenient to authorities," one reader thought. Others, such as former Iraq hostage Norman Kember, criticised the example set by the prince in undertaking active military service. Labour's apparent campaign to rile its own side continued with its support for a large programme of post office closures, its determination to give police the power to detain terrorism suspects without charge for 42 days and — most bizarrely of all — culture minister Margaret Hodge's criticism of the Proms for being elitist. She was taken to task in a letter from cellist Stephen Isserlis. But Gordon Brown did stand firmly with the liberals in resisting pressure to abandon a bill that would allow advanced embryo research to go ahead. The rising number of casualties caused by Israeli military action in Gaza made peace seem as distant as ever. Meanwhile in Northern Ireland, Ian Paisley was preparing to step down as first minister after a successful year of power-sharing, leading one reader to say he felt lucky to be born in Creggan and not Gaza. But the continuing sensitivity of the Troubles was revealed in an exchange of letters over the definition of terrorism. Heathrow's Terminal 5 opened to much fanfare — and a lost-luggage crisis.

March 1

Jonathan Freedland argues for a US-style separation between the executive and the legislature at Westminster. This would carry a lot more weight if the US legislature had at any time since 2000 successfully checked, balanced or scrutinised the executive, or had passed vital legislation that was not vetoed by the president, or countermanded by his "signing statements".

John O'Dwyer
Steeple Claydon,
Buckinghamshire

March 1

Since it must have been one of their blokes that started it (Groin turns into no-go zone for luckless Italians, February 28), what do the Italians say for "Spectacles, testicles, wallet and watch"?

Tim Grollman
London

March 1

The blast of war blows in our ears

I applaud Jon Snow of Channel 4 for attacking the decision by news media in Britain and elsewhere to keep quiet about the deployment of Prince Harry in Afghanistan in return for interviews and coverage to be shown after his return to the UK ('I think this is as normal as I'm ever going to get', February 29). In doing so, the media insulted their profession and the prince. News should be reported when it happens, not when it's convenient to authorities. The interviews now being rushed into print and on air seem stilted and unreal because they were so carefully staged. Better to have caught the prince briefly at work in Afghanistan without mention of his location or unit. It was a bad deal for the media and the prince, who seems only to want to be an ordinary soldier, an admirable desire.

Ron Odgers
Hove, East Sussex

• To protect "bullet magnet" Prince Harry and those around him, newspapers ganged up with the Ministry of Defence to decide what readers should and should not know. Why stop there? The entire royal family, as representatives of our country and, by implication, its deeply unpopular foreign policy, are bullet magnets. May I suggest a news blackout on all activities of all members of the royal family, for all time? This will help ensure their safety, and give the rest of us a break.

Zoe Fairbairns
London

• So we are back to the middle ages — a young prince has to prove his manhood by killing other young men. These days it is not even face to face but by calling down an air strike. What example is this to other young men? Is this the way to win hearts and minds in Afghanistan? Better if the prince had joined a friend of ours doing humanitarian work there.

Norman Kember
Pinner, Middlesex

March 3

Parenting stakes and career ladders

Until the age of 38 I enjoyed, in many ways, sexual and economic equality with men (The world is still organised to meet the wishes of men, February 28). I had my own house, a decent job and a fairly autonomous life. By 38 I was broody, desperate even, to have a baby and acquired four males — a son, a husband and twins, in that order. Keeping my brain cells intact and a foothold in the outside world has proved very tricky. I have been plunged into social and psychological conditions of mothering that are actually worse than my mother encountered in the 1950s. Social mobility has meant no grandparents to call on and no extended family networks for support. Lack of funding for nannies, the tyranny of the 3pm school gate and the isolation of the modern nuclear family means that, in this so-called post-feminist era, I have little more choice than my own mother. My marriage, my sense of self and my career have all had to take place in the narrow margins that motherhood permits.

Bev Gold
Cambridge

March 3

Mark Lawson asks us to "imagine a world in which the doctor was able to hand out gym member-ship ... a labrador ... a creative kind of placebo" (Comment, February 29). Doctors can already prescribe gym membership for depression. Pet therapy is also a possibility.

Celia Richardson
Mental Health Foundation

March 3

We're told "shock-waves ... had enough force to knock the head off of the model of Dr Crippen" at Madame Tussauds (The great quake of '08, March 1). "Off of"? Has the editorial team enough force to get its journalists to knock the "of" off of "off"?

Mario Petrucci
London

March 3

Brainless invertebrates washed up on the Costa Brava (Scientists warn of new plague of jellyfish, February 29)? We expats have feelings, you know.

Andrew Harvey
Figueres, Spain

March 4

I would like to add one thing to Alan Clayson's obituary of Mike Smith (March 3). After its release in 1964, Glad All Over was adopted as an anthem by supporters of Crystal Palace FC. The pause between "I'm feeling" and "glad all over" provided an excellent opportunity for two beats of improvised percussion. Palace fans still sing the song, whether at Selhurst Park or at the away supporters' ends of grounds when the team is on the road.

Professor John Bryant
Exeter, Devon

March 4

Israel, Gaza and shattered hopes for peace

We are horrified at the escalating Israeli attacks on Gaza, the bombardment of a population under siege (Israel defiant as Gaza toll rises, March 3). Since last Wednesday more than 90 Palestinians, including 19 children, one a two-day-old baby, have been killed by the Israel Defence Forces; 63 civilians died in their homes on Saturday as a result of bombing attacks by the Israeli air force.

In a clear threat of genocide and ethnic cleansing, the Israeli deputy defence minister, Matan Vilnai, has said that the Palestinians are risking an invasion of Gaza and a "shoah" (Hebrew for disaster). It is time for the international community to speak out against the policies of the Israeli government, which are in open breach of the fourth Geneva convention and international law. Their actions constitute a war crime.

Peace will never be achieved through a policy of death and destruction. Peace will only be achieved by the Israeli government stopping its brutal siege of Gaza, ending its illegal occupation and abiding by international law.

Geoffrey Bindman, Victoria Brittain, William Dalrymple, Baljeet Ghale President, National Union of Teachers, **Antony Gormley, Bruce Kent, Betty Hunter** General secretary, Palestine Solidarity Campaign, **Miriam Margolyes, John Pilger, Corin Redgrave, Michael Rosen and 18 others**

March 6

Acts of cultural supremacy

Margaret Hodge is to be congratulated for having chosen the least appropriate of all musical events for her ill-advised attack (Hodge attacks Proms, March 4). The Proms are celebrated worldwide for their appeal to all possible audiences, from the most dedicated classical music anorak to the first-time concertgoer of any age or background. Had she singled out one of the opera houses where a dinner jacket and bottle of champagne are required audience accessories, there might have been some point to her claims; but to attack the world's most popular classical music festival is ridiculous.

I very much doubt she has ever stood with the dedicated Prommers, listening intently to music ranging from medieval to hardline contemporary. Having played several times at the Proms, I can testify to the unique atmosphere engendered by such open-minded concentration; every year, the festival reaffirms the joy that music can bring to people everywhere.

Interesting, too – and wearily predictable – that the minister should choose to attack a classical-music institution. She wouldn't dare attack a concert by a rap artist for failing to appeal to the vast majority of British listeners, for fear that it might lose her votes. We classical musicians resent having the art that we love assigned to one particular class of society. It is neither the players nor the promoters – and certainly not the music itself – who are responsible for this; it is a position thrust upon us by the mindless twitterings of people who understand absolutely nothing about music.

Steven Isserlis
London

March 4
How did Prince Harry escape the legendary army haircut?

Allan Horsfall
Bolton, Lancashire

March 5
Mario Petrucci (Letters, March 3) asks whether your editorial team can get its journalists "to knock the 'of' off of 'off'". "'Of' off of 'off'"? "'Of' off of 'off of'", surely?

Roger Mullis
London

March 5
A signwriter was writing a new sign above the shop of John Smith And Son. Just as he got to the word "Son", John Smith came out and said: "Could I have a little more space between the word Smith and And and And and Son".

Mark Yoxall
London

March 6

I was going to comment on Ian Paisley's stepping down, but after reading Seumas Milne's excellent article (To blame the victims for this killing spree defies both morality and sense, March 5), I realise that, as bad as it was in the north with Paisley, I feel lucky I was born in Creggan and not Gaza.

Michael Nash
London

March 6

When playing Glad All Over (Obituary, Mike Smith, March 3) at a Christmas party, my uncle tried to get everyone to "break step" because he was convinced we'd all go through the bouncing floorboards in his flat and end up in Grandma's bedroom on the floor below.

Penny Claridge
Limpsfield, Surrey

March 7

Keep the plinth as an art showcase

We believe that the rotating programme of contemporary art on the fourth plinth in Trafalgar Square is the best public use for the plinth and should continue (The new embraceable Britain, G2, February 18). The series of commissions on the plinth presents 21st-century London as a forward-looking, dynamic and progressive city with a rich heritage. It is one of the things which contributes to London being a world leader in the field of visual arts.

It has captured the public's imagination and generated debate about the value of public art. It has reached thousands of young people who every year submit their own creative and often profound ideas for public sculpture. It is free and accessible, showcasing world-class contemporary art to many people who live in or visit London.

The recent proposal that a single sculpture, however fine, should stand for all time on the fourth plinth seems to us to limit rather than extend the impact of public art in the city. We therefore wish to express our strong support for a continuing commitment to the rotating programme on the plinth.

Iwona Blazwick Whitechapel Gallery, **Michaela Crimmin** Royal Society of Art, Fourth Plinth Commission Group (FPCG), **Tamsin Dillon** Art on the Underground, FPCG, **Mark Jones** Victoria & Albert Museum, **Jay Jopling** White Cube, **James Lingwood** Artangel, **Gwyn Miles** Somerset House, **Sandy Nairne** National Portrait Gallery, chair FPCG, **Grayson Perry** Artist, FPCG, **Julia Peyton-Jones** Serpentine Gallery, **Sunand Prasad** Penoyre & Prasad, FPCG, **Nicholas Serota** Tate, **Moira Sinclair** Arts Council London, **Jon Snow** Channel 4 News, **Bill Woodrow** Artist, FPCG

March 7

Post Office should put public service before profit

Jenni Russell (We're all poorer for making the Post Office turn a profit, March 5) highlights the dangers facing the postal service as a result of accelerating post office closures. Unfortunately, the situation is worse than presented: according to Postcomm, there have been over 5,000 closures since 1997. This contrasts with only 500 closures in 1969-97. We do not expect our hospitals or schools to make profit and need to recognise the Post Office network for what it is: a valuable public asset which requires government investment. While profitability is an issue, it has not been helped by the withdrawal of government services, such as Girobank and more recently TV licences. This has been exacerbated by Post Office management's apparent preoccupation with running the network down rather than as a successful business.

The Post Office performs a valuable social role which should remain centred on the provision of and access to government services for all. The network also forms an integral part of Britain's mail service and as such is linked to the universal service obligation. Ken Livingstone's legal challenge to further closures, and campaigns across the country to save offices, should speak loud and clear to politicians. Let's invest in the great assets of our network before it's too late.

Billy Hayes
General secretary, Communication Workers Union

March 7

Re short world leaders (G2, March 4): Omar Bongo of Gabon trumps them all, standing at 5ft tall. Since Fidel Castro stepped down, President Bongo also holds the distinction of being the world's longest-serving leader. Bongo took power on December 2 1967.

David Crossan
Paris

March 7

Your Guide to DIY (March 1) fired my wife's enthusiasm and a raft of projects has suddenly appeared, necessitating suspension of my daily crossword-solving sessions in the Red Lion. Thanks.

Chris Jermyn
London

March 8

Mark Yoxall's letter (March 5) had far too much space between

"Smith" and "and" and "and" and "And" and "And" and "and" and "and" and "And" and "And" and "and" and "and" and "Son".

John McElhatton
Salford

March 10
So, Canadian detectives are baffled by the three feet washed up on Vancouver's beaches (Report, March 6)? Three feet? Surely a job for the Yard?

John Smith
Sheffield, South Yorkshire

March 10
I have news for Simon Hoggart (March 8). There is a teapot orbiting the sun. It's in my kitchen cupboard.

Dr David Philpott
London

March 10
"For solutions, turn to Obituaries" (Chris Maslanka's puzzles,

March 10
Practical tests for ID card scheme

I have just read Edwin Black's 2001 book IBM and the Holocaust: The Strategic Alliance Between Nazi Germany and America's Most Powerful Corporation. What I learned most from it was how important it is to oppose the collection and storage by the state of too much data on individuals (Smith targets public sector in ID card hard sell, March 7).

Without IBM's Hollerith machines, storing data on every individual in Germany and beyond, the Holocaust would have been impossible. This is why it is so important to oppose the government's ID card scheme. Consider how grateful the Nazis would have been to have had such technology.

Brian Abbott
Cork, Ireland

March 10
Arms treaty could save millions of lives

The capture of the notorious Viktor Bout (Report, March 7) will come as heartening news to many who have lost loved ones in the war zones where he is suspected of running guns. The conflicts ravaging central Africa have claimed millions of lives since the mid-1990s — including that of my sister, Charlotte Wilson, a British aid worker shot dead by Burundi rebels in December 2000. These wars have been massively inflamed by the flood of cheap guns and ammunition from European dealers, among whom Bout was the most infamous. This point was not lost on my sister's killers, who told her: "It's the white supplying the weapons in Africa — now you're going to feel what it's like."

Those who worked hard to expose Bout have done us all a service.

Richard Wilson
London

March 11

Other perspectives on the Troubles

I have to agree with Ian Jack (My silence about the terrorists was only partly cowardice, March 8) on one point: political memories are usually selective. My sister, Mairéad Farrell, is a "martyr" to her comrades and a "terrorist" to the Guardian and the British establishment. On the other hand, the English imperialist Lord Pym was a "man of great decency and principle" according to Gordon Brown.

Lord Pym had the innate task of carrying the white man's burden. And my dear sister should have accepted her place to be a second-class person in a sectarian hellhole created by her British betters.

Ian Jack prefers to ignore that the IRA have put down their arms, while the British imperialists continue to carry their burden to Iraq, Afghanistan … Yes, they will pursue their righteous cause to the death of the last native with the assistance of their killers in the SAS etc.

Brendan Behan summed it up quite succinctly: "It's easy to spot the terrorist. He's the one with the small bomb."

Niall Farrell
Galway, Ireland

March 8). Are these the ultimate answers?

Colin Virden
Ashbourne, Derbyshire

March 11
While "For solutions, turn to Obituaries" might be amusing, the Saturday March 1 suggestion: "Solutions on p???????" was more in keeping with the spirit of Chris Maslanka's puzzles (Letters, March 10).

David Reed
London

March 11
After a fitful night trying to de-rattle our bedroom's ageing sash windows, at 6.42am I looked out into our street, where I could make out through the driving rain a man heading for the station, leaning into the gale-force wind, riding a unicycle! I felt very proud to be English.

Ken Starkey
London

March 11

We don't expect police officers, firefighters, nurses etc to wear their uniforms when off-duty (Attack on nurse triggered order to wear civilian clothes, March 8). Why, therefore, should we encourage members of the armed forces to wear their uniform in their free time?

John Norton
Kingston upon Thames

March 12

We heard on Saturday that Bush continues to endorse waterboarding. We read on Friday (Spain drops extradition attempt against Guantánamo torture pair, March 10) that two British residents were so badly injured while in US custody in Guantánamo that they are unfit to stand trial. The description of their injuries is horrific. Let such crimes never cease to horrify, and

March 12

Hearing Beethoven

As usual whenever the topic of "choosing deafness" comes up — as a deaf bioethicist I find it comes up with depressing regularity in academic circles — proper debate is being scuppered by polarised views of the lives that are at stake (The hearing's difficulties, March 11). It's rarely a question of being either hearing or deaf, with deaf people impoverished because they are completely excluded from all auditory experience. Hearing people, like John Humphrys in his interview with Tomato Lichy, seem to think that "but you can't hear Beethoven" is the killer argument. I have zero hearing in one ear and about 5% in the other; I enjoy the experience of music — and I've had a lot of it, married to a musician for 20 years — via sound, vibration and movement. I play the saxophone no worse than anyone else who took it up at 40.

It's true that I can't hear Beethoven like you do, but then you can't experience music like I can either — and what I do hear is arguably closer to what Beethoven heard. What infuriates many deaf people more than anything is the absolute refusal by hearing people to imagine that our experience may be not just a depleted version of theirs, but worth something in its own right.

Dr Jackie Leach Scully
Newcastle University

March 12

Violence and political change in Northern Ireland

I would ask Niall Farrell (Letters, March 11), the brother of the leader of the IRA active service unit killed in Gibraltar, a similar question to that I asked Patrick Magee when he came to Brighton a while ago to explain why he bombed the Grand hotel. Has Mr Farrell ever asked whether the rights and values his sister was fighting for justified the destruction of human life?

For many on the left the answer should, logically, have been no. Whatever injustices the British did in Northern Ireland since partition, they were trivial compared with atrocities in places like Yugoslavia, which the left regarded either as justified or as a lesser evil than the western military intervention that stopped them. Where is Northern Ireland's equivalent of the massacres at Srebrenica or Vukovar, or the merciless shelling of Sarajevo? How do even the Shankill Butchers compare to Arkan's Tigers? What did the British do in Northern Ireland that could have been serious enough to put before the UN security council or the international criminal court? If Mr Farrell is at a loss for an answer in terms of genocide or crimes against humanity then he has to face the fact that his sister was an aggressor and possible war criminal.

Michael Petek
Brighton, East Sussex

March 14

Hypocrisy surrounding 'terrorist' label

Michael Petek (Letters, March 12) wrongly assumes I was a supporter of the IRA's military campaign. However, I can't abide the hypocrisy of those who label my sister, Mairéad Farrell, a "terrorist" but do not apply the same term to those who oversaw the sinking of the Belgrano, the slaughter of

let us never forget how our government connived so shamefully for so long.

Margaret Drabble
London

March 12

Blasphemer! The one true teapot (Letters, March 10) is in MY kitchen cupboard! This worshipper of false teapots shall be damned in the pantry of penitence for eternity.

Nicholas Hilken
Wolverhampton

March 12

All these new sins promulgated by the Vatican (New sins should come with better guidelines, March 11) seem to me to be a modern reinterpretation of existing ones. When will they come up with an original sin?

Tony Stowell
Tetbury, Gloucestershire

March 14

Can we send a delega-
tion from the Black
Country to ask that
the Vatican adopt
seven Dudley sins
(Letters, March 12)
– camplin', gawkin',
ivver-ovverin',
werritin', waggin',
pullin' maygrums, and
gerrin' on me wick?

Chris Bond
London

March 14

There are too many
false teapots (Letters,
March 12). I am the
Guardian of the One
True Teapot, with a
capital T. By my name
ye shall know me.

Colin Philpott
Farnborough, Hampshire

March 15

Celestial teapots
(Letters, March 14)?
What's wrong with
good old-fashioned pie
in the sky?

Ian Short
London

the innocents in Iraq through UN sanctions, the invasion of Iraq and the executions in Gibraltar. The IRA's war is over, but not that of the "great powers" – so I hope Mr Petek (and Ian Jack for that matter) will be in London tomorrow, just as I will be in Dublin, marching against the imperialist warmongers in Iraq.

Niall Farrell
Galway, Ireland

March 15

Abandon plans for 42 days' detention

In October last year the prime minister made a promising speech in favour of preserving our civil liberties and extending them further. He argued for respecting the freedom of citizens to be protected from arbitrary treatment by the state and said: "The very freedoms we have built up over generations are the freedoms terrorists most want to destroy." It is in agreement with these words that we today call upon the prime minister to abandon plans to extend pre-charge detention of terrorist suspects to up to 42 days, from the current limit of 28 days (Labour MPs revolt over 42-day detention, March 1).

It has become clear, as this debate has proceeded, that there is no consensus on the case for an extension of detention powers. Rather, it has resulted in a broad consensus among independent and expert opinion outside government that no convincing case has been made. We feel that the Home Office is underestimating the damage this legislation could do: to our struggle against home-grown terrorism; to preserving individual liberty; and to the reputations of the United Kingdom and the Labour party as forces that seek to protect and advance human rights.

We are concerned that these measures will once again polarise opinion, with damaging results. In particular, they are likely to undermine the efforts of those involved in the difficult task of building confidence in the intelligence work and policing efforts among all British citizens and British Muslims in particular on which our security depends. The parliamentary joint committee on human rights said the plans were "an unnecessary and disproportionate means of achieving the aim of protecting the public". We agree entirely, and call on the government to withdraw the measure, while renewing its commitment in seeking to build a broad consensus on national security and anti-terror strategy.

Sunny Hundal LiberalConspiracy.org, **Fareena Alam** Q-News, **Yasmin Alibhai-Brown, Lisa Appignanesi, Timothy Garton Ash, Anthony Barnett** openDemocracy, **Geoffrey Bindman, Yahya Birt** City Circle, **Jon Bright** OurKingdom, **Martin Bright** New Statesman, **John le Carré, Tufyal Choudhury** Durham University, **Peter Facey** Unlock Democracy, **Dr Catherine Fieschi** Demos, **Conor Foley, Pam Giddy** Power Inquiry, **Jeremy Hardie** Open Democracy Foundation, **Gavin Hayes** Compass, **Bob Hepple QC, Paul Hilder** Avaaz.org, **Ed Husain, Helena Kennedy QC, John Jackson, Sunder Katwala** Fabian Society, **Francesca Klug** LSE, **Hari Kunzru, David Marquand, Prof Tariq Modood** Bristol University, **Fuad Nahdi** Radical Middle Way, **Susie Orbach, Philip Pullman, Ziauddin Sardar, Dr Ghayasuddin Siddiqui** Muslim Institute, **Gillian Slovo, Prof Quentin Skinner** Cambridge University, **Juliet Stevenson, Prof Stuart Weir** Democratic Audit, **Timothy Winter** Cambridge University

March 17
Jonathan Powell on Tony Blair (Weekend, March 15): "He would get up at 4 o'clock in the morning and write in his underpants." No wonder it took him a long time to learn how to use a computer.

Bryan Morgan
Worksop, Nottinghamshire

March 17
I deny the existence of the One True Teapot (Letters, March 14). I think this makes me an ateaist.

John Taylor
Epsom, Surrey

March 18
If John Lewis's prices are the benchmark for publicly funded house-hold items (Never knowingly undersold: the MPs' guide to setting up home on expenses, March 14), why do Department for Work and Pensions staff administering social fund grants for

the poorest still use the Argos catalogue?

Neil Bateman
Ipswich, Suffolk

March 19
The gay old people's home (Shortcuts, G2, March 17) is an excellent idea. How I wish someone would open a home for old Guardian readers.

Anne Amison
Codsall, Staffordshire

March 19
In our house we have the One True Coffee Pot (Letters, passim). Please withhold my name and address, as I'm trying to get my children into a Teapot school.

Name and address withheld

March 20
I was delighted by the letter from Anne Amison from Codsall (March 19) suggesting a care home for

March 19

The courtesies of coca culture

Rory Carroll's use of the word "boisterous" in a sentence beginning with the statement that Peruvian "politicians munched on the raw ingredient of cocaine" is unfortunate (Peruvian politicians in coca protest, March 15). It associates the mastication of coca leaves with activity uncharacteristic of what the article rightly points out as the sacredness surrounding coca culture in the Andes.

People in Aymara- and Quechua-speaking communities in Andean countries observe certain courtesies on meeting an acquaintance; a reciprocal exchange of a personal item, a little coca bag, takes place so that you take a few leaves from my bag and I take a few leaves from yours. A quiet exchange of news information follows the addition of the leaves to the quid in one's mouth. The attitude is one of contemplation. At the end of the meeting, one usually adds new leaves before taking one's departure.

People often masticate coca in a period of studied calmness before undertaking strenuous activity such as mining or herding, which more often than not take place at altitudes well in excess of 4,000m above sea level. The cultural behaviour associated with the highs reported from taking cocaine could not be more different.

Dr Penelope Dransart
Reader in anthropology, University of Wales, Lampeter

March 20

Red-green alliance to save us from Boris

It could not be further from the truth to say
that there are no serious differences between the
contenders in the London mayoral election (The
weary and warier, March 18; Ken and Boris play Big
Brother, March 19).

The choice between Boris Johnson's nightmare
vision and our policies could not be clearer.
Boris Johnson opposed the minimum wage, and
supported George Bush in opposing the Kyoto
treaty. He would scrap the affordable housing
requirement and the £25 CO_2 charge on gas
guzzlers, and has called the low-emission zone to
cut air pollution "the most punitive, draconian
fining regime in the whole of Europe". He backs
nuclear power and nuclear weapons.

Because Boris Johnson's anti-green and anti-
social agenda is a throwback that means he cannot
be trusted with London's future, we have come
together to call on our supporters to use their
second-preference votes for each other. The choice
is very clear – go backwards with Boris Johnson,
or make sure London continues to have a green
mayor by voting for our candidacies.

Sian Berry Green party candidate
Ken Livingstone Labour party candidate

March 24

Human rights and realpolitik in Tibet

I was to be an Olympic torch-bearer in Thailand
on behalf of the Green World Foundation, an
NGO concerned with environmental education.
Although I had reservations due to China being the

Guardian readers. I
hadn't known there
were any other
Guardian readers in
this Tory stronghold.

Fiona Taylor
Codsall, Staffordshire

March 20

Teapot devotees
(Letters, passim) should
note that Huddersfield
is home to the Teapot
Chapel Mosque.

John Duffy
Huddersfield,
West Yorkshire

March 21

A few years ago a
Guardian headline
read "Why we are
obsessed with Sting's
tantric sex". I wasn't,
and don't know what
tantric sex is. Now
you have a headline
reading "Why we love
to hate Heather" (G2,
March 20). I don't. The
first person plural is
almost always wrong
in headlines.

Fred Sedgwick
Ipswich, Suffolk

March 24

The choice for opera fans is not only between high London prices and flying to a European capital (Letters, March 22). In less than three hours by car/bus/train they can be in a capital with a fantastic theatre built with opera in mind. Last week cute folk could see Bryn Terfel in Falstaff for £15. In Scottish and other English cities there will be other gems — but why are we telling the Londoners?

Maggie Pierce
Cardiff

March 25

John Mortimer famously defined tantric sex (Letters, March 21) as being like waiting at home for a delivery: "You stay in all day but nobody comes."

Michael Clarke
Godalming, Surrey

second largest carbon emitter, I felt that positive engagement on environmental matters was the best course of action. In view of recent events in Tibet (Pelosi urges world to condemn China over crackdown, March 22), I have now withdrawn. As a Buddhist, I cannot participate when China has shown a disregard for human rights, refuses to enter into a dialogue with the Dalai Lama and has no regard for world opinion. China is using the Olympics as an attempt to encourage the world community to endorse its regime. I understand that I am the first torch-bearer to withdraw from carrying the flame, which should be a symbol of peace, not oppression.

Narisa Chakrabongse
Chairperson, Green World Foundation

March 24

Verse by the yard for Downing Street Bard

The story of the unknown poet who wrote in uncomplimentary terms about Gordon Brown (At Downing Street upon the stair, I met a man who wasn't Blair..., March 21) saw me diving into my history books. Two lines of satirical poetry — "The cat and the rat and Lovell our Dog, / Rule all England under the Hog" — saw a nationwide witch-hunt in 1485 as Richard III sought to find the author. The cat was Sir Thomas Catesby, the rat Sir William Ratcliffe. The dog was Thomas, Lord Lovell. The hog was Richard himself. It perhaps should be noted by the anonymous poet of 2008 that his or her ancestor-in-wit, William Collingbourne, was tracked down and hung, drawn, castrated and quartered. He kept his wit to the end. After being brought down barely alive from the gallows, and at the moment of disembowelment, he said with his last breath: "Oh, Lord Jesus! More trouble."

Jon Buss
Ipswich, Suffolk

• Obviously Brown wrote it. What better way to keep ministers in line than to have them all under suspicion of disloyalty?

Geoff Wicks
Derby

March 24

MPs with principles

Much as I admire Martin Bell's achievements as an anti-sleaze campaigner, it really will not do for him to continue to imply the behaviour of all MPs is beyond the pale (Police halt inquiry into disgraced MP, March 21). Some of us (many of us?) do not believe there is one rule for us and another for everybody else. Indeed it is a matter of record that some of us were against the disgraceful moves to exempt MPs from freedom of information regulations put forward by a group of senior MPs last year. I agree that there is a real need for external regulation, and many MPs are already committed to greater transparency and accountability. But the case for change – so vividly illustrated by the Conway case – is not helped or assisted by pretending that all MPs are trying to defend the status quo.

Mark Hunter MP
Lib Dem, Cheadle

March 26

No need to spend 2 hours 7 minutes getting from London to Cardiff for cheap opera (Letters, March 24). Lille is only 1 hour 24 minutes away.

JR Batts
Banbury, Oxfordshire

March 27

I was pleased to read that the totally delightful, completely beautiful and utterly seductive No 1 Ladies' Detective Agency was rubbished by your TV critic (March 24). As the Guardian rubbishes everything I write for TV, I am beginning to think that I'm not so bad after all.

Guy Hibbert
Tilting Ground Productions

March 27

I am alarmed to read of the proposal to drop three letters from the Portuguese alphabet, with the letters p, c and h likely to be "consigned to orthographic history" (Report, March 26). I fear on my next visit the atmospheric second city of Oorto, the ancient university centre of Oimbra and many other places I have loved in Ortugal will be, well, just not quite the same.

Enda O'Doherty
Dublin

March 27

I note that Gordon Brown and Nicolas Sarkozy will sign an "entente atomique" at the Emirates stadium this week (Report, March 22). It gives a whole new meaning to the term nuclear arsenal.

Mark Fletton
Exeter, Devon

March 27

I recommend walking barefoot over bubble wrap (Get your socks off, G2, March 25), but it needs to be the kind

March 26

Science, ethics and the embryo bill

The attacks on the proposed revision to the 1990 Human Fertilisation and Embryology Act are reminiscent of the debates about in vitro fertilisation (Scientists say Catholic clergy inflaming embryo debate, March 25). It was 20 years ago this week that my father Patrick Steptoe died, and nearly 30 years since he was involved in the birth of the first IVF baby, Louise Brown. Then — as now — scientists were accused of tinkering with the sacred building blocks of life and the creation of monsters. It is worth remembering that IVF did not lead to disaster, but has brought incalculable joy to millions of families from all religions. Embryo research has an outstanding opportunity to advance therapies for the serious diseases that afflict so many men and women in their later years. Patrick always championed the relief of suffering and the rights of patients to benefit from scientific progress and would certainly have supported these amendments.

Professor Andrew Steptoe
University College London

March 29

Travellers' camp

OK, so somebody explain to me what's wrong with a group of Travellers setting up camp on their own land near a government minister's house (We've nowhere else to go, say Travellers, March 26)? Did they invade somebody else's country, amass extravagant expenses, lie to parliament? Oh no, that's the preserve of pampered politicians. Or are the Travellers merely trying to live a lifestyle they have preserved against the odds for centuries?

All the Travellers I have met while researching my new book have been hard-working, welcoming, charming people with strong family networks. Some of these "outraged" opponents of the settlement should calm down and go and talk to their new neighbours. I guarantee they will be pleasantly surprised. Come on, live and let live.

Alan Gibbons
(Children's author), Liverpool

March 31

Brazil sugars the pill on biofuels

It should be made clear that there are considerable differences between biofuels in terms of greenhouse gas emissions (Biofuels: a solution that became part of the problem, March 25). Sugarcane is by far the most productive, cost-efficient and carbon-saving feedstock for biofuel production. Sugarcane ethanol allows for a 90% reduction in emissions, compared with petrol, and its energy balance is 8.3 to one, ie for every unit of energy used in production eight units of energy are created. Gains in agricultural productivity in Brazil have led to a simultaneous increase in ethanol and food production. Brazil now produces enough ethanol to power 45% of its passenger vehicles using only 3.4m hectares, or 1%, of its arable land. This production is located mainly in the centre-south of Brazil, 2,500km distant from the Amazon. Brazil's ethanol production is expected to triple by 2020, but the increase will require only 6m additional hectares, only a fraction of the 30m hectares of degraded pasture currently available. Thanks to hydroelectric power and to

with large bubbles for the ultimate in podalic pleasure. Removing greenhouse insulation in late spring provides a good opportunity.

Meg Morton
Leeds

March 28
President Sarkozy calls for *fraternité* (President pays tribute to Britain and calls for 'brother-hood', March 27): what this country needs is more *liberté* and more *égalité*.

Anthony Evans
London

March 29
Why can't Brits do launches? Millennium Dome – no invitations sent out. Millennium bridge – too wobbly. London Eye – tech-nical problems. Every computer system the government has installed ... Now T5 (Terminal 5 in chaos on opening day, March 28). A triumph if you

don't mind sleeping
on the floor and doing
without luggage.

Daphne Romney
London

March 29
I'm looking forward
to an in-depth article
on Angela Merkel's
husband, the quantum
chemist and professor
Joachim Sauer. I
imagine it will be far
more edifying than
the ridiculous sexist
froth (yes, women can
be sexist too) we were
treated to in the article
about M Sarkozy's
latest acquisition (Je
Thames, March 28).

Helena Forsyth
Edinburgh

biofuels, approximately 45% of Brazil's total energy
mix is comprised of renewable sources, compared
with the EU's average of 6.7% and the UK's 2%.

Felipe Costa
Embassy of Brazil

March 31
Review migrant and asylum systems

While it's good to see the nastiness and brutishness
of the gangmaster system exposed (Gangmaster
loses employment licence, March 22), you really
only describe the tiny tip of a gigantic iceberg:
financial, physical, emotional and sexual abuses
of migrant workers are rampant in our country
– and not just by gangmasters. The Gangmasters
Licensing Authority is often helpless to do
anything about even the crassest abuses because
they are outside its remit, which excludes directly-
employing farmers and workers in all occupations
except agriculture and horticulture.

The advent of the woefully underresourced
GLA has only caused abusers and exploiters to
shift their business into the care, hospitality and
building industries: there is hardly a hospital, care
home, restaurant or factory without gangmaster
involvement. We have a choice: either the GLA
needs much more power, resources and people to
do a much more thorough job on the gangsters
who abuse foreigners and British workers alike, or
do away altogether with this horrendous system of
institutionalised abuse and let jobcentres deal with
immigrant workers.

Rev David de Verny
Ecumenical chaplain with new arrival communities in
south-east Lincolnshire

April 2008

The gathering storm over Labour started to reach a critical mass — and all over 10p. The abolition of the lowest 10p-in-the-pound income tax band, to fund a cut in the main rate from 22p to 20p, had been one of Gordon Brown's last acts as chancellor. Even as the change came into effect, Brown seemed to be in denial that this amounted to a tax increase for many of the poorest taxpayers. Eventually a package to offset the losses was put together which satisfied parliamentary rebels, led by Frank Field. But Labour's reputation for economic competence and commitment to fairness both took a severe knock as the local elections approached. The party began to fear that Ken Livingstone's reign as London mayor could come to an end, helped by the unabashed support for Boris Johnson from the Evening Standard, the capital's main paper. The death of the much-respected MP Gwyneth Dunwoody and the prospect of losing a safe seat added to the gloom for Labour; plans for ecotowns and cadet corps in schools did little to win back the core vote. The wider economic impact of the credit crunch began to be felt, and rising world food prices — partly driven by speculators — raised fears of famine in developing countries. Many European countries were embarrassed by the progress of the Olympic torch and/or the pro-Tibetan protests that followed it. Nick Clegg was embarrassed over revelations about his personal conquests. Readers were unembarrassed about eating apple cores.

April 1

Could you please pass the word around the City of London that I would willingly try to bring any bank to its knees for a fee considerably less than that promised to Adam Applegarth (Former Rock chief in line for £760,000 payoff, March 31).

Frances Worsley
High Peak, Derbyshire

April 2

Gordon Brown and Carla Bruni-Sarkozy (Calling Carla: Brown enlists first lady to give Britain style, April 1), an obvious April Fool contender, but 30 women sleeping with Nick Clegg (Clegg tots up sex encounters in GQ interview, April 1)? How gullible do you think we are?

Sonal Shah
University of Birmingham

April 2

Diana inquest verdict

I have followed the Diana inquest closely and been absorbed by the contradictory evidence. I simply cannot accept that the coroner has any right to withdraw from the jury the opportunity to find that she was "unlawfully killed" by a third party (No evidence Diana killed by MI6, coroner tells jury, April 1).

While I can appreciate that no evidence to implicate the Duke of Edinburgh has emerged, there certainly is evidence for unlawful killing by a third party other than the paparazzi or Henri Paul. As Michael Mansfield QC has repeated throughout, it is for the jury to determine the truthfulness or otherwise of the evidence.

The jury will now not be able to pass their verdict on the contradictions in the evidence surrounding Henri Paul's postmortem, Diana's engagement and pregnancy, the claims of her friends, employees and family, or the less than convincing evidence of the security service and police officers, who failed to provide relevant evidence to the coroner at the earliest opportunity.

Dr Rory Ridley-Duff
Sheffield

April 4

Boris: my new ideas for London

It seems bizarre to accuse a candidate of failing to attend election hustings for mayor of London in the week that I've attended two consecutive televised public hustings (A diary clash, a prior engagement, the wrong issues. Boris Johnson shuns mayoral hustings, April 2). Last night, when all three mayoral candidates participated in an important housing hustings, you missed the opportunity to report on some of the new ideas I am bringing forward to reduce housing waiting lists and deal with the crippling cost of housing in the capital. Indeed, your readers would have benefited from full reports of the 12 hustings at least some mayoral candidates have been involved in so far.

As for the Labour mayor, it is indeed disappointing that he has already chickened out of three important hustings – at the UK youth parliament, the Federation of Small Businesses and, most tellingly, a hustings in Islington on how to deal with gun and knife crime.

Unfortunately, Time Out changed the date of one hustings and made it impossible for me to attend. Instead, I will be cross-examined by local newspaper editors – the sort of scrutiny that the mayor is shying away from.

Indeed, Londoners are increasingly asking: where's Ken? He should hear how Londoners are calling time on his tired regime and want a fresh approach to solving London's problems.

Boris Johnson
Conservative candidate for London mayor

April 4

Protecting data and the public interest

Your report on the Data Protection Act (PM seeks retreat on bill to outlaw press spying, April 1) did not mention that the media industry is absolutely united in its opposition to jail sentences for journalists for breaches of the act, especially as

April 2

Supposedly green fuels shipped across the Atlantic and back, the PM wants to let newspapers buy our personal data, there's a GCSE in nail art, and Boris is ahead for London mayor. Shouldn't you go easy on the April Fool's jokes?

Mike Robinson
Leeds

April 2

Liverpool John Lennon Airport has, as part of its logo, the phrase "Above us only sky", taken from Lennon's song Imagine. Perhaps British Airways (BA brings in hundreds of volunteers to tackle baggage mountain, March 31) may like to adopt another phrase from the same song: "Imagine no possessions".

John Shaw
Liverpool

April 2

Maybe Mugabe is
just taking time out
to get votes from his
superdelegates (Secret
Mugabe meeting
ponders military move
or fixed result – but
not an admission of
defeat, April 1).

Dr Sandy Wilson
Raglan, Monmouthshire

April 2

Thanks, Alan Pickup
(Starwatch, March 31),
for locating the Teapot
in Sagittarius.

Tony Purcell
Chelmsford, Essex

April 3

Jamie Oliver might
profit from studying
David Kynaston's
Austerity Britain
1945-48: A World to
Build (Now Jamie
Oliver wants Britain
on a wartime diet,
March 29). Kynaston
quotes a frustrated
1940s housewife:
"Our rations now are
1oz bacon per week,

the threat of unlimited fines already lies on the
statute books. All newspapers, local, regional,
national – including the Guardian – and the
major television outlets are opposed to the idea of
two-year sentences for journalists doing their job.

Let it be stressed that the industry unequivocally
condemns payments to private detectives illegally
"blagging" private information, but the Data
Protection Act is drawn so widely that a journalist's
first steps in checking a story – which may or may
not be of public interest – could be a breach of the
act. The chilling effect on responsible journalism
of the threat of jail goes without saying. While the
industry is doing all it can to address the concerns of
the information commissioner, it is vital that those
who believe in the freedom of the media oppose
this draconian and disproportionate measure.

Bob Satchwell
Executive director, Society of Editors

April 5

Eclectic roster on Play for Today

From 1967 to 1973 I was producer of The Wednesday
Play, later renamed Play for Today when it was
moved to Thursdays. Graeme McDonald and
I shared the output, which, in retrospect, was
amazingly large. Between 1969 and 1973 I produced
53 plays, the bulk of which were specially written.
I subsequently wrote a book called Play for Today,
in which the genesis of the plays and their authors
and directors are described.

Mark Lawson (One-hit wonders, G2, April 2)
deals only with the tail end of the series and
ignores the important input of my boss, Sydney
Newman, a charismatic Canadian imported

by director general Hugh Carleton Greene to make contemporary programmes on the North American model, in contrast to the "anyone for tennis" style. Sydney wanted us to follow American writers such as Paddy Chayevsky, Reginald Rose and Gore Vidal with hard-hitting drama based on strong realistic subjects. Although there was a clique of leftwing writers and directors, like Ken Loach and Tony Garnett, we were an eclectic lot. And contrary to Lawson's contention, there were women writers. Nemone Lethbridge, a lawyer married to an ex-convict, wrote three plays, Faye Weldon two; Julia Jones wrote four. Among the others were Brigid Brophy, Vickery Turner and Joan Henry.

My best-known production, Edna the Inebriate Woman, about a bag lady, written by Jeremy Sandford, was much used for fundraising for the homeless. William Trevor wrote many scripts, and other writers included John Osborne, the sociologist Tony Parker, David Rudkin, John Mortimer, Alun Owen, Peter Terson, Roy Minton, Don Shaw, Barry Reckord and Willis Hall.

Hanging above my desk, I have a certificate for my contribution to the 1968-69 NET Playhouse series (broadcast on US television) which won an Emmy for outstanding dramatic series. So Kevin Spacey could well have seen Play for Today in the US.

Irene Shubik
London

April 5
Poor show by Labour on tax

A year ago Labour abolished the 10p tax band, a change which comes into effect on Sunday, in

3lbs potatoes, 2oz butter, 3oz marge, 1oz cooking fat, 2oz cheese … 1lb jam or marmalade per month and ½lb bread per day." Just about enough to stretch Jamie's creative imagination for one single meal.

Anne Currie
Richmond, North Yorkshire

April 4
There is a sound economic logic as to why the poor can face marginal tax rates of 70% while the rich can be demotivated by rates of 40% (Letters, April 1). Money, like anything else, has a marginal utility that diminishes the more you already have. So while someone with little money may work hard for an extra £1, even though they only get to keep 30p, a wealthy person may not bother earning that extra £1 unless they can keep over

60p. This is all very unfair, but economics isn't called the dismal science for nothing.

Dr Hillary Shaw
Harper Adams University
College, Shropshire

April 4

How much more interesting your survey could have been if Nick Clegg and the passersby had been asked for a qualitative rather than a quantitative response to the "people I have slept with" question (Between you, me and the bedpost, G2, April 2).

Anne-Marie Quigg
Halifax, West Yorkshire

April 4

"If…" version 2.4.6234 (G2, April 2) is possibly the most scabrous and insulting thing I've ever read. Well done.

Steve Perry
Aylesbury,
Buckinghamshire

the full knowledge that 5 million households on low incomes would be negatively affected (Brown fights revolts on tax and alcohol duty, April 4). For a year MPs did nothing about it. A little media coverage at five minutes to 12 triggered a Labour motion, only for it to be withdrawn.

Those like myself who earn little and who are proud not to receive state benefits will have a substantially increased chunk taken from their already miserly pay package in order to fund what benefits society as a whole. We have a party and a government that has shown its commitment to a new form of social justice: single out low earners who are financially self-reliant for higher taxation than anyone else and make them pay. My view on social justice is different. Labour just lost a vote.

Bettina Reiber
London

April 7

Listen to our body language

As the "heavily pregnant" woman who kneeled nearly naked in a metal stall to remind viewers of how mother animals are totally commodified, abused and denied their every desire on factory farms, I am surprised by Julie Bindel's curious interpretation of my actions – though I suppose if she thinks that a heavily pregnant woman is a sex symbol, perhaps I should be flattered as well (Who is this supposed to help?, G2, April 4).

It smacks of the very paternalism that Bindel purports to oppose to tell women what they can and cannot do with their bodies. I have a mind of my own and I can decide how I want to express myself. Individuals, driven by their beliefs, have used their bodies to convey messages since Lady Godiva rode naked on a horse to protest against taxes on the poor.

Other animals are made of flesh, blood and bone, just like humans. They have the same five physiological senses, the same capacity to feel pain, and they value their lives. They are our "cousins", as Richard Dawkins puts it, and being compared to them is no insult.

Peta campaigns work because they force people to look, think and, most importantly, take action.

Noemie Ventura
Campaign coordinator, www.peta.org.uk

April 8

Fanning the flame of discontent

How many people are aware that the modern torch relay (Arrests, fights, jeering: Olympic spirit flickers amid the chaos, April 7) was introduced by Carl Diem, president of the organisation committee for the 1936 Olympics in Berlin, as part of an effort to turn the games into a glorification of the Third Reich?

Adolf Hitler said: "Sporting chivalrous contest helps knit the bonds of peace between nations. Therefore may the Olympic flame never expire."

Patricia van den Brink
Herne, Germany

April 8

Understanding Travellers' traditions

Libby Brooks is wrong to say those of us who oppose illegal sites do not understand the Traveller

April 5

Oh good grief, as Charlie Brown would have said; now the government wants a league table of adventure playgrounds (Youngsters to assess local facilities, April 4). Another example of only valuing what is measurable (instead of measuring what is valuable). Let's hope the children use measures like numbers of trees climbed, acreage of grazed knees, and the one we as boys used, height of piss up the wall.

Rick Hall
London

April 5

BBC News, July 18 2005: Malaysia 'teapot cult' attacked (http://tinyurl.com/572kr3). Probably stirring things up again (Letters, passim).

Ike Ginn
Nottingham

April 7

The Guardian's Tom Service (Just don't call me cool, G2, April 2)? Sounds interesting. How do I sign up for it?

Ken Atkin
Richmond, Surrey

April 9

I was very pleased to read (How to... eat an apple, Weekend, March 22) that there are people other than myself who eat the entire apple including the core. I have never known anyone else apart from my mother who did this. I cannot understand why "it is the older generation" when, to the best of my knowledge, I am the sole representative of the core eaters. I am 70 and have done it all my life, but would be interested to know if there are others, whatever their age might be.

Gwyneth Raymond
Grange-over-Sands,
Cumbria

way of life (Our view of house and home allows no place for Travellers, April 3). Basildon district provides over 100 authorised sites and pitches, more than any other local authority in Essex, and has a long tradition of being home to Gypsies. But this has also made us a target for illegal sites, with Dale Farm in my constituency now reportedly the largest in Britain. There comes a point at which protection of the green belt must be taken seriously: we cannot have one law for the settled community and another for Travellers.

John Baron MP
Con, Billericay

April 9

Urban regeneration still the right course

Simon Jenkins' article on the dangers of ecotowns is both right and important (Comment, April 4). Over the last decade we have focused on the regeneration of our towns and cities, not least by constraining development on greenfield sites. The result has been urban renaissance in cities as diverse as Manchester, Bristol, Southampton and Sheffield. We have not always got things right – the quality of some of our urban design too often leaves a lot to be desired and we have not built enough affordable new homes. But we have secured the economic and social regeneration of many urban communities, while at the same time protecting our environment. The government can take much of the credit for the success of this policy approach.

By contrast, the government's planned ecotowns threaten to be the thin edge of a wedge. There will be significant damage to both urban and rural environments, including increased road congestion and carbon emissions. The simple fact is that car-dependent greenfield developments will never be as sustainable as regenerating existing urban areas.

By continuing the regeneration of our towns and cities, we can use the increasing tax base to further strengthen our existing infrastructure — schools, utilities, public transport. There is plenty of space left in urban Britain to meet almost all our residential and commercial development needs. It is not always easy to achieve that regeneration, but future generations will not thank us if we change direction now.

Richard Rogers
Rogers Stirk Harbour & Partners

April 9

Give politicians credit for the crunch

Larry Elliott is right to finger the banks for their role in the current global financial crisis (We're in a winter of discontent again — but this time big finance is the villain, April 7). But others are more culpable, because they gave away extensive powers and defaulted on obligations to act as guardians of the nation's finances: politicians, including chancellors and finance ministers, and central bank governors. We the electorate are also culpable as we were willingly duped by the finance sector and its "guardians" into believing that there were no risks and only gains to be made from the deregulation and creation of "easy money".

Sure, the finance sector pushed for the deregulation and privatisation of credit creation. But it was politicians — from Nixon through

April 9
At Deene Park, Northamptonshire, there is a teapot on top of an obelisk. Is this a rallying point for cult followers (Letters, passim), or to guide in the flying saucers?

Susan Kellerman
Leeds

April 9
Ken Atkin (Letters, April 7) asks how to sign up for "the Guardian's Tom Service". Perhaps his local vet could oblige?

Stewart Easton
London

April 10
I was one of those arrested for attempting to run alongside the Olympic torch with a Tibetan flag (Thousands protest as Olympic flame carried through London, April 7). During the protest, brought to an abrupt end by the police, I found myself

in the company of 12 Chinese torch attendants. Given that the cream of China's security agency are likely to be men with colourful CVs, why was it that such individuals were allowed to jog through our streets to defend a giant cigarette lighter?

Ben Stewart
London

April 10

I'm 55 and I thought I was the only apple-core eater (Letters, April 9). I eat the apple down to the core. Then I start eating it again from the base, biting across at right angles to the length of the core, to leave only the stalk. This way you don't seem to notice the crunchy bits and the seeds!

Steve Tompkins
Matlock, Derbyshire

Heath, Callaghan, Thatcher, Reagan, Clinton and Blair – who had the power to deregulate through legislation. They were often richly rewarded for their efforts, with Tony Blair's highly paid advisory role to the US bank JP Morgan but the latest example. If we are to regain control over the banks, avoid nationalising losses and ensure market discipline prevails, it will be vital to hold the feet of politicians to the fire – before they retire.

Ann Pettifor
Fellow, New Economics Foundation

April 11

Anti-mayor reports are hardly Watergate

Do we need still more proof of most editors' blinkered desire for the "hot" story about failure or mismanagement in preference to anything which those in power achieve, however slowly? Yes, apparently we do. And so this year's British Press Awards have "honoured" Andrew Gilligan as Journalist of the Year for his "investigative" reporting into allegations of fraud at the London Development Agency (Report, April 9)

Yet three years ago, as councillor for the ward containing the Green Badge Taxi School – one of Gilligan's "scoops", and two of whose executives have now been arrested (for fraud) – I repeatedly approached the Evening Standard with the story. But the paper repeatedly rebuffed my efforts – and those of the building's new owner – to bring the story to a wider audience. Three years later, with the paper's blood up as it charges into battle against London's mayor, the story – precious little investigation required – is unearthed and run. This was no Woodward-Bernstein achievement. This was simple archive work, with a little accountancy on the side.

Now every paper has a right to support one candidate over another. But what the Standard is doing isn't support – it's a vicious, repetitive attack on one (who has his faults), and a beatification of the other (who has no experience or proven abilities). Even two days ago its headline accused Livingstone of receiving a "secret donation" in 2004 – though Gilligan's text offered not a single proof of this "secrecy". In a city with only one serious local paper (the freesheets are just celebrity tattle), this shoddy, personalised journalism is genuinely anti-democratic. If this deserves an award, God help us all.

Jonathan Myerson
Former Labour councillor, Lambeth

April 11

Speculation fuels food price rises

Over the past decade we have seen asset bubbles burst in the dotcom industry, developing-country stockmarkets (the latest is China) and now a colossal housing bubble in the US and Europe (We are in the worst financial crisis since the Depression, says IMF, April 10). The victims have largely been the middle and working classes of the wealthier west. But the new victims of the unregulated flows of international capital will be the poorest households on earth. Amartya Sen taught us that reduced purchasing power rather than a lack of food availability causes hunger and malnutrition. The recent terrifying increases in food prices (Food price rises threaten global security – UN, April 9) mean the poorest households in the developing world, surviving on

April 11
Next to my name on my national travel pass (Letters, April 7) it says "expiry date November 21 2012". Is this a government strategy for solving the pensions crisis?

Doug Meredith
Manchester

April 11
I am five and a half. I eat the whole apple. I eat the seeds and the stalk (Letters, April 10).

Ivor Nash
London

April 12
You state "ITV1 and Channel Five both insist their public service obligations are no longer viable" (Leaders, April 11). I cannot speak for ITV, but as far as Five is concerned this is emphatically not the case. Our schedules include two early evening news programmes, three

hours of predominately UK-produced programmes for children every day and a wide range of factual programming in peak time. We are committed to continuing with such a mix in the years ahead. Five is proud to be a public service broadcaster, and that is how we see our future.

Jane Lighting
Chief executive, Five

April 12
Re expiry dates (Letters, April 11), the music magazine fRoots tells potential subscribers: "A subscription implies that the magazine will be sent to the subscriber until one of the three expires."

Mark Holmström
Norwich

April 12
Halve your apple (Letters, April 11) with a cut through the equator, not through

tiny fixed incomes, will be hungry right now. In a few months our TV screens will show the pot bellies of children with kwashiorkor and the emaciated faces of mothers and children ravaged by malnutrition and infection. Many will die unnoticed. Food price rises cannot simply be explained by crop yields or the expansion of the use of agricultural land for biofuels. Speculation in agricultural commodity markets runs in parallel with the rising costs of gold, oil and essential metals.

Gordon Brown is right to call for concerted action by the G8. Food commodities should be insulated from speculators and hedge funds who profit as prices rise, and again when they fall in a few months' time. Anyone profiting from this volatility will do so at the expense of the lives of thousands of mothers and children.

Anthony Costello
Director, UCL Institute for Global Health

April 12
Bog-standard changes

In describing the BFI's decision to create two gender-neutral toilets for the London Lesbian and Gay Film Festival as a scandal (The great gender-neutral toilet scandal, G2, April 10), Julie Bindel is perhaps creating a storm in a toilet bowl. Gender-neutral toilets were created following audience requests for facilities, and we've heard nothing but positive feedback from all sections of the audience, including many queer women. There are no urinals in these toilets so, for those who care about such things, there is no question of improper exposure to users of the facilities. Other toilets are equally close to the busy bar area, and our female audiences are as well-catered for as ever with a choice of whether to use gender-neutral or women-only. This innovation has been so well-received, we are considering making it a permanent fixture.

Now let's talk about the films ...

Sandra Hebron Head of BFI Festivals, **Brian Robinson** Senior programmer, London Lesbian and Gay Film Festival team

April 14
Award for Gilligan

It is difficult to understand the point Jonathan Myerson is making in his letter (April 11). Is he suggesting that a major investigation into the scandal of how public money went missing should be suppressed because there is a mayoral election taking place? Surely this is the exact time when public figures need to be made accountable for mismanagement. It was only following revelations by our reporter Andrew Gilligan that audits took place and the police were brought in to investigate. As the British Press Awards judges who this week made Andrew Gilligan Journalist of the Year said: "He is one of Britain's most courageous journalists, uncovering abuses at the heart of government and society that affect millions of people. There is no one else like him."

Doug Wills
Managing editor, Evening Standard

April 15
Speaking up for inheritance tax

The core mission that should underpin progressive politics is that we should not inherit our life

the poles of stalk and calyx. This shows each half to have five segments, to be separated by five more cuts to each half, giving 10 parts – the apple is a decimal fruit. The pips now fall off the inside-out fruit, and can be eaten, discarded or planted. Each of the 10 segments has two pieces of papery pericarp – nasty if caught between the teeth – which can be economically shaved off and discarded. Discard the stalk and enjoy the rest – four apples feed a whole maths class.

David Simmonds
Canterbury, Kent

April 12
It's all very well eating apple cores complete with the pips but, as my mum would say, don't come crying to me when an apple tree grows out of your ear.

Steve Pinder
London

April 14

As a person who is nearly 70 I am frequently lacking in energy, so after reading that artificial colours can provide a boost of hyperactivity I am going to start eating more mushy peas (Food watchdog seeks ban on six artificial colourings, April 9).

Irene Marshall
Beeston, Nottinghamshire

April 15

In your debate between Simon Jenkins and Richard Harries (Atheist versus bishop, April 12), it was not always easy to understand who was the atheist and who was the man of faith. One thing the two contributors do have in common, however, is that they are both members of the Human Fertilisation and Embryology Authority. Neither is likely to be opposed

chances at birth: our opportunities should depend on our efforts, not who our parents are. That is why the government is right to make ending child poverty the great cause of our times. Yet this ambition was undermined by the government's retreat in the face of a rightwing challenge over inheritance tax (This buffeted prime minister must stop scrambling at every puff of wind, April 11). Progressives must react to prevent any further inheritance tax reductions which again prioritise the richest, over the poorest, in our society.

Inheritance tax matters because it is one of the few tools which directly reduces inherited inequalities. Those arguing against it must know they will entrench social immobility. People across Britain who seek a fairer society must ensure they are campaigning for a fair and progressive tax system as an essential means to ensure a more just society.

Much of the opposition to inheritance tax is based on misinformation. There is a public perception that this is an unfair tax that large swaths of the population must pay. In fact, for the past few years, only the very richest have paid it – around 5.4% of estates. We must explode these politically motivated myths and make the public case for the fairness of this tax. So government must make the case for a fair and progressive tax system to ensure opportunities are made equal.

However, we cannot leave government to act alone. In this hostile political environment we believe that other public figures must speak up and make the moral case too: campaigners across the political divide should unite in challenging the perception that inheritance tax is somehow unfair. We must scrutinise all parties' tax proposals to ensure that the claims they make of wanting a fairer society stand up, and continue to campaign to narrow the gap in life chances.

Sunder Katwala Fabian Society, **Professor John Hills** LSE,
Professor Julian Le Grand LSE, **Richard Titmuss** LSE,
Professor Ruth Lister Loughborough University, **Professor David Miller** Oxford Universtiy, **Professor Peter Townsend**,
Alf Dubs House of Lords, **Brendan Barber** TUC, **Kate Green**
Child Poverty Action Group, **Will Hutton** Work Foundation,
Fiona Mactaggart MP, Terry Rooney MP Chair, pensions
select committee, **Clare Short MP and 23 others**

April 16

Correction: Richard Titmuss

Richard Titmuss could not have signed the letter to the Guardian supporting inheritance tax (April 15) since, sadly, he died in 1973. The error presumably arose because of a mistranscription of the name of the chair that I am privileged to hold at the LSE and that is named after him. However, I am certain that, as one of the outstanding thinkers of the 20th century and a committed egalitarian and social democrat, he would have signed it if he had been in a position to do so.

Julian Le Grand
Richard Titmuss professor of social policy, LSE

April 16

Don't bring war into our classrooms

The possibility that New Labour may "expand military cadet corps in English secondary schools" (Report, April 7) is deeply depressing. On October 1 1930, Einstein, Freud, Thomas Mann, HG Wells, Bertrand Russell, Jane Addams and the Society of Friends, among others, warned the world

to embryo research, nor to the creation of embryos using animal eggs. Next time you rent a bishop go for a Catholic and you will get a more robust debate.

Josephine Quintavalle
Comment on
Reproductive Ethics

April 15

"There's plenty of boys that will come hankering and gruvvelling around when you've got an apple, and beg the core off you; but when they've got one, and you beg for the core and remind them how you give them a core one time, they make a mouth at you and say thank you 'most to death, but there ain't-a-going to be no core." — Mark Twain, Tom Sawyer Abroad (Letters, passim).

Don Callister
Sheffield

April 16

According to my French diary, May 2 is St Boris's day. If that turns out to be an omen, it may serve us right for having elections on May 1 instead of keeping it as the workers' holiday.

John Arthur
London

April 18

Susie Grimshaw (Shortcuts, G2, April 15) is put out, it seems, that some travel writers spend mornings having leisurely breakfasts before deciding which restaurant to go to that night. And her point is? Breakfast and dinner are the only good bits about being a travel guidebook writer, which is otherwise an unremitting slog of tedium and hackery – apart from lunch, obviously. And cocktails. I didn't realise, however, that I was supposed to have

just after the Kellogg-Briand pact had repudiated war as an instrument of national policy: "There is a ... stark contrast between the peace declarations of governments and the maintenance and extension of military training of youth. Military training is the education of the mind and body in the technique of killing. It is education for war ... The older generation commits a grave crime against the younger generation if in schools ... youth are educated, often under the pretext of physical training, in the science of war."

At nearly 90, I definitely belong to the older generation. But, as I look back on a career devoted to education for life, which included helping to found the Open University, I beg the government not to expand education for war.

(Sir) Roy Shaw
Hove, East Sussex

April 17

Giant leap for frogs

Like all illegal immigrants, tree frogs are evidently exploring clever new ways to get in (How tree frog hopped to UK, April 12). Concealing themselves in spinach bags is clearly an advance on the more blatant techniques formerly used. In summer 2000, waiting for luggage at Gatwick, I was surprised to see a tree frog riding confidently around the carousel on a suitcase. It was swept off by the rubber curtains into the dead zone in the middle, and I gravely embarrassed my teenage children by leaping over the luggage to rescue it. It was hungry and dehydrated, and must have been in the airport for some days. A raucous male, he has enjoyed luxury accommodation in our conservatory ever since, having outlived two younger (captive-bred) companions I bought him. Like Popeye the spinach immigrant he is a European tree frog, and — also like Popeye — we named him after the place he was discovered, Gatwick.

Anthony Cheke
Oxford

April 19
Can Jay-Z stop the rain at Glastonbury?

Just thought I'd throw in my tuppence worth (Glastonbury denies reports rapper Jay-Z is to pull out, April 14). There is another far more pragmatic reason that I and quite a few of my white middle-class friends aren't going to Glastonbury this year. It's not the lineup. There's always a hoo-ha about this year's lineup: "You should've been here last year, it was so much better last year." I wouldn't mind seeing Jay-Z. He's got to be better than Oasis at Glastonbury 2004, headlining Friday night. My mum with a ukelele would've been better than Oasis at Glastonbury 2004. And I quite like them. No, I'll give you a clue. It pissed down in 2004. It pissed down in 2005. Only once, but the torrent was biblical. And it just pissed down the whole pissing time in pissing 2007. I'm 40 this year and the gamble is just too much. GlaxoSmithKline themselves couldn't produce a stimulant stimulating enough to artificially make me forget the pissing horror of three pissing days cold and wet in a pissing field.

Justin Missingham
London

sex with the waitresses. Perhaps that's where I've been going wrong.

Jules Brown
Alvém, Portugal

April 19
Steve Harmison (Sport, April 15) put it succinctly when he said: "I've got broad shoulders and I'll take it on the chin. People are sticking their fifty pence in every day but I'm sure that down the line it will be someone else's turn." It's a good job that cricket isn't a game of two halves.

Peter Quinn
Helperby, North Yorkshire

April 19
Duncan Campbell's note on the often-changed name of the Merseyside village of Lunt (Diary, April 11) reminds me of the former Crewe Alexandra midfielder Kenny Lunt (now back at Gresty Road on

LETTERS TO THE EDITOR

loan), known to some
fans as Lenny.

Paul Wilkinson
London

I can close my eyes
and see my late grand-
father standing with
his back to the fire. He
always used a sharp
knife to eat his apple
(Letters, passim),
removing the peel in
one long ribbon. He
would then slice off
pieces of apple, which
he transferred straight
to his mouth from
the knife. He went
right down to the
pips, throwing away
just the last little bit
plus the stalk into the
fire behind him and
replacing the knife on
the mantelshelf.

Carole Underwood
Kendal, Cumbria

April 23
Where would we be
without the Guardian?
I had no idea of the
underlying reason

April 19

How I'll put London back on track

John Vidal makes baseless criticisms of my plans for
London's public transport and cutting congestion
in the city (Centre of attention, Society, April 9). I
do not plan to privatise London Underground, but
believe it should be run in exactly the same way as
London's successful bus network and the award-
winning Docklands Light Railway. The tracks,
trains and stations will all remain Transport for
London property, and TfL will set the fares and
service standards and would take the fare box,
while a contractor would be paid a fee to deliver
the service.

My tram proposals are fully costed at a total of
£779m and over 10 years, on a busy route, they are
cheaper than buses. Trams are safe and popular,
and independent analysis has shown that, because
they run on rails, they require three times less
energy than vehicles such as buses with tyres on
tarmac. My proposals would provide badly needed
extra capacity on routes between the city centre
and Deptford, Stratford, Camden and Brixton,
bringing substantial regenerative benefits to these
and other areas on the routes.

Finally, on congestion, while Ken involves himself
in political posturing with his £25 congestion charge
for gas-guzzling cars, he is, in the same package of
measures, allowing smaller vehicles exemption
from the charge. This will create jams, longer
journey times and thus, according to Friends of the
Earth, potentially even more pollution. I propose a
£10 charge for all cars coming in from outside the
city, with specific measures to protect shopping
and business centres on London's periphery. It is
these long-distance commuters who create the

most pollution and I will use the money raised to improve public transport in the outer boroughs.

Brian Paddick
Liberal Democrat candidate for London mayor

April 22
MP's caring call

Gwyneth Dunwoody (Obituary, April 19) was a true politician who other politicians could do well to follow. A few years ago, one Sunday evening when television programmes were dire, I switched to BBC Parliament. Watching Dunwoody chairing a transport select committee, I was drawn to the discussion about transport and the disabled. Realising that there was very little "disabled" input, I wrote to her pointing out that the problems of travelling for the physically disabled, in our case to Ireland, both by air and ferry, were well nigh impossible.

Two days later the phone rang and we were met with "Dunwoody here, can I speak to Mrs Keat?" She was so interested in what we had to say – the first time our disabled son has received such high-powered interest. Her request that we send her a report to include in the document was granted, and for all I know that is just what happened.

Anne Keat
Corsham, Wiltshire

April 23
Cheap shots at Varna are unworthy of you

I am 29 and a manager at a multinational company based in Bulgaria. I felt offended, hurt and indignant

for the fig roll crisis (Shortcuts, G2, April 21). Particularly stressful or traumatic events in my life require two consecutive packets.

Sheila Oliver
Stockport, Cheshire

April 24
I agree that the archaeological museum in Varna is first-rate (Letters, April 23), but it's also the first museum I've ever seen that has a sign saying "no guns" as well as the more common "no photographs". No doubt it was there to reassure visitors, but it didn't quite have the intended effect on me.

David Bradbury
London

April 26
David Bradbury (Letters, April 24) doesn't need to go as far as Varna to be refused entry for carrying a gun. A

notice at the Science Museum in London has banned them for at least a year.

Kate Byrne
London

April 28

The author of the letter about exploding coconuts (April 24) is not alone! See www.chickenarmpits. blogspot.com/2005/04/ mystery.html.

PD Butcher
Gloucester

April 28

Noise like a gunshot? Bounty hunters?

Sue Johnston
Newcastle upon Tyne

April 28

The Guardian Science Course – Part 1: The Universe (April 26) would appear to leave little scope for subsequent parts.

Les Hearn
London

when I read Tanya Gold's article ('I am starting to love this dirty town', G2, April 21). Gold has reflected Bulgarian reality through a perspective distorted by the far-fetched, imperialistic British humour. As a Bulgarian who has visited Varna many times, I would say that this description doesn't make it seem as if the town is in Bulgaria at all.

I object to the way the author has exaggerated her experiences to make the article more amusing. I think that a world-famous and serious newspaper like the Guardian should not allow such an unserious representation of a country's tourism, especially when the country puts a lot of effort and money into providing comfortable and unforgettable holiday experiences to British tourists. The article borders on the ridiculous. A well-respected newspaper should not rely on cheap, low-level humour to entertain its readers.

So, considering the whole absurdity of the situation, I hope you will make the best use of your British irony and sarcasm, and excuse us for being so touchy. With all respect to you and your British culture.

Stanimir Andonov
Sofia, Bulgaria

April 26

We were right to drop 10p amendment

David Abbott accuses me of giving in too soon (Letters, April 25). The Labour amendment to the budget was not to restore the 10p tax, but for compensation measures. The government does not know who the 10p losers are. It is now trying to locate them. There are likely to be different packages of compensation, and payments will have to offset average losses. There cannot be 5.3m separate deals. Each package will be backdated to April this year. In attempting to maximise the numbers helped, the government will be seeking better long-term means of help. What more would be achieved by holding out? The government's promise to protect the lower-paid was the message Labour MPs wanted to get out as early as possible for the local elections.

Frank Field MP
Lab, Birkenhead

April 30

We're not celebrating Israel's anniversary

In May, Jewish organisations will be celebrating the 60th anniversary of the founding of the state of Israel. This is understandable in the context of centuries of persecution culminating in the Holocaust. Nevertheless, we are Jews who will not be celebrating. Surely it is now time to acknowledge the narrative of the other, the price paid by another people for European anti-semitism and Hitler's genocidal policies. As Edward Said emphasised, what the Holocaust is to the Jews, the Naqba is to the Palestinians.

In April 1948, the same month as the infamous massacre at Deir Yassin and the mortar attack on Palestinian civilians in Haifa's market square, Plan Dalet was put into operation. This authorised the destruction of Palestinian villages and the expulsion of the indigenous population outside the borders of the state. We will not be celebrating.

In July 1948, 70,000 Palestinians were driven from their homes in Lydda and Ramleh in the heat of the summer with no food or water. Hundreds

April 28

In the article about discrimination against women (You're fired, G2, April 23) you say "names have been changed". Any chance of telling us the real name of the little shit you called Alan Sugar?

Ray Chalker
London

April 29

If the strike by workers at Grangemouth in defence of their pensions is going to cost so many millions of pounds, that would have funded their pensions for years (Global pressure as Grangemouth turns the taps off, April 28). Or perhaps that's too simple?

Mick Taylor
Leeds

April 29

I thought the Sisters had liberated me from quickly (!) running up clothes on the Singer for myself and the family into the early hours (How to make your own clothes, G2, April 28). What next? Rubbing two sticks together to cook roadkill?

Jennifer Mann
London

April 30
Sharing apples (Letters, April 26) is all very well, but as Shaw observed: "If you have an apple and I have an apple and we exchange these apples then you and I will still each have one apple. But if you have an idea and I have an idea and we exchange these ideas then each of us will have two ideas." So let's continue sharing ideas about apples!

David Jaques
Oxford

died. It was known as the Death March. We will not be celebrating.

In all, 750,000 Palestinians became refugees. Some 400 villages were wiped off the map. That did not end the ethnic cleansing. Thousands of Palestinians (Israeli citizens) were expelled from the Galilee in 1956. Many thousands more when Israel occupied the West Bank and Gaza. Under international law and sanctioned by UN resolution 194, refugees from war have a right to return or compensation. Israel has never accepted that right. We will not be celebrating.

We cannot celebrate the birthday of a state founded on terrorism, massacres and the dispossession of another people from their land. We cannot celebrate the birthday of a state that even now engages in ethnic cleansing, that violates international law, that is inflicting a monstrous collective punishment on the civilian population of Gaza and that continues to deny to Palestinians their human rights and national aspirations.

We will celebrate when Arab and Jew live as equals in a peaceful Middle East.

Cllr Jonathan Bloch, Ilse Boas, Prof Haim Bresheeth, Mike Cushman, Dr Linda Edmondson, Colin Fine, Brian Fisher, Bella Freud, Uri Fruchtmann, Stephen Fry, Claire Glasman, Tony Greenstein, Michael Halpern, Abe Hayeem, Rosamine Hayeem, Anna Hellman, Joan Horrocks, Deborah Hyams, Selma James, Riva Joffe, Yael Oren Kahn, Les Levidow, Peter Levin, Deborah Maccoby, Daniel Machover, Prof emeritus Moshe Machover, Miriam Margolyes, Mike Marqusee, Harold Pinter, Roland Rance, Sheila Robin, Prof Steven Rose, Mike Rosen, Prof Jonathan Rosenhead, Leon Rosselson, Sabby Sagall, Alexei Sayle, Monika Schwartz, Amanda Sebestyen, Sam Semoff, Linda Shampan, Sybil Shine, Prof Frances Stewart, Inbar Tamari, Ruth Tenne, Martin Toch, Stanley Walinets, Martin White, Ruth Williams, Gerry Wolff, Sherry Yanowitz and 54 others

May 2008

The international community and the west in particular was left on the sidelines wondering how to respond to crises in Zimbabwe and Burma. The threat to an already threadbare democracy in Zimbabwe posed by delayed election results and growing violence against the opposition to Robert Mugabe attracted a letter of protest from Václav Havel and Nobel prize winner Doris Lessing, who was brought up in the country. Aid to those affected by massive floods in Burma was hindered by the reluctance of the secretive ruling military junta to allow in foreign aid workers. Many even mooted armed intervention if necessary. Diplomacy finally had some effect, but not before huge, and possibly unnecessary, loss of life. Food price rises also came home, with indications of people switching to low-cost retail chains such as Aldi. The Guardian reported the death of Pauline Campbell, a tireless campaigner for penal reform – and tireless writer of letters to the newspaper (one example from October 24 2007 appears in this book). Cherie Blair took time out to promote her autobiography, with some eye-catching revelations about contraception that rapidly became a cause for euphemism. A young writer won a small campaigning victory when mighty Port Vale FC agreed to join the battle for Fairtrade footballs. And readers were inspired by our science booklets – to finally get to grips with how to pronounce "quark". It's a start.

May 1

Does anyone else know the trick of sharing an apple (Letters, passim) by pressing firmly with one's thumbs on either side of the stalk end until the apple breaks neatly in two? My grandfather taught me how, and more than half a century later it never fails to surprise those who watch me do it.

Maggie Butcher
London

May 2

I thought taking drugs was supposed to shorten your life (Albert Hofmann, inventor of LSD, dies at 102, May 1)?

Steve Ralph
Portsmouth

May 2

As a regular Glastogoer I have no problem with Jay-Z topping the bill (Report, April 29) but if, as forecast, he is to be introduced

May 1

United against all forms of bigotry

The passage of time seems to have clouded Julie Burchill's memories of Rock Against Racism/ Anti-Nazi League in the late 1970s (Letters, April 28). Was Tom Robinson ducking the question of homophobia when he sang his anthem Glad to Be Gay at the Victoria Park carnival in 1978? The Anti-Nazi League launched "gays and lesbians against the Nazis" groups, and we produced thousands of badges with the same slogan – were we ducking the issue?

The three main RAR reggae bands were Steel Pulse, Aswad and Misty in Roots. It's a simple challenge, Julie: name one of their songs which is homophobic. Homophobia in some elements of reggae developed much later. Why just pick on reggae artists? Were white punk bands free of prejudice? During RAR plenty of people challenged women's oppression. I remember marching behind a "Women against the Nazis" banner on my way to the Brockwell Park carnival and listening to the punk band the Au Pairs talking about women's rights at an RAR meeting. The RAR magazine, Temporary Hoardings, also ran several articles challenging sexism.

To mention in the same breath the celebration of the history of an anti-racist struggle with the rantings of the BNP is a disgrace – we are defending multiracial Britain; they want to destroy it.

Last Sunday's Love Music Hate Racism Carnival was not a nostalgia trip. At its core was tens of thousands of people sending a powerful message against the very real threat of bigotry, racism and fascism today.

Martin Smith
Organiser of the Love Music Hate Racism carnival

May 2

We must support the people of Zimbabwe

We are very concerned at the deepening crisis in Zimbabwe and at the pace at which matters of utmost constitutional importance are progressing (Zimbabwe braced for presidential run-off, May 1). The people of Zimbabwe have expressed their democratic will for the future of their country. They have the right to see it announced and implemented as a matter of the most urgent priority. The continuing delay has thrown a shadow over an electoral process and casts doubt on the integrity of the authorities charged with implementation. Post-election violence has already compromised any continuing electoral process; to inspire confidence all electoral processes must be transparent and must operate within the framework of the constitution.

We call upon all who can bring influence to bear to ensure that the rule of law is upheld. This includes the right of all the people of Zimbabwe to cast their votes free of coercion by threat of violence, forcible removal or detention. It also includes the right to see their vote at the ballot box transformed into a democratically elected and accountable government. The world is united in admiration for the patience of the people of Zimbabwe in pursuing the democratic path to renew their country. However, the patience of the world is running out in waiting for their wishes to be honoured by the current government of Zimbabwe.

Václav Havel Former president of Czechoslovakia/Czech Republic, Doris Lessing Nobel laureate, Bill Morris Former general secretary, TGWU, David Puttnam Film producer, Kenneth Roth Executive director, Human Rights Watch

on stage by the festival organiser, I trust Michael Eavis will stick to the proper English pronunciation of Jay-Zed.

Brian Highley
Newton Poppleford, Devon

May 3
Matt Dunham's photo (Sport, May 1) of Didier Drogba and Ricardo Carvalho tenderly cradling Frank Lampard's pale and exhausted body was a truly remarkable piece of sports photography. I'm sure I was not the only one to see echoes of Michelangelo's Pietà in this image.

Alan Gavurin
London

May 5
Informative as the Science Course inserts have been, they have failed to answer the important question raised in Part 4 (May 1). Why, if "quark" is to

LETTERS TO THE EDITOR

rhyme with "fork",
isn't it spelt "quork"?

Colin Harrison
Chesterfield

May 6

There was one other
person who should
be acknowledged as
helping save Pinter's
career after the with-
drawal of the Lyric
Hammersmith's
production of The
Birthday Party
(Fighting talk, Review,
May 3). The late
Stephen Joseph, who
founded Britain's first
theatre in the round,
read the script and
immediately invited
Pinter to come to his
theatre and direct
the play himself. The
production, with a
cast that included
the young Alan
Ayckbourn as Stanley
and myself as Lulu,
was, I believe, Pinter's
first as a director.

Faynia Williams
Brighton

May 2

Reasons to celebrate the state of Israel

Rather than sitting piously in their green rooms,
ivory towers and Holland Park homes pontificating
about all that is wrong with Israel, why don't the
signatories of your letter (April 30) do something
positive towards achieving the laudable goal of
Arab-Jewish harmony they apparently yearn
for? Daniel Barenboim's Divan orchestra, which
brings together Palestinian and Israeli youngsters,
provides a shining example of what might be done.
I for one will be celebrating the birth of a nation
intended to be a haven for Jews after millennia
of butchery, persecution and genocide, much as I
would that of a prodigal son that I hope may one
day return to reason.

Mark Glanville
London

May 5

The real achievements of 1968

Geoffrey Wheatcroft, who "sat on the touchline
watching with ironic detachment", thinks 1968 was
a waste of time (It was fun, but 1968 left us sybaritic,
self-absorbed and ruled by the right, May 1). Those
who protested against Vietnam did not think it a
waste of time, nor those who took to the streets after
the murder of Martin Luther King. Nor those who
battled with the police in Warsaw or resisted Russian
occupation in Prague. I could add those arrested for
forming illegal trade unions in fascist Spain, the
students massacred in a police ambush and ignored
by the media assembled for the Mexico Olympics,
the first protesters in Northern Ireland and, of

course, the millions of French workers who took part in the biggest general strike in world history. In fact, 1968 was part of a long chain of insurgency that went on until the mid-70s, culminating in the collapse of the fascist regimes in Portugal and Spain. Not bad for "a brief orgasmic thrill".

Of course, many of the gains were rolled back. That was what the coups in Chile and Argentina were about. That was what Thatcherism and Reaganism were about. That is what the transformation of women's liberation into sexual commodification is about. The conclusion, surely, is not that it was wrong to fight, but that we have to fight again. As the French activists said, "Ce n'est qu'un début" – it was only the beginning.

Chris Harman
Editor, International Socialism

May 8

Maltby and the BNP

Your correspondent Chris Marshall (Letters, May 7) asks whether it is significant that a BNP councillor was elected in Maltby, Rotherham, where he lives and which is in the S66 postcode area I identified as representative of England in my book Welcome to Everytown. The S66 postcode was chosen because it has a typical spread of inhabitants, so it does not surprise me that BNP voters are represented there too. What the election of the BNP there reflects is not, I think, endemic racism, but a feeling by white working-class voters that they are the forgotten ones and that the mainstream parties don't care for them or their views. That is why it is important that those who chose to vote for the BNP are not assumed to be intolerant bigots, even if you think

May 6

Colin Harrison asks why "quark" rhymes with "fork" (Letters, May 5). Murray Gell-Mann found the word in Joyce's Finnegans Wake, in a sentence spoken by seagulls: "Three quarks for Muster Mark!" Its appeal was that there were indeed "three quarks" in his sub-atomic model. In an interview, it was said he felt that "quarks" was "seagull-speak" for "quarts" (of beer), and that the rhyme should follow. The fact that the passage contains several other rhymes with "Mark", and that it's question-able how a seagull with a Dublin accent would pronounce the word, did not trouble him.

Bill Evershed
Kidlington, Oxfordshire

May 6
Try asking Kirsty Wark.
Robert Maclean
London

May 7

This time Steve Bell (If…, G2, May 5), in putting Brown down, cruelly misses the point. Brown "more popular than Adolf Hitler"? Brown, hugely unpopular, is a decent politician without charisma. Hitler, hugely popular, was an evil politician with charisma.

Paul Oestreicher
Hove, East Sussex

May 8

I was relieved to read that Fay Goodwin experienced Philip Larkin's displeasure with photos taken of him (Photographer's papers reveal image-conscious Larkin, May 7). In 1972 I accompanied my future wife Frances Hill to Hull, where she was to interview Larkin for the TES. He was decidedly disgruntled to learn that I was there to take his picture. When he saw the end

the leadership of the BNP are just that. The more the attempts of poor, white Britons to be heard are dismissed, the stronger the BNP will become.

Julian Baggini
Bristol

May 9

It's no use droning on about airships

I was intrigued by George Monbiot's ruminations on airships, but even the pessimistic note he struck was not pessimistic enough (If there is a God, he's not green. Otherwise airships would take off, May 6). The Hindenburg disaster of 1937 was only the last in a long line of calamities. In 1921 the British airship R38 broke up over Hull, killing 44 of the British-American crew. A year later the US army's Roma blew up, killing 34 men. In 1925 the US Navy dirigible Shenandoah ran into a squall over Ohio and fell apart, killing 14. In 1930 the pride of the British airship fleet, the R101, crashed in flames in France with 54 passengers and crew on board. Eight survived. In 1933 72 men died when the US Navy's biggest airship, Akron, came to grief, followed two years later by the Macon.

Airships are, by their nature, vulnerable. Even if kept aloft by non-flammable helium, they will be lighter than the fluid in which they move and therefore at the mercy of the weather. Nor can they climb above the weather without the gas expanding to wreck the structure. Airships are a dead-end technology, suitable only for low-level work or tourist jaunts.

George Rosie
Edinburgh

May 10

A few questions for Coca-Cola to answer

Interesting to see Lauren Branston defending Coca-Cola against "alleged misdeeds in the past" (Letters, May 8). Especially as I visited India last month to research the current accusations levelled at the company. Lauren and Coca-Cola have not been able to reply to these serious questions about their business practices. So here are a few of them, in the hope that I can get a reply now.

1) Didn't Coca-Cola sponsor the TERI foundation, which carried out the "independent report" Lauren refers to?

2) Despite this potential conflict, the report noted the company's refusal to give crucial documents and data needed for a proper assessment of the company; are you going to make this data available?

3) The report says the company's efforts to deal with the water crisis in Kala Dera rely on rainwater harvesting — the company's much-vaunted solution to its water consumption problems. However, the report also notes that rainwater harvesting relies on rainfall, so can you tell me where this rainfall comes from in a drought-prone area, ie a place with not much rainfall? Even the report concludes that the company's efforts are "unlikely to be meaningful".

4) The report lists possible options to address the water crisis in Kala Dera — one of those is to shut the Coke plant down. Any chance you will follow the report's advice?

5) Should I send other questions for Lauren to answer via the Guardian letters page?

Mark Thomas
London

result he told my wife it made him "look like a dishonest Kilkenny land agent".

Leon Arden
London

May 9

Please spare us the witty headlines for the next three weeks (Tories train their sights on Crewe, May 5). For years the local football team has been "derailed", "shunted into the sidings" etc.

Leo North
Crewe, Cheshire

May 9

Marcel Berlins (G2, May 7) cautions us against involving children in courts and councils. Decisions about their lives should be left to the maturity and good judgment of adults, it seems. Does he read the papers?

Nick Lee
Leamington Spa,
Warwickshire

May 10

Why does the horse have a bridle, a symbol of possession and control (Plan for Britain's biggest sculpture, May 8)?

David and Elaine Stott
New Milton, Hampshire

May 12

How prescient of the late Gwyneth Dunwoody to say some months ago that the components of Metronet would only receive future public transport contracts "over her dead body" after their debacle on the London Underground modernisation contract. Here we are, just a couple of weeks after her funeral, watching the contracts for the upgrading of the M25 being awarded to a consortium of Atkins and Balfour Beatty — otherwise known as Metronet (Report, May 9).

Stewart Rotherham
Nottingham

May 12

The myth that is hawks v doves

How sad that Simon Jenkins should have such muddled views on the so-called battle between songbirds and raptors (Comment, May 9). The only real battle is between virtually all Britain's birdwatchers, ornithologists and conservationists on one side, and a small but vocal lobby group, with a vested interest in reducing raptor populations, on the other. Most people aren't "pro-raptor" or "anti-songbird", but simply have a basic understanding of population ecology. The "genocidal carnage" does not — indeed cannot — exist. Predator numbers wax and wane according to the availability of their prey, not the other way around. Here in Somerset, as in the rest of Britain, the songbirds that most often fall prey to sparrowhawks, such as tits and finches, are thriving. Those in decline, like the skylark, linnet and corn bunting, are suffering as a result of decades of environmentally disastrous farming methods, not because they are being killed by raptors. The conservation debate is complex, with no easy answers. So for Jenkins to weigh in referring to raptors as "cannibals" is not just unhelpful, but dangerous. It offers support to the tiny minority of raptor-haters, while deflecting attention from the real problems faced by the songbirds we all cherish.

Stephen Moss
Mark, Somerset

May 13

Meritocracy is not dead — sadly

Is meritocracy dead (Networked from birth, G2, May 9)? If only. John Harris and a number of the people he interviewed have misunderstood what meritocracy means as defined by the late Michael Young, who invented the word, in his book The Rise of the Meritocracy, published in 1958. The book was a satire, meant to be a warning against what might happen to Britain between 1958 and the imagined final revolt against the meritocracy in 2033. As Young explained in the Guardian in June 2001, objecting to Tony Blair's misuse of the word in many of his speeches: "It is good sense to appoint individual people to jobs on their merit. It is the opposite when those who are judged to have merit of a particular kind harden into a new social class without room for others ... With an amazing battery of certificates and degrees at its disposal, education has put its seal of disapproval on the many who fail to shine from the time they are relegated to the bottom stream at the age of seven or before."

Young, creator of innovative institutions such as the Open University and NHS Direct, was as opposed to rule by a public school posse as he was to a meritocracy – now in politics still largely white and male – based on an ability to pass exams. "It is hard indeed in a society that makes so much of merit to be judged as having none," he wrote. "No underclass has ever been left as morally naked as that." One of the Young Foundation's projects is Learning Launchpad, re-engaging in education and apprenticeships young people dismissed as failures by a meritocratic system soaked in snobbery towards the vocational.

Yvonne Roberts
Young Foundation, London

May 12
Has anyone noticed that the sun has shone continuously since Bo Jo was elected as London's mayor (Hard work and easy on the jokes as Robo-Boris takes control, May 10)?

David Joss Buckley
London

May 12
If there really was "one young staffer swishing through the building in formal black tie, coat and tails", he will get short shrift from Boris, who knows about these things. Tails are worn with a white tie. Black ties are worn by waiters.

Mike Turner
Teddington, Middlesex

May 13
Carrion feeders red kites may be, but I had an excited call from my friend regarding one bird's errant behaviour (Letters, May 12). She

was hanging out her washing yesterday morning, and a red kite swooped down and took away a green, silky blouse in its talons. This seems more like seagull manners to me.

Helen Kingsbury
Marlow, Buckinghamshire

May 14
Red kites' practice of stealing washing to line or decorate their nests (Letters, May 13) has been long recognised. Helen Kingsbury's friend should have heeded the warning in The Winter's Tale: "when the kite builds, look to lesser linen".

Steve Sheppardson
Bromley, Kent

May 16
Neil LaBute (Dead Lepers? Sounds like my kind of show, G2, May 13) says he greatly admires the title Vertical Smile,

May 13

A case of bridles revisited

Jonathan Jones (My kingdom for a horse, May 10) places Mark Wallinger's proposal for a great white horse on open land at Ebbsfleet in the tradition of the ancient chalk horses cut into the landscape. In execution, however, it surely has more in common with the literal-minded sculptures – at St Pancras, among others – that he deplores. This horse, measured and modelled to the nth degree, requires no imaginative response, whereas the Angel of the North and Serena de la Hey's Willow Man, beside the M5, are successful because their subtle suggestions invite a second, longer look. They, like the chalk figures, are truly "dream images" connecting us to our environment. With Mark Wallinger's horse, what you see is what you get: the bridle is entirely appropriate.

Sally Jaine
Totnes, Devon

May 14

Criminalising the music industry

At 16 I became a professional session musician. Before the age of 18 I recorded on tracks such as Tainted Love (keyboard), Electric Avenue (bass), Walking on Sunshine and dozens more. I toured as support for acts such as Meat Loaf and Motörhead. I earned around £50,000 a year, around 20 years ago. Under the government's new provisions that all under-18s must be either in school, training or employment, my career would have been illegal and I would have a criminal record for pursuing it. My career path – not unusual then, nor today – is one that appeals to the disaffected and the poor but talented. By criminalising this, the government will be criminalising the entire music industry and the people who earn billions for Britain.

Heather McDougall
Cullercoats, Tyne and Wear

May 16

We are working flat out to help Burma

Simon Jenkins was right to acknowledge the problems of getting aid into Burma but was wrong to suggest we are sitting on our hands (Comment, May 14). We are working round the clock to get assistance to those who need it. Airdrops can help, but they depend upon expert teams on the ground getting the aid where it needs to be. Indeed, key supplies such as safe drinking water cannot be delivered via airdrops. Our focus has to remain on securing the distribution of aid to those that need it. The UK's aid pledge has risen to £17m, which is expected to help at least 370,000 people by providing clean drinking water, basic healthcare and shelter. The first plane carrying British aid landed in Rangoon on Wednesday carrying plastic sheeting to make tents for 9,000 families. More UK flights are arriving throughout this week.

On a diplomatic level, we will continue to use every possible channel, including our position as chair of the UN security council, to make clear to the regime its responsibility to act now to save lives. The prime minister has spoken to Ban Ki-moon and we are encouraging him to call an emergency summit similar to that which followed the 2004 tsunami and the 2006 Pakistan earthquake. UK ministers Mark Malloch Brown

the original name of the play Happy Now? The playwright, however, did not originate this title. Prefaced by "The", it was the name of a novel by the author of The Manchurian Candidate, and was considerably more daring in 1971. Book reviewers were in a real dilemma about whether to explain it and how. I am sure the late Richard Condon, an immensely genial man, would have been greatly amused to know that it was used again, by a playwright named Lucinda Coxon.

Rhoda Koenig
London

May 16
So Cherie Blair's "fourth pregnancy was caused by her being too embarrassed to bring her contraception to Balmoral" (Gloriously tragic, G2, May 13).

I'd have thought that, having grown up in Edinburgh, Tony Blair would have known the meaning of "getting off at Haymarket".

Alessandra Asteriti
Culross, Fife

May 17

Given that Cherie grew up in Liverpool, one wonders why she didn't make Tony get off at Edge Hill (last station before the Liverpool terminus at Lime Street) rather than Haymarket (Letters, May 16).

Paul Clein
Liverpool

May 19

The problem with the Blairs is not which station Tony failed to get off at (Letters, May 17) but that both are at East Ham, ie one stop short of Barking.

John Brooke
Bewdley, Worcestershire

and Shahid Malik have been in the region, visiting Thailand and Singapore to support international discussions. Gordon Brown has set out clearly our position. No options should be ruled out, including the responsibility to protect, but legal debate should not delay us – the imperative is to act to save lives. The best way to do that is for the Burmese regime to open up and cooperate with the international community.

Gareth Thomas MP
International development minister

May 17

We still believe Labour can win

More than a decade ago we were all lucky enough to work as foot soldiers within the Labour party as staffers at Millbank Tower or supporting MPs in opposition. We had a front-row seat as Labour renewed itself to regain the trust of the electorate. We all support the current Labour government with the same level of commitment that we did when the party spent 18 years out of office.

Since the local elections this month there has been much talk of Labour's time in government coming to an end, with the Tories now ready for office in the same way Tony Blair's team were over 10 years ago. Nothing in our view could be further from the truth. Tony Blair by 1997 had achieved two fundamental goals: he had not only reconnected his party with the public, but he also outlined an eloquent progressive programme for government, having won the argument for change within the party. David Cameron has only achieved some of the former, has produced comparatively little significant policy and has only papered over cracks within the Tory party. We do not underestimate the government's problems, but 11 years on from 1997, it is still the Labour party which offers the big answers to the big questions facing this country. That is why the prime minister and Labour's talented team of ministers are more than capable of winning the next general election. We wish him the best.

David Bradshaw Regional editorial, **Dan Clifton** Broadcasting officer, **Huw Evans** Regional press officer, **Tristram Hunt** Rebuttal researcher, **Alice Hunt** Rebuttal researcher, **Sophie Linden** Assistant to David Blunkett, **Joe McCrea** Assistant to Frank Dobson, **Chris McShane** Media researcher, **Adrian McMenamin** Head of rebuttal unit, **Benjamin Wegg-Prosser** Assistant to Peter Mandelson, **Margaret Mythen** Health policy officer, **Bridget Sweeney** Events officer (positions listed are those held in 1997)

May 17

For Pauline

It was with considerable sadness that I read of the untimely death of Pauline Campbell (Report and obituary, May 16). Julie Bindel (Women, G2) paid a moving tribute to her brave and tireless campaigning on the urgent need to stop the tragic rise in the deaths of vulnerable women in custody. Following the death of her only child, Sarah, at HMP Styal in 2003, I invited Pauline to speak to probation staff recently. One aspect of her talk was her obvious fury at the government for refusing to fund families attending death-in-custody inquests. This was recommended in one of its own reports (the Corston review).

Pauline felt deeply that this injustice needed to be addressed. Napo will do all it can to ensure

May 20

Charlie Brooker (Attention all boring people: do not ever try to chat with me. Any attempt to do so will be met with silence, G2, May 19) might like to learn the response of my late grandfather when he made his first visit to a new barber in Whitley Bay. When he was asked: "How would you like your hair cut?" He replied: "In silence." The man with the clippers never inquired again.

Phil Penfold
Doncaster, South Yorkshire

May 20

Ah, the ironies of New Labour-style meritocracy: Edward Timpson is not fit to be the next Crewe and Nantwich MP because of who his parents are, but Tamsin Dunwoody is because of who her mother was (Llamas an animal too far as campaign becomes a circus, May 17).

Antonio Arnal
Leatherhead, Surrey

May 21

Simon Jenkins draws attention to the wonderful durability of the book (When it comes to kissing and telling, you can't beat this 15th-century gadget, May 1). We agree. That is why we are so perturbed by our university management's decision to clear 60,000 of the things from our library shelves and ship them to their campus in China. There, we understand, they will not be available to students to read, despite having been paid for with considerable amounts of taxpayers' money. Apparently, if we really need a book, it might be sent back overnight by plane. Readers will not need reminding of the

this happens for Pauline's sake and all those other families whose loved ones are "dying in the care of the state".

Mike Guilfoyle
Greater London Napo

May 19
Fairtrade footballs

As part of a geography project we looked at how much the children who make footballs are paid in the third world. Each of our class then wrote to senior figures at clubs and at the English FA to ask them to buy professional-standard Fairtrade balls, which cost £35 to £38 instead of about £60 for non-Fairtrade ones. The people who make Fairtrade balls earn an extra 20p per ball (80p more per day). Three months on we've had only three replies. The FA said it had a contract with Umbro so can't buy Fairtrade. It said Umbro "meets all the regulations", but did not say what that means. Someone from Alex Ferguson's office wrote to say he was too busy to bother with such things. It's sad that the people running the game seem to think they are too important to make sure everyone involved can afford enough to eat.

Sarah Whale
Class 7JE, King Alfred school, London

May 20
Post offices in rural areas

Country Diary (May 2) mentioned the unfortunate need for longer journeys to post offices in rural areas, and I have objected to the Post Office about its proposals to close our local Leven Valley post office, which is also the only shop in the village. I pointed out that its proposed action in this case would probably lead to an extra 370,000 car miles per year being travelled by locals, with a consequent large jump in carbon emissions. Its response was that the government "do not require Post Office Ltd to take environmental impact into specific consideration". If this is true, it seems to be an astonishing case of the left hand being out of touch with the right, given the government's aim of reducing the UK's carbon footprint.

Professor Peter Matthiessen
Ulverston, Cumbria

May 20

Real legacies of Blair, Brown and Smith

My old workmates from the 1997 election (Letters, May 17) seem to have fallen into the first trap of politics — don't believe your own propaganda. The best stuff we implemented after the 1997 victory was nothing to do with Blair or Brown; it was the legacy of John Smith — minimum wage, trade union recognition, social chapter, national devolution, regional development agencies etc. The Brownite stuff (independence for the Bank of England and lax regulation of the financial sector) and the Blairite stuff (permanent revolution in schools and hospitals, tougher on crime than its causes) all looks far less attractive in retrospect. Then there is the elephant in the room of foreign policy. Seven wars in seven years — and what happened to being at the centre of Europe?

More important than the policy failings of Brown — on pensions, post offices, tax relief for the

absurd environmental costs of all this, on top of the educational losses.

Dr KH Adler, Dr M von Buelow, Dr G Dodd, Dr C Haase, Dr R Lutton, Dr S Mawby, Dr F Meyer and Dr C Taylor Faculty of arts, University of Nottingham

May 22

Many thanks to Sarah Whale and her classmates (Letters, May 19) for bringing the Fairtrade footballs scheme to our attention via your pages. In the case of League clubs, such as ours, the Football League decides which brand of football shall be used and under which contractual terms. We wholeheartedly support their efforts to persuade the Football League to investigate whether it is possible to start using such Fairtrade footballs for all League matches, and we have now written to the Football

League expressing that support.

Glenn Oliver
Director, Port Vale FC

May 23

In the light of the letter (May 21) about books from the University of Nottingham's library being shipped out to China, my husband will not now be returning the copy of Warrender's The Political Philosophy of Hobbes, which was due back on November 18 1967. Up until now he'd still been meaning to get round to it.

Dr Sarah Hale
Birkbeck College,
University of London

May 23

Phil Penfold's grand-father's reply to the barber to cut his hair "in silence" (Letters, May 20) is included in a book of Greek jokes called Philogelos (laughter-lover)

dead while increasing tax on the poorest workers – and something even I didn't realise until last year's floods, is just how hopeless he is as a politician. We live in a democracy; you have to go out and meet people and understand them (even the Chinese leader has understood this).

Wake up – the "nice decade" is over. Labour will lose the general election whenever it comes. We are facing the same squeeze that the Tories faced in 1997. Who would have thought that the Conservatives would be the first post-Thatcherite party? The changes we need to make have to be done quickly. We must have a new leader very soon so that defeat can be mitigated, giving us a small chance of regrouping; the alternative is we go into oblivion with Brown.

Nick Matthews
(Labour's policy officer for trade and industry and employment in 1997), Rugby

May 21

Commercial break for low-cost Aldi

Yes, Aldi sells quality products at low prices (Cheap chorizo, anyone?, G2, May 15). Yes, it offers special one-off ultra-cheap deals. And it wastes no space stocking 92 varieties of yoghurt. But there are even more compelling reasons for shopping at Aldi. The company completely bypasses the brands promoted by massive and expensive advertising campaigns. You won't find Kellogg's, Heinz, Coca-Cola, Walkers or Flora. Instead you may be (briefly) baffled trying to find Aldi's unadvertised equivalents. In deserting Tesco and Asda, you can show that you reject the gross consumerism and debased values of such advertising. Children will not find the global brand names which taint childhood with their addictive imagery. The enormous overheads of the advertisers and the mega-supermarkets are thus cancelled out at a stroke. I've also been impressed that my local Aldi sells locally produced vegetables and fruit. It's a significant environmental attraction. Don't be put off by the spartan surroundings. You will be saving more than mere money.

Maurice George
Ormskirk, Lancashire

May 24

Playground acting in the Premier League

I am a headteacher of a north London primary school and have just witnessed the most depressing of scenes. During a 20-minute playtime football game between 30 or so kids on our tarmac strip, the kids acted out, as they do, what they'd seen during the recent battles in the Premiership and in Moscow. On at least three occasions I saw a child drop to the floor as if he or she had been poleaxed by some external force and roll around in supposed agony clutching a leg or holding head in hands in obvious mock distress. The pained facial expressions were superb! As team members gathered around, they comforted their team-mate and then eventually carried the player to the side of the pitch.

I watched unconcerned as I knew what was coming next as, on each occasion, the "injured" child returned immediately to the pitch to resume the game. I wonder how long it will be before "doing a Drogba" becomes a common part of their playground language?

Steve Hilborne
London

published in the fourth century AD.

Michael Bulley
Chalon-sur-Saône, France

May 23
An interesting side-effect of living in the city with the highest proportion of broad-band internet connections (Fears of digital divide groundless as online access soars in rural areas, May 22): I am now finding that nine out of 10 families involved in the funerals I conduct have the facility to send me by email tributes and readings for me to use during the service. The advantages of this are mutual: I get text which is typed and therefore legible, and they get to use my ink and my paper!

Fr Chris Collins
St Aidan's Vicarage,
Sunderland

May 24

Meg Hillier MP, minister for identity (Letters, May 23)? Never heard of her.

Chris Armstrong
Ipswich

May 26

The mind boggles at hospital staff observing "a bare below the elbows dress code" (Deaths from MRSA and C difficile in individual hospitals are revealed, May 23). Surely elbows to wrists is sufficient?

John Kilburn
York

May 27

I am so glad that Hadley Freeman stood up for Princess Beatrice (In praise of Princess Bea's style — even the butterfly hat, G2, May 20). I have just returned from a wedding in Seville where every second person was wearing a butterfly hat. Have

May 27

Don't get carried away, David

Before David Cameron lets his euphoria run amok (Triumphant Cameron: New Labour is dead, May 24), may I remind him of another "famous victory"? In 1981 I won a byelection for the Liberal-SDP Alliance in North West Croydon. We knocked the Tories off their perch and boasted that we had "gone home to prepare for government".

Just under two years later the Tories regained the seat and the government had not been budged an inch; in fact it took another 14 years to get rid of them. Byelections are more often than not protests, not declarations of future intent.

Bill Pitt
Broadstairs, Kent

May 28

Moscow scores with United fans

Returning from Moscow as a happy Manchester United fan (Moscow highwire act allows United to state credentials, Sport, May 24), I feel compelled to say a big thank-you to the Russian government. The arrangements in Moscow were superb and not at all the "gulag" scenario predicted by some of the British media. To start with, while Uefa was ripping us off with a compulsory £11 transportation fee and the travel companies were charging a grand for day trips, the Russians came up trumps by waiving the visa requirements, thus saving us £95 each. In Moscow the wonderful metro was opened up, free of charge, to all fans to make sure we got back to our hotels, coaches or trains after the match.

The security arrangements were awesome, if

initially scary. As we left the stadium it was all pretty relaxed, but, lest we forgot to behave ourselves, ranks of police, on foot, with dogs and on horses, paraded nonchalantly down the street. Parked nearby, just to press the point home, were two huge water cannons. But I felt safer faced by a powerful but disciplined force than I do when confronted by twitchy cops with riot shields. And once we got on the metro we were accompanied by very friendly police who helped everyone decipher the Cyrillic signs on the stations and were happy to have their photos taken with scarves, flags and the inevitable two fingers behind the head.

The ordinary Russians we met were an absolute delight. When a group of us became stranded at the wrong terminal of St Petersburg's Pulkovo airport the locals ensured that we got free transport to the right place. I just hope Rome can match Moscow next year.

Howard Stones
Otley, West Yorkshire

May 29
Why Finkelstein was rejected

Your article about Norman Finkelstein's exclusion from Israel (US academic deported and banned for criticising Israel, May 26) claims that Finkelstein was refused tenure at DePaul University for attacking pro-Israel supporters, such as me. This is entirely false. Finkelstein's denial of tenure was based on his lack of scholarship and professionalism. The minority report written by three members of the political science department lays out the basis for his tenure denial.

Finkelstein and his followers have access to

female columnists forgotten the fun of being young and trying out different fashions? May I suggest these people visit bodygossip.org, which is concerned with all the unpleasantness regarding the female form and how that is affecting female children.

Philippa Jecchinis
London

May 28
Sandi Toksvig says she doesn't know who came up with the solution to the Israel/Palestine situation that involves getting one side to draw in the border and the other side to choose which half they want (Just one question, G2, May 27). Well I believe it was me. That was certainly the joke I wrote for the stage version of Grumpy Old Women. You never know, it might get implemented as an

actual policy and bring peace to the region. I'd very much like the world to know that I was responsible for the idea! If anyone else claims that they came up with the joke too, maybe one of us could draw a line through the joke and the other one choose which part of it we want to take credit for.

Richard Herring
London

May 30
The Toksvig-Herring algorithm has been used by my family for well over half a century as a way of sharing cake fairly between children. It is expressed more simply as "you cut − I choose".

Dermot J O'Donovan
West Ewell, Surrey

this minority report, but they have deliberately suppressed it, releasing instead a rebuttal to the report, while withholding the report itself. I have challenged Finkelstein to release the report, which he is entitled to do, but he has refused.

The result is that newspapers such as yours mischaracterise the reason for his tenure denial, in a way they would not be able to do if they had the minority report available to them.

On the merits of his exclusion from Israel, I categorically disagree with Israel's decision. Finkelstein should be allowed to speak in Israel. His views should be exposed to the marketplace of ideas, where they will be rejected as they have in most other parts of the world.

Alan M Dershowitz
Harvard law school, Cambridge, Massachusetts

May 30

The reason I was denied tenure is no secret

Professor Dershowitz (Letters, May 29) alleges the justification for denying me tenure is contained in a secret departmental report I have suppressed. The decision was made by the president of DePaul University. He provided an extensive written explanation, and also issued a public statement when we reached a private settlement. The latter statement acknowledged that I was an "outstanding teacher and prolific scholar". Both the president's letter and the public statement are posted on my website, and have been widely quoted.

Norman G Finkelstein
New York

June 2008

Elections and their aftermath dominated the month. In the US, Hillary Clinton finally conceded defeat in the Democratic primary, Barack Obama becoming the first African-American presidential candidate for a major US party. In Zimbabwe, Morgan Tsvangirai, leader of the Movement for Democratic Change, pulled out of the presidential runoff vote as Robert Mugabe's Zanu-PF and its backers ratcheted up the levels of violence and intimidation against MDC supporters. June may have given electoral respite to Labour, but the coalition of dissatisfaction with the government grew ever wider. Attacks came from the left over education, health reforms and poverty, and David Hockney protested about the "cultural vandalism that contaminates New Labour". Wider criticism over civil liberties also increased, focused by the decision of the shadow home secretary, David Davis, to resign his seat and fight a byelection over plans to extend detention without trial to 42 days, ID cards and other civil liberties issues. Some unlikely alliances formed, with iconic leftwinger Tony Benn supporting Davis's fight, the CBI backing Polly Toynbee's defence of Labour's polyclinics and leading employers endorsing the government's educational diplomas. The Irish threw a spanner in the works by rejecting the Lisbon treaty on EU reform, Bo Diddley died and boozy parties on tube trains marked the last night of legal drinking on the London underground.

June 3

Could somebody explain the difference in column inches devoted to a few hundred "revellers" partying on the underground (Parties and arrests on tube at closing time, June 2) to celebrate/ deplore the banning of alcohol, compared with nearly 10,000 people marching from Hatton Cross to Sipson to protest against the building of a third runway at Heathrow? Is the moral of the story that peaceful marches are not worth taking notice of, but damaging six tube trains and injuring policemen is news-worthy?

Mary Crawford
London

June 4

Given the relative numbers of men and women among the existing statues in London, the fourth

June 4

Art and indecent images of children

The no-smoking policy in mental health institutions is outright cruelty, imposed by an unthinking and blind political elite (Letters, May 30). They are now getting into trouble with images, as I said they would (Pictures and power, March 27). But no one was prosecuted for the NHS advert with the image of the boy with a fish-hook in his mouth that had to be withdrawn. Why not? Now they are moving into very dangerous territory. The suggestion that drawings of children should now be prosecuted is mind-blowing in its ignorance (This loophole is real. But the remedy is really perverse, May 31). I am out of step with the mean spirit of our age. I told a friend I had been to a house in Lincolnshire where in three rooms there must have been pictures of a few hundred naked children and a lot of naked adults as well. He looked shocked until I told him they were painted by Antonio Verrio between 1688 and 1698, at Burghley House in Stamford. I detest the cultural vandalism that contaminates New Labour. I hope they go – and soon.

David Hockney
London

June 4

Labour's efforts to reinvent itself

I read John Harris's outburst against my tentative suggestion about putting a little more money in the pockets of Britain's workers with some amusement (Instead of reviving New Labour, the party must now drop this Blairite rot, June 2). John may be right, but if every idea is to be machine-gunned out of the sky by columnists, how on earth does Labour, old, new, and yet-to-be-born, reinvent itself?

Denis MacShane MP
Lab, Rotherham

June 4

Hey, Bo Diddley

It's a shame that the most succinct account of the enormous influence of Bo Diddley I've ever read should be in your obituary (June 3). In 1995 I saw Bo on the same night that people were camping outside Virgin Megastore for tickets to see the Rolling Stones (who owed Bo a great deal) — but at the Clapham Grand tickets to see him were still available while he was playing. Bo Diddley, in just two sides of his first record, encouraged the British beat groups to break away from the 12-bar format of rock'n'roll and develop what would eventually become hard rock, from which everything from heavy metal to punk derived. For fans of any of those styles, Bo's death is not the end of an era, it is the end of the era. I expect tributes to start pouring in from the surviving members of the Stones, the Who, the Kinks, David Bowie, the Smiths and all those who have had hits based on his music without Bo ever receiving a penny.

Steve Wilson
London

June 5

Hemingway the Poet

The two poems by Ernest Hemingway which your story calls "unpublishable at the time because

plinth in Trafalgar Square (Comment, May 24) must surely be used for a statue of a woman. We already have the Unknown Soldier — why not the Unknown Housewife?

Professor Jan Pahl
Canterbury, Kent

June 4
Sometimes wit and imaginative rhyming (Letters, passim) combine: "When love congeals / It soon reveals / The faint aroma of performing seals / The double crossing of a pair of heels / I wish I were in love again" (Richard Rodgers, again). And note the subjunctive.

Professor Alan Alexander
Edinburgh

June 4
Surely 42 (Letters, June 3) is the product of a government at sixes and sevens?

Ted Dougherty
London

June 5

It was Lorenz Hart, not Richard Rodgers, who created the rhymes in I Wish I Were in Love Again (Letters, June 4). It was Lorenz Hart, not Ella Fitzgerald, who created the rhymes in Manhattan (Letters, May 22). Lyricists, like writers in every sphere, are always the last to receive their proper due.

W Stephen Gilbert
Corsham, Wiltshire

June 5

So Linda Grant was a budding feminist in 1969, bravely wearing her trouser suit to work. Pity it didn't last. "Hillary Clinton," she writes (G2, June 3), "a woman who does not possess good legs ... " Now, while I can see that Hillary Clinton would not make a useful US president, she can walk, can't she?

Marjorie Sachs
Boyle, Co Roscommon,
Ireland

of their rudeness" (When Hemingway turned his hand to verse, June 4) were published in 1924 and 1925, in English, in a German avant-garde magazine, Der Querschnitt. (They were republished in 88 Poems (1979), the first authorised collection of Hemingway's poems, with an informative introduction by Nicholas Gerogiannis.) In Green Hills of Africa (1935) Hemingway tells how, on safari, he encountered an Austrian who was interested in modern literature:

"Hemingway is a name I have heard. Where? Where have I heard it? Oh, yes. The dichter (poet). You know Hemingway the Poet?"

"Where did you read him?"

"In the Querschnitt."

"That is me," I said, very pleased.

Tom Stoppard
London

June 6

Obama's ticket to the White House

Much of what your article says is true (How Hillary Clinton turned an air of certainty into a losing run, June 4). But the irony is that someone you call "out of step with voters" got more votes than Obama in the primaries, or at the least – by any method of counting – a statistically equal number of votes. And it's not unimportant that she won in large "swing" states. Looking at the electoral college, there is no doubt but that in the election against John McCain we Democrats would rather win the states Hillary won than those which Obama won.

This is true in spite of the disorganised Clinton campaign, the alleged liabilities of her husband,

and the air of "inevitability and entitlement" for Barack Obama which his supporters and much of the press adopted and cultivated as early as February, after which she won more voters' endorsements than did Obama. Clinton deserves more respect than she is being given.

That said, as a Democrat who has anxiously looked forward to the end of the Bush era, I will vigorously support Obama, whose style and grace I do appreciate, and I hope he will make good use of Clinton and John Edwards in the general election campaign.

Kendric E Smith
Atlanta, Georgia, US

Mood music

June 6

Your review of Paul McCartney's Liverpool Sound concert at Anfield (Star distraction: McCartney banishes culture blues, June 2) seemed to miss the beat. Not only was it more about the city's finances than the musical content, it was out of tune with the facts. There is no shortfall in the budget for European Capital of Culture 2008. The Liverpool Sound concert was cost-neutral — with £300,000 donated to charity. As to deprivation, Liverpool is fighting a 40-year decline, but it is also celebrating £5bn of investment in projects like the Echo Arena, Liverpool One District, and the new Museum of Liverpool. The city is proud that more than 3 million people have been to a cultural attraction or event so far this year, with all box-office records being broken. If that is a "difficult tenure", we will have to redefine its meaning. So, while your review was fine when sticking to familiar music,

June 6

The letter from WS Gilbert (June 5) reminded me that after Arthur Sullivan received a knighthood, his librettist (a certain WS Gilbert) also complained that lyricists were always the last to receive their proper due. Are they related? I think we should be told!

Geraint Jones
St Albans, Hertfordshire

June 6

Oscar Hammerstein suffered the same lack of recognition as a lyricist as Lorenz Hart. Jerome Kern's wife was being introduced at a social function. "Her husband wrote Ol' Man River," announced the hostess. "Oh no," interjected Hammerstein's wife, "my husband wrote Ol' Man River; her husband wrote 'da da da-da'."

John Wurr
Kingsbridge, Devon

June 7

The Bronze Woman Monument, designed by Ian Walters but completed after his death by the sculptor Aleix Barbat, will soon be ready for installation. However, the utilities companies are telling us that the site in Stockwell, south London, is too near a gas pipe, so we are looking for a new home. What better place to celebrate the contribution of Caribbean women to British society than the empty plinth in Trafalgar Square (Letters, June 4)?

Linda Bellos
Chair, Bronze Woman
Monument Project

June 7

Imagine my surprise and delight on hearing on local radio that the new manager of Manchester City is to be Marcuse! This position will perhaps compensate the great

it was way out of time with the new mood music sweeping the city.

Phil Redmond
Creative director and deputy chairman,
Liverpool Culture Company

June 9

Taking the temperature on polyclinics

Polly Toynbee is right to point out the contradictions in much of the BMA's hyperbole against NHS reform. The CBI has been pressing for greater flexibility in the primary care system, not least because restricted opening times means the UK economy loses far more working hours through doctors' appointments than through industrial action.

We have been told variously that we are arguing for privatisation (when, as the article makes clear, most GPs are private sector contractors), that we are seeking to destroy the jewel in the crown of the NHS (when many, especially in deprived communities, get a very poor service) and that we should just stay out of the argument – despite the fact that business taxes help pay for the service and our employees use it.

The sole criterion for change should be about service improvement. As that is clearly happening in areas such as Camden and Derby, where the private sector is successfully running surgeries, ideological objections to bringing in new providers are misplaced.

Dr Neil Bentley
CBI director of public services

June 9

Public services must give value for money

Seumas Milne (A mania for tax cuts at any cost defies public opinion, June 5) says those Labour MPs who want the taxpayer to get value for money are pushing an aggressive agenda to slash the public sector. He asks: "Who is listening to the voters?" Well, perhaps it's those very MPs who knock on doors and talk to their constituents in their advice surgeries who do, rather than draw conclusions from reading opinion polls. Talk of left-right divides fills comment pages, but it means nothing to a generation of voters whose politics were shaped long after the fall of Thatcher. The world has moved on – and the message from the electorate is that there is a debate to be had about the role of the state, improving the efficiency of public services and how they are paid for.

Voters, like Labour MPs, do believe in good public services. But the public rightly demand value for money too. It's their cash and they want to know what it is spent on. Labour must respond to these concerns and engage in the debate over how we finance our public services and whether the users of those services get a good deal. Not to do so would be the quickest way of abandoning vital services to the slash and burn of a Conservative government.

Gisela Stuart MP
Lab, Birmingham Edgbaston

June 10

Fireworks – my night with Silvio

I do wish Alexander Chancellor had bothered to read what I actually said in my book about the

man for having been left out of the German team against the Greeks in the Monty Python sketch, his place presumably having been taken by "surprise inclusion" Franz Beckenbauer.

Sarah Hayes
Manchester

June 7
William Schwenk Gilbert was – I am delighted to report – finally knighted in 1907, a quarter-century after his collaborator (Letters, June 6). But I am no kin to him. I own, however, that I do flourish my W (for William) in part because of its pleasing resonances.

W Stephen Gilbert
Corsham, Wiltshire

June 10
On the cover of yesterday's G2 you ask "Where are the women running the arts?" Clearly Maddy

Costa doesn't think of television drama as an art, and therefore doesn't mention that women run drama at three main terrestrial channels (Jane Tranter at the BBC, Laura Mackie at ITV and Tessa Ross at Channel 4). Perhaps the headline – Thinking outside the box – was a deliberate double entendre?

Mark Shivas
London

June 10

Good for Philip Pullman in leading the resistance to age banding of children's books (The week in books, Review, June 7). For more than 22 years my novel Journey to Jo'burg has been in print with two UK publishers. Illustrations in the trade edition give the book a younger look, while photographs in the educational edition indicate older readers.

visit Tony and I paid to Silvio Berlusconi's home in Sardinia in 2004, instead of basing his remarks on hoary old myths and an invented quotation of an interview I gave recently to an Italian newspaper (So now we know. God gave Tony Blair the strength to invade Iraq – but he didn't say it was right, G2, June 6).

According to Mr Chancellor, what I told the Italian journalist in relation to the visit was that it was "one of the most thrilling" of all my "freeloading holidays". In fact all I said was "I have never spent an evening like the one I spent at Signor Berlusconi's house in Sardinia", an entirely different statement.

First, it was only "an evening" that we spent in Sardinia – less than 24 hours in fact. It was not a holiday. Our family holiday that year was in Tuscany, where we had left the children during the brief visit to Sardinia. There was a particular purpose in Tony agreeing to the visit at that time, having turned down every one of the many similar requests by the Italian prime minister over the years. Tony was hunting for IOC votes in the hope of London winning the bid to host the Olympic Games in 2012 and Italy was a key player in the IOC. He felt if there was any influence that Signor Berlusconi could exert over the Italian IOC delegates, it would be worth it.

And I *have* never spent an evening like it. We were treated, among other things, to a major firework display, which ended with "Viva Tony" being emblazoned across the sky, and found ourselves taking part in a singalong accompanied by an orchestra which had been flown in for the occasion. Not the sort of evening either of us were anticipating.

Cherie Blair
London

June 10

War to Windrush

Spike Lee's comments about Clint Eastwood (Dirty Harry comes clean, June 6) were perfectly timed. The Imperial War Museum's tribute to black servicemen and women, From War to Windrush, opens on June 13. We also need to reflect on the appalling absence of black servicemen and women from British films about the second world war. There is no trace of any of our leading postwar black actors, including Earl Cameron, Errol John and Cy Grant, in film classics like The Cruel Sea, The Colditz Story, Reach for the Sky, Dunkirk and Battle of Britain. Cy Grant joined the RAF as a navigator in Bomber Command in 1941, and was a PoW in Germany for two years. He is featured in the new exhibition. Hopefully this exhibition, and my exhibition at the nearby Cuming Museum, Keep Smiling Through, which honours black Londoners on the home front, will encourage visitors to broaden their knowledge of the subject. Film-makers take note.

Stephen Bourne
London

June 11

Labour needs a vote against 42 days

It is with enormous sorrow that I must urge friends in the House of Commons to vote against the government's proposal for 42-day pre-charge detention today. As a criminal barrister with many years' experience of terror trials, I have no doubt that the provisions — even with the hopeless purported last-minute "concessions" — are wrong in principle, unnecessary and counterproductive

I receive letters from all ages. Will the same text now be branded with different age classifications? Not as absurd as the original banning of the book in apartheid South Africa, but still daft.

Beverley Naidoo
Bournemouth

June 10
My reaction to fathering a big baby — Megan Grace, 10lb 10oz — was one of concern over possible complications mixed with the kind of pride that arises from growing the village fete's largest marrow (Rise of the sumo baby, G2, June 9). I loved becoming a dad and, being a certain kind of male, I liked geeking out about percentiles.

David Curl
Southampton

June 11
Thanks to the letters page of the Guardian

(June 9) I now know where to stand on the question of polyclinics. If Save Our NHS is against them and the CBI is in favour then they have to be another step on the road to privatisation.

Dr David Pollard
Hove, East Sussex

June 11
Your Euro 2008 schedule (Sport, June 7) read: 1945 Germany v Poland. Surely that should have been 1939.

Steve Till
Bishop's Sutton, Hampshire

June 12
What a crossword (June 11)! Clues about masturbation ("No stains made by wankers"), untipped cigarettes, motorway service stations and animal cannibalism. It makes me proud to be a Guardian reader (4-5,6).

Greg Hetherton
Hove, East Sussex

to the community cohesion that yields vital intelligence in these cases.

I was particularly alarmed to hear that my name may have been dropped by members of the government as someone supportive in principle but concerned about the detail of "safeguards". This could not be further from the truth. The essential "safeguard" in a civilised legal system is that you are promptly informed of the accusation against you.

As a long-standing member of the Labour party, I am also very worried about the political folly of this divisive policy. I had long hoped that my party could begin to win back the many members and voters alienated by the war on terror and war in Iraq. Voting against 42 days would be a good way to start.

Helena Kennedy QC
Doughty Street Chambers, London

June 12

The success stories behind 'failing' schools

That young Ed Balls is at it again (I will close up to 270 failing schools to improve standards, says minister, June 10). There are apparently 638 schools attended by poorer, disadvantaged or unselected students where only around 30% get the five GCSEs at A-C level, including maths and English.

With a bit more maths and history, Balls might celebrate the remarkable increase in students passing what was originally a matriculation exam designed for around 10% of the school population, which became from 1952 to 1987 the O-level exams designed for some 20%. Now, hooray, even in so-called failing schools nearly 30% acquire the equivalent at GCSE level, and the non-failing schools do even better. And what a shame he's using it all to hammer schools, teachers and local authorities again, and continue breaking up our state education system via academies and trusts. Will all these new agents running our schools – private companies, charitable foundations, religious and voluntary organisations – really help us get a better-educated population, not to mention a cohesive society?

Professor Sally Tomlinson
Senior research fellow, education dept, Oxford University

June 12

How mathematicians lost the plot in the City

Mathematicians who cite the fact that 25% of maths graduates have recently got jobs in finance as evidence for the usefulness of their subject should curb their enthusiasm (Letters, June 7). The coverage of the credit crunch in the financial press has identified the widespread use of mathematical models of risk as one of the contributory factors. The point is that, however sophisticated the maths, these models are only useful as far as their underlying assumptions correspond to economic reality. Problems occur when enough investors in the same markets – all using the same mathematical models and the same assumptions – try to adopt the same hedging strategies, which no longer work because they are all on the same side of the market. The sophisticated mathematics is suddenly not enough because the models are no longer valid representations of reality.

Professor Dennis Leech
Economics department, University of Warwick

June 12
"Why women enjoy old age more than men", it says on the cover of G2 (June 11). It depends on the old men, I suppose.

Monica Neville
Aberdeen

June 13
I don't want to detract from the seriousness of the case of the woman who was apparently able to get the money to do away with her husband from a "home improvement loan" (Report, June 11). But it did start me wondering if I could have done without the double glazing.

Maggy Rengert
London

June 13
If the inhabitants of Cyprus are called Cypriots, can the inhabitants of Lesbos not call themselves Lesbiots to avoid confusion (Lesbos

islanders go to court
in bid to reclaim the
word lesbian, June 10)?

Francis Jones
London

June 14

Does David Davis
realise how much
it costs to hold a
byelection? I read
somewhere that Crewe
and Nantwich cost the
Treasury over £2.7bn.

Chris Bond
London

June 14

A woman goes into
a bar and asks for
a double entendre
(Innuendo: did she give
him one too many,
G2, June 12). So he
gave her one. A sound
engineer observes the
encounter. So he gave
her 1, 2. A bandleader
decides to join in. He
gave her 1, 2, 1, 2, 3, 4.
Oh dear, that doesn't
work, does it?

Bill Ashton
Director, National Youth
Jazz Orchestra

June 13

Parliament on trial over 42 days decision

In a democracy members of parliament are accountable to the people from whom their authority comes and to whom they are ultimately accountable. Apart from the broad political choices that have to be made in a general election, issues sometimes arise where it is right and proper that MPs should take the opportunity of consulting their own constituents formally on major questions.

Legislation that would allow people to be jailed on suspicion without charge for 42 days repeals Magna Carta, and could easily be extended to cover anyone whom it was claimed might threaten national security. The parliamentary vote in support of this was only won after the whips had imposed the most rigid three-line whip upon Labour MPs who, in a free vote, would almost certainly have defeated it (Desperate Brown scrapes through, June 12).

David Davis's decision to take this issue back to his own constituents and ask for their support for his stand against this law is absolutely right.

Cynicism about politics is now widespread, and the Haltemprice and Howden byelection, fought on the question of civil liberties, will restore public confidence in parliament, which increasingly seems separated from the people it was elected to serve.

Tony Benn
London

June 14

Labour's failed anti-poverty strategy

How must the government respond to the news about rising poverty (Up. Up. Up. Child poverty, pensioner poverty, inequality, June 11)? Successive governments have ratified different human rights treaties and the UK has repeated its commitment to those treaties. They include the rights to an adequate standard of living and to social security.

The key element in a new strategy is to raise universal child benefit and state pensions, not just to the 1997 percentage of average earnings but 33% or 50% higher. Child poverty would be reduced by a third of a million at a stroke and pensioner poverty by a similar figure. The cost could be covered by a percentage increase in tax from the highest incomes, or from inheritance and capital gains tax. This would be acceptable to many with rapidly appreciating high incomes.

All OECD countries have substantial public social security systems. The most successful in reducing poverty rely predominantly on universal or group schemes, which are invariably more efficient and less costly to administer than means-tested benefits, including tax credits. But these schemes also contribute to social integration, link the generations and support those who cannot be expected to earn their way out of poverty.

Because they are a right they do not operate as a disincentive into paid work for the economically productive in households. Cast as one element of a global development strategy to reduce child and pensioner poverty in low-income countries by establishing social security systems, they can also symbolise — especially to the liking of the British prime minister — a necessary new direction in world political leadership.

Peter Townsend
Professor of international social policy, LSE

June 14
Why refer to "shark-infested waters" (Leaders, June 12)? Sharks do not infest water, they live in it — it's their home. If people choose to enter the water as uninvited guests they take the risk of becoming the shark's next meal.

Avril Murray
Ulverston, Cumbria

June 16
"King John did not have Islamist militants in mind when he signed the charter" (The Magna Carta question, June 11). Actually, according to some sources, he was thinking of becoming one himself. Matthew Paris records John sending a delegation to the sultan of Morocco, offering to convert to Islam in exchange for military help. The sultan, noting a lack of spirituality, politely declined. The authenticity of the story may

be in question, but it's an intriguing idea.

Jeremy Muldowney
York

June 17
So Hadley Freeman thinks facial hair "does not get most ladies' motors going" (Ask Hadley, G2, June 16). Nonsense – a man without a beard is like profiteroles without the chocolate.

Josephine Billingham
Brighton

June 18
That my asymmetric brain size is shared with lesbians (Report, June 17) gives rise to a frisson of free-willed lobal raciness matched only by the thought of my gay colleagues' predilection for wee-frilled robal laciness.

Fr Alec S Mitchell
Manchester

June 16
The EU's democratic deficit

Fintan O'Toole completely misread the no vote in Ireland (The fear factory devastated Ireland's flaccid political class, June 14). It is invariably described as an incoherent alliance of left and right nationalists. In fact Eurobarometer polls show that the Irish have been and continue to be among the most enthusiastic Europeans. In October 2007 three-quarters of those polled in Ireland agreed "that EU membership is a good thing". This compares with just 34% of Britons.

The common thread that drew together the seemingly incoherent worries of the Irish groups campaigning against the Lisbon treaty is democracy. The left didn't want to cede power to Brussels to determine health policy, the liberal right didn't want to cede power to determine tax, conservative Catholics didn't want social policy regarding abortion or euthanasia determined by the EU. Whether the Lisbon treaty in fact ceded this power to the EU is a matter of debate – a debate the yes side didn't entertain. But there was a common fear that democracy was under threat.

If the EU responds to the concerns of its supporters it can extricate itself from this problem. If it chooses to ignore these concerns it will deepen the divide between the political elites and the citizens. This will leave us vulnerable to the rhetoric of populist nationalist parties and all that goes with it.

Dr Eoin O'Malley
School of law and government, Dublin City University

June 16

Why Britain needs 'peasant farming'

George Monbiot (These objects of contempt are now our best chance of feeding the world, June 10) champions highly productive "peasant farming" for delivering food security in the south. Peasant has long been a derogatory term in the UK, but the model of smaller-scale family farms is as relevant to food security here as for developing countries.

It was the diversity of generally smaller, mixed farms that fed Britain when policymakers' blind faith in the global market to supply the majority of the country's food and fuel was scuppered by the German U-boats. Instead of recognising this, postwar governments, lobbied hard by the agrochemical industry, set UK agriculture on the path of increased specialisation, mechanisation and dependence on fossil-fuel derived inputs. Consequently, the resilient infrastructure of mixed farms, regional processors and local markets, which should have been seen as a national strategic resource, was decimated.

From a majority of 500,000 in 1945, less than 10,000 mixed farms remain today. With those farms we've lost the people with the knowledge and skills to work the land — 12 farmers and 37 farm workers have left the land on average every day for the past 60 years. Today it's not a limited threat of torpedoes we face, but the much greater, global and enduring challenges of climate change and harder-to-extract, more costly oil. Fertiliser prices have doubled over the past year, predicted to hit £500 a tonne by the end of the year. The "super-efficient", highly mechanised, labour-light but oil-heavy farms promoted by agribusiness are neither environmentally nor economically

June 20

King Abdullah II of Jordan has just been awarded the degree of doctor of civil law by diploma at the Sheldonian Theatre, Oxford. Last month three judges upheld Abu Qatada's appeal against deportation to Amman on the grounds that he was likely to face a terrorism trial based on evidence from witnesses who had been tortured (Radical preacher released on 22-hour curfew, June 18). Are we talking about the same place?

Dr Stephen Wilson
Oxford

June 20

My grandfather used to say that a kiss without a moustache was like an egg without salt (Letters, June 17). My grandmother's thoughts on the subject are unrecorded.

Barbara Freeman
Leicester

June 23
Your article about the
Rausing family (G2,
June 19) was replete
with pop psycho-
analysis and cliches.
The Rausings are an
extraordinarily affec-
tionate family and
immensely generous
to the world around
them. You may sneer
that Hans Rausing,
the patriarch, moved
his family to Britain
in the 1980s because
taxes were lower than
in their native Sweden.
But thank goodness
he did! Britain has
gained immeasurably
from the Rausings'
presence here and the
untold millions that
the family has given to
philanthropic causes.
They should be
cherished.

William Shawcross
London

June 24
The Guardian's
speculative story about
ITV's submission
to Ofcom (June 23)

sustainable. If the UK government was serious
about providing its citizens with a secure food
system, it would learn from past emergencies and
look to the best practical modern models available
– namely organic, rotational, mixed farming that
relies more on solar power (sunshine, clover and
crop rotations) and human inputs of labour and
knowledge to build fertility.

Robin Maynard
Campaigns director, The Soil Association

June 16

David Davis: a strange friend of liberty

The notion that David Davis is a libertarian (Davis
faces byelection battle with former Sun editor,
June 14) will provoke hollow laughter from
Britain's gays and lesbians. Davis has opposed
every freedom extended to gay and lesbian people,
from the freedom to register one's partnership to
the freedom to serve one's country. He has one
of the worst voting records in the Commons on
such matters. Like most Conservatives, Davis is
very selective about whose liberties are worthy of
support. He supports greater rights for suspected
terrorists but not extending basic freedoms to
peaceful and law-abiding gay and lesbian people.

Ben Bradshaw MP
Lab, Exeter

June 18

Academies, music and elitism

Until recently Pimlico school was the only state
school offering students a full musical education.

It was allowed to select 10% on musical ability and offered children 90 minutes of instrumental teaching per week plus opportunities to play in orchestras, chamber groups and jazz bands.

On June 10 Ed Balls announced a list of 638 "failing" schools. Pimlico (37% GCSE A*-C) was not on it, but two of Westminster's existing academies – Westminster (17%) and Paddington (25%) – were. But strangely, it is Pimlico that has been placed in special measures and is in the process of being made into an academy. Equally odd, (Conservative) Westminster council has written a lease which bans selection of any kind, so the sponsor cannot continue the course in its present form. The music staff and parents have campaigned against this, but the council believes the course's excellence to be "elitist" and is adamant it should cease.

The closure of this successful school and its dragooning into the academy programme has denied the only opportunity for poor, talented, musical children to future generations of inner-city kids.

Professor Andrea Vicari
Trinity College of Music; head of jazz, Pimlico school

June 20

Divisions and unions in the church

Every single British Christian should look in the mirror and ask themselves if there isn't something more important to worry about than two queer priests marrying (Archbishops criticise gay clerics' ceremony, June 18); like, say, Darfur, Afghanistan, child-trafficking, the need to stop cluster bomb use? I and my lover just celebrated our 32nd anniversary and still feel no need to ape dumb

bore the misleading headline: "ITV seeks to cut public service output before digital switchover." Can we be very clear: digital switchover has already happened – 90% of UK homes now have digital multichannel television.

Michael Grade
Executive chairman, ITV

June 25
Having tabled a previous early day motion regarding the accountability of Network Rail, I welcome your coverage of the Co-operative party's People's Rail campaign (Report, June 23). Like many people, I am tired of train delays, with no one taking responsibility when things go wrong. I have tabled another EDM in the Commons to gather the support of fellow MPs. I urge readers to show their support for the

campaign by visiting the website at www. peoplesrail.org.uk

Don Touhig MP
Labour and Co-operative,
Islwyn

June 25

ITV1 did not withhold copies of the Prince Philip documentary because we feared a mauling by Mark Lawson and his mates (Eek! Who let the critic in?, G2, June 24). We were unable to send out tapes because the films were being edited right up to broadcast. True, when the critics watched them, they sneered. But we were far more interested in the opinions of the 5 million viewers who tuned in.

Jeff Anderson
Controller, current affairs
and documentaries, ITV1

June 25

Re Paul Ince being named the Premier League's first black

breeder rituals such as marriage, but so what if others do? Get a grip, for goddess's sake.

John Gill
Skopelos, Greece

June 21

Into the snake pit

When I purchased tickets for the match between Surrey and Kent at the Oval last weekend I foolishly did so in the anticipation of watching some cricket. Instead I had to watch the boorish behaviour of a sizable number of the crowd who seemed more interested in building beer snakes out of plastic cups. M Cross (Letters, June 17) seems to believe that the actions of the stewards and police in putting a stop to this "fun" will deter the public from going. Well I hope he's right. Try building a beer snake down the local or at a football match and see how well it's received. For those who feel the need to become Sir Norman Foster after a few pints there is a simple solution. Set aside an area for snake builders behind the main stand. Include a sand pit with buckets and spades, and a paddling pool full of small plastic balls. This would leave those of who want to see the cricket – and that rare thing, a Surrey victory – in peace.

Ian Burch
Sidcup, Kent

June 23

Labour dilemmas put in context

The Labour party needs to reconnect with its core voters, forge a new progressive coalition and secure a fundamental shift of policy towards equality, fairness and social justice, involving a massive housing drive empowering local councils to build homes for let at affordable rents, promoting trade union rights, investing in and expanding public services, ending privatisation, withdrawing troops from Iraq and Afghanistan, and rejecting the proposal to renew Trident. These policies have been promoted on Labour's national executive committee by the four constituency members on the Grassroots Alliance slate. Individual members of the party will be receiving voting papers for the national executive. Members should vote for Mohammed Azam, Ann Black, Peter Kenyon, Christine Shawcroft and Pete Willsman. I shall be retiring from the NEC in October because of advancing years.

Walter Wolfgang
Richmond, Surrey

June 24

Zimbabwe's people deserve better

While Morgan Tsvangirai's decision to withdraw from a "violent, illegitimate sham of an election" (Report, June 23) is understandable, the decision will set a dangerous precedent. Opposition parties throughout Africa, especially in Kenya, Nigeria, Democratic Republic of Congo, Uganda and Ethiopia, where violence has accompanied rigged elections, could also boycott future elections, potentially making the use of violence the only means of changing governments.

The UK and other donor countries should not focus on Robert Mugabe as the only problem in Africa. It took centuries for British democracy

English manager (Report, June 23), for rugby league fans it's "been there, done that". Forty-five years ago, Roy Francis became the first black professional coach in any British team sport, managing Leeds and overseeing them to victory in the 1968 Challenge Cup and the league in 1974-75.

John Pearson
Leeds

June 26

In Alfred Hickling's review of Monkey (June 21), he wrote: "The character of the Monkey usurped the narrative ... which is rather like the Scarecrow taking top billing in the Wizard of Oz." What's wrong with that?

Hilton McRae
(currently rehearsing as the Scarecrow in the Wizard of Oz at the Royal Festival Hall)
London

June 27

In April, I was interviewed by Aida Edemariam about the book The Mitfords – Letters Between Six Sisters. In the piece published in the Guardian (Hitler, my sisters and me, G2, May 23), Edemariam said "in wartime, for example, which Diana spent in Holloway prison for treason". This extraordinary statement is untrue. My sister was never tried for any offence, let alone treason, but was imprisoned under the rule called 18B in Holloway for over three years. I cannot allow this false statement to stand.

Deborah Devonshire
Bakewell, Derbyshire

June 27

Clive Stafford Smith says "there is a clear reluctance within the record industry to discuss the use of music as torture"

to take root. It is too much to expect Zimbabwe and the rest of Africa to fully embrace western liberal democracy in just 50 years. Democracy cannot take root and flourish without other democratic institutions. More emphasis needs to be put on establishing independent judiciaries, state security forces and civil services, and an electoral commission in Africa.

Sam Akaki
London

June 26

Harsh verdict on yob nation

I thought Max Hastings was bang on (If we endorse yob behaviour in role models, we'll become a yob nation, June 23). It is out of hand: the terror of losing celebrities from successful shows; a surrender to the power of the lowest common denominator; and the remarkable demolition of the notions of excellence and justified elitism. Our generation and the one behind us have got this wrong.

Melvyn Bragg
London

June 27

Nuke-free England

If true, the withdrawal of US nuclear weapons from Lakenheath in Suffolk is to be welcomed (US removes its nuclear arms from Britain, June 26). But the silence from Westminster is deafening, particularly since the government now claims to be a "disarmament laboratory" for the world. The failure to publicly announce this decision is in keeping with the nuclear secrecy that prevails. Or perhaps the US air force simply removed them without telling the government, possibly by mistake. Senior US air force heads are still rolling from an incident last August when nuclear weapons were unknowingly flown from North Dakota to Louisiana.

It also means that though Britain's nuclear weapons support infrastructure is based in England (the warheads are designed and built at Aldermaston and maintained at Burghfield), there are no longer any permanent nuclear weapons stationed there. It's ironic that all the weapons (submarines, missiles and warheads) are based in anti-nuclear Scotland, while pro-nuclear England has become almost nuclear weapon-free. Gives a new slant to the West Lothian question.

Dr Ian Davis
Consultant, British American Security Information Council

June 27

In praise of Ramsay

Max Hastings (Comment, June 23) seems to have brought out all the other little Colonel Blimps (Letters, June 26). There are nuances to my mind in Gordon Ramsay's foul-mouthed feedback. First, it's driven by his high standards in the kitchen; second, it's driven by passion — for which I can forgive a lot; and third, there's genuine warmth to it. My impression is that he's a decent human being with leadership qualities, whose calibration of the loss of impact of obscene language is far more in tune with current mores than Max. From here to stabbings, diminished public realm, yoof of today etc is a bit of a leap. Crime is going down, youth

(Welcome to 'the disco', G2, June 19). We can reassure him that the Musicians' Union takes this issue very seriously. We will be putting forward a motion to the International Federation of Musicians executive committee at their October conference with a view to securing international condemnation of this use of music in interrogations.

John Smith
General secretary,
Musicians' Union

June 27

Actually the Scarecrow (along with the Tin Woodman) did take top billing in Baum's 1902 stage adaption of The Wizard of Oz, devised as a showcase for the popular double act of Montgomery and Stone (Letters, June 26).

Harry Robertson
Edinburgh

June 28

Further to the letter from the Duchess of Devonshire (June 27), rule 18B was part of the Emergency Powers Act (1939) and allowed the imprisonment of suspected Nazi sympathisers without trial – effectively revoking habeas corpus. It's a good job that similar legislation founded in fear and hatred couldn't find its way on to the statute books now.

Mark Redhead
Oxford

June 30

Your flattering profile of David Davis (G2, June 27) eulogised his record as a fighter for civil liberties. It failed to mention his support for the return of hanging and the repeal of the Human Rights Act, and his opposition to the recent extension of gay rights.

Peter Walker
London

is as irreverent and challenging, in a modern way, as the youth complained of more than 2,000 years ago. When they go too far, I continue to face them down in public, directly and warmly (Ramsay would be proud) and they respond just fine. Young people are vital and fun and trying to wind us up: it's their job.

Phil Wolsey
Wallingford, Oxfordshire

June 27

Diplomas are a win-win qualification

The CBI seems confused on the diploma (CBI tells Balls to abandon diplomas, June 23). We, like thousands of employers, have volunteered our time to support the development of the qualification because we see it as a once-in-a-lifetime opportunity to break down the pernicious and damaging divide between academic and vocational educational routes, and to build employability skills into the curriculum. We support the diploma because it has been developed with employers, and will involve employers at the heart of its delivery, to better prepare young people for work. The diploma will help fill skills gaps across industry, including in science and languages. It's good news for young people and good news for UK plc in a fast-changing world.

Alan Jones Toyota, **Will Butler-Adams** Brompton Bicycle, **Tony Cohen** Nsure, **Chrissie Dunn** Manufacturing Diploma Development Partnership, **Simon Hogg** Scanlaser, **Andy Puttock** BT, **Douglas Oakervee** Crossrail, **Mike Stapleton** Compass Group **and five others**

July 2008

As the government announced tough new checks on those receiving incapacity benefit, the often grim reality of a life on benefits was graphically outlined in letter from a welfare recipient — and many readers were moved to offer help. Meanwhile the 60th anniversary of the greatest welfare reform of all, the National Health Service, passed quietly. The legal system was in the news at home, courtesy of a television series which upset lawyers, while international law secured a notable victory with the capture in Serbia of alleged war criminal Radovan Karadzic; hiding behind a beard and a false name, he had been practising alternative medicine. And motor racing executive Max Mosley won his privacy case against the News of the World, which had published details of his racy personal life. When David Cameron's bike was stolen from outside a supermarket as he bought his supper, what exactly this meal is seemed a more important question for readers than how someone who can't lock his bike properly could keep the country secure. His reputation remained barely dented, while the prime minister's was shredded by the SNP in the Glasgow East byelection. David Miliband used a Guardian article to throw his hat into the ring as a potential replacement and received support from Gordon Brown — of Farnham, Surrey. And readers took an interest in soon-to-be Wimbledon champion Rafael Nadal's habit of tugging at his underpants in between points.

July 1

There was pandæmonium at home after your recent article ('More than just a pumped-up ß': Germany celebrates recognition of the letter ß, June 27). You say that æ is a Scandinavian vowel. It is not — it is Anglo-Saxon, like me.

Ælfleda Bishop
Exeter, Devon

July 2

It has come to our attention that our colleague, the Scarecrow, has been implying that he is the starring role in The Wizard of Oz at the Royal Festival Hall this summer (Letters, June 26). In fact we, the Lion and Tin Man, carry the entire story and the Scarecrow is merely a subplot. We are sorry he seems to have an inflated sense of his importance. He is clearly clutching at

July 1

Foundations of strong communities

Simon Jenkins is right to rail against the architectural atrocities committed in the name of social housing, although he misses several points (This icon of 60s New Brutalism has its champions. So let them restore it, June 20). The social impact of getting rid of these places is vast, and their replacement is both environmentally damaging and expensive, aggravating the shortage of affordable homes. Slum-clearance programmes have created a legacy of alienation, dislocation and worklessness. Often the biggest problem facing large social housing estates is that they are poorly managed and under-maintained, highlighting the need for local services that respond to small problems before they escalate. The communal areas of estates are the most neglected, yet they are crucial to children's play and people feeling safe together.

It takes many decades to lay down foundations for a strong, mixed community. Wiping out estates accelerates the pace of social unravelling. Of course tenants in poorly managed and under-repaired places will "vote" for demolition if they are promised a lovely new home, but false promises have devastated millions of families' hopes. We must not repeat these mistakes.

Anne Power
Professor of social policy, LSE

July 2

Guilty verdict on BBC

The BBC's Criminal Justice serial is not the basis upon which one can draw any sound conclusions about our system of justice, as Marcel Berlins points out (Writ large: TV's legal fictions don't do the profession justice, June 30). The drama shows barristers acting in breach of their professional obligations. In episode two a QC encourages a client to provide a false defence to a court — a grave breach of professional conduct that would be grounds for the barrister to be struck off. The Bar Council is very concerned at this portrayal of a profession which works to the highest ethical standards. Peter Moffat, the writer, appears to have missed the real story. Publicly funded criminal defence practitioners continue to serve the public in the most difficult circumstances. Even though the system is chronically underfunded, they act to the highest standards. Counsel's first duty is to the court and to the interests of justice. Criminal justice is not a game and it is a travesty to suggest practitioners see it in that way.

Timothy Dutton QC
Chairman, Bar Council

July 5

The way ahead for the NHS at 60

Polly Toynbee (For all the hyperbole, Bevan would have approved of this, July 1) rightly points to Nye Bevan's realism over an NHS where "expectations will always exceed capacity". He would not have approved of the waves of managerialism and market values that have dogged its last 25 years. But despite the Conservatives' introduction of the internal market in the 1990s, the care ethos has survived, and it is still free.

The privatisation agenda would have disturbed his socialism — the cheap accounting trick of the

straws, as he hasn't got a brain.

**Gary Wilmot and
Adam Cooper**
London

July 3

If anyone still doubts Christopher Hitchens when he says water-boarding is torture (Shortcuts, G2, July 2), they should watch our 90-second film (www.unsubscribe-me.org).

Sara MacNeice
Amnesty International UK

July 3

Perhaps Germaine Greer is overinter-preting Bob Dylan's lyrics (Arts, G2, June 30). When asked what his songs were all about, the Minnesota Minstrel replied: "They're all about three minutes."

Dr John Doherty
Vienna, Austria

July 4

So the Scarecrow, Lion and Tin Man all claim to be the star of The Wizard of Oz (Letters, July 2). They should be careful – Dorothy has a lot of friends out there.

Brian Hartigan
Banstead, Surrey

July 4

Are the producers of the West End musicals closing soon after opening (Report, July 3) Bialystock and Bloom?

Matthew Thompson
Stockport

July 4

Am I the only one to notice that Nadal has a problem with his undies? Or is it the lack of them that is causing the problem?

Jo Soper
Trevillick, Cornwall

July 5

Scandinavian or Anglo-Saxon vowel? Greek or Latin diphthong?

private finance initiative and the concept of selling health services for the profit of shareholders would have had him ranting on the parliamentary benches. The "choice" agenda, however, could break the last goodwill strand that keeps the service going. Intuition tells us that "choice" is a false premise for healthcare. All we want is to be treated soon, safely and locally.

In health, as in education, the recycling of ideas is inherent. We have seen the polyclinic before – it was called a cottage hospital. Restructuring and rationalisation phased them out over the last 10 years.

Today is the 60th anniversary of changeover day in 1948. My institution has no celebration planned, sadly; but I hope the Guardian has something to remind us that there is a survivor of some radical thinking 60 years ago, albeit the creation of a now "embarrassing" and unpopular political paradigm.

Jonathan Hauxwell
Cross Hills, North Yorkshire

July 7

Nuclear insurance policy

Twenty years ago last week, the USS Vincennes shot down Iranian Airlines Flight 655 from Bandar Abbas to Dubai inside Iranian airspace, killing 290 civilians. How an Airbus A300 can be mistaken for an attacking F-14 remains without explanation. Or apology. How would the US react if an Iranian warship shot down a Boeing inside American airspace? Does that bear thinking about?

It's high time that the US and its closest allies were judged by the same standards as other nations less endowed with overkill capability and the arrogance that goes with it. The careful handling of North Korea and the fate of Saddam Hussein make it clear that the US government has inhibitions about getting tough with nuke-equipped regimes. The reverse also holds true, so who can blame the Iranians for wanting some radioactive insurance?

Alexander Upatov
St Petersburg, Russia

July 8

Reversing the polarity of Doctor Who's doodah

I hate to say it, but Russell T Davies sounds uncannily like those nasty C of E clergymen in his attempt to justify preserving the apostolic succession of all-male Doctor Whos ('Amy Winehouse would be a great Doctor', Media, July 7). His squeamish reference to female genitalia seems to echo the discomfort of the priesthood over women's bodies. Saying that dads would find it embarrassing to explain how a male Doctor could regenerate as a female is bizarre. Since when did any sane parent ever try to explain any of the – ahem – implausible elements of a Doctor Who episode to their children? If they really wanted to know, you'd just have to say that they'd reversed the polarity of the doodah. Come on, Russell, you'll have to do better than that!

Lucy Whitman
London

July 9

More tips for cutting food waste

Gordon Brown belatedly recognises the grossly wasteful nature of our society but hits out at

Digraph? I think you'll find that Ae (Letters, passim) is a small village a few miles north of Dumfries.

Douglas Richardson
Edinburgh

July 7
Southern Cross, a large operator of care homes for the elderly, is struggling to meet a repayment for a £46m loan (Report, July 1). Last December its management shared personal windfalls of £36.6m. Any connection?

MJ Erskine Wallis
Oxford

July 7
Regarding Nadal's shorts (Letters, July 4), the old Lancashire term to describe his behaviour is "taking in washing".

F Kelly
Tarporley, Cheshire

July 8
I am sure professional

broadcasters will have many stories to tell of Charles Wheeler, but my favourite dates from the defection of Kim Philby at the height of the cold war (Obituaries, July 5). Wheeler was asked whether he was surprised at Philby's treason. "Not really," replied Wheeler, "I never really trusted him. He was the sort of fellow who ... smiled at breakfast, that sort of thing." A great loss, fondly remembered.

Christopher Frew
Edinburgh

July 8

So the French have an escargot shortage (Report, July 7)? Well, I'd offer them mine from my back garden, but I eat them myself with butter, garlic and parsley. The recipe is from Elisabeth Luard's European Peasant Cookery. Delicious!

Joe Alessi
London

the wrong target (UK is wasting far too much food – Brown, July 7). Of course individuals could waste less food. However, the real culprits are retailers who deliberately advertise, package and manipulate pricing to persuade shoppers to buy more than they need or can consume.

The average person is bombarded with over three hours of television adverts a week. Unsurprisingly these do not recommend buying only what we need but urge us to buy, buy, buy. Supermarkets have no interest in fulfilling the real needs of their customers – they simply aim to sell as much as they possibly can. Indeed the more food the customer throws away, the more profit the supermarket makes! But hey, that's capitalism.

Mike Davies
Chair, Alliance for Green Socialism

July 10

The economists' guessing game

As one of the 364 economists who signed the famous protest against Margaret Thatcher's deflationary purge, I agree with Simon Jenkins when he debunks the pretensions of economics, though not with his endorsement of Thatcherism (When the going gets tough, the economists go very quiet, July 9). There is, indeed, a crisis in modern economics, but it goes well beyond failures of modelling and management. Economists have forgotten, if they ever knew, that markets are embedded in forms of social life that are not themselves governed by market "laws" and that the biosphere is a living ecosystem, not a limitlessly exploitable resource. As a result, contemporary economics offers neither a persuasive account of our collective life experience nor wise guidance for tackling the problems of our dysfunctional society and degraded environment.

David Purdy
Stirling

July 10

The case against anonymous witnesses

Having spent three decades defending rape survivors, we are aghast at the witness anonymity bill now before parliament (There can be no fair trials with this perjurer's charter, July 8). Rape survivors are anonymous in the media, not in the witness box.

This bill proposes that the accused should not know who is accusing them, and therefore should not be able to challenge or appeal the evidence against them. The excuse is that some witnesses are afraid to come forward. But for every such case there are many where witnesses do come forward but they are not interviewed and/or their evidence is lost or dismissed or they are not called to give evidence in court. We have seen case after case destroyed by police and CPS bias and inefficiency. This is not only true of reported rape, with its shocking 6% conviction rate. Racist assaults, for example, have a 7% conviction rate.

We are now helping a rape survivor facing a workplace disciplinary procedure based on anonymous accusations. She believes the man who raped her is behind them, but cannot defend herself since her accuser cannot be challenged. To extend such grotesque injustice to the criminal courts would destroy any hope of justice.

Some of the rape victims we fight for are asylum seekers who have fled dictatorships where the

July 9
We are deeply concerned for the health of Joe Alessi (Letters, July 8): English garden snails are not true escargots, and are not, alas, edible – otherwise my wife and I would be enjoying them too.

Michael Law
London

July 9
I am a firm supporter of women's ministry to the highest office (Report, July 8); however, I hope that when women bishops emerge they do not have to wear the ridiculous hats that male bishops now do.

Rev Dr Laurie Blaney
Basildon, Essex

July 10
I'd like to thank Mr and Mrs Law for their concern (Letters, July 9). I can assure them that common English garden snails are safe

to eat, providing you keep them in a bucket for about 10 days so they can purge themselves of any harmful plant life they may have eaten. During this time, I also like to fatten them up with fresh herbs. Bon appetit!

Joe Alessi
London

July 11

Perhaps the schism in the Anglican church is better described as a cleavage (Church of England synod votes to allow women bishops, July 8).

Malcolm Stewart
Edinburgh

July 11

Jonathan Hauxwell (Letters, July 5) is quite wrong to describe the private finance initiative as "a cheap accounting trick". It is extremely costly.

Roger Broad
London

word of the police is enough to get people locked up for any crime, guilty or innocent. The same will be true in Britain if anonymity prevails.

Cristel Amiss Black Women's Rape Action Project
Ruth Hall Women Against Rape

July 11

Bags delayed, not lost at Terminal 5

Taking a pop at Terminal 5 has become a pastime in some quarters, but this does not justify your assertion that the terminal is "losing more than 900 bags a day" (Report, July 10). These bags are not lost. They are bags of passengers connecting between flights which become delayed in the transfer process, often for the simple reason that the incoming flight was late. The large majority of these delayed bags are flown by other carriers into other terminals for transfer to a British Airways flight and are not the fault of BA or T5.

The performance of BA at Heathrow airport has significantly improved since moving to T5. Its new baggage system has also allowed us to reprocess delayed bags through security more quickly and, very often, have them ready for the next flight to the relevant destination, reducing the inconvenience to customers.

Delays to transfer bags are a routine feature of every hub airport in the world. The problem is compounded at Heathrow because its lack of spare runway capacity makes it the most vulnerable to flight delays in Europe. More runway capacity would mean fewer late bags.

Willie Walsh
Chief executive, British Airways

July 12

Plane stupidity

Willie Walsh's case for a third runway at Heathrow (Letters, July 11) appears to be disappearing down the same chute as the 900 bags that his terminal loses each day. With his economic arguments floundering – both the Economist and the Conservatives now oppose further expansion – his justification is becoming increasingly imaginative. Incredibly, Walsh is now using BA's own incompetence to bolster his position, claiming "more runway capacity would mean fewer late bags".

Last year more than 8 million passengers flew between Heathrow and destinations easily reachable by train. A total switch to rail on these routes would free up 12% of the landing and take-off slots at the airport. With major harmonisation of timetables and a coordinated booking system announced by European rail operators for 2009, train travel will be a faster, more convenient, cheaper and far less climate-damaging alternative on these routes. Electrified rail will be the solution to Europe's transport needs into the 21st century.

Joss Garman
Co-founder, Plane Stupid

July 12

Little grey snails and Roman escargots

As someone who has worked professionally with snails for over 30 years, let me correct some misunderstandings (Letters, July 9). English garden snails are indeed not the same as the snails commonly thought of as restaurant escargots. However, they are closely related and quite edible,

July 12

Thank you for your article on Dorothy Tyler at the 1948 London Olympics (G2, July 10). Her Olympic career was, in one way, most unlucky. She won silver in 1936 and 1948, clearing the same height as the gold medallist each time. The rules on who should win if athletes tied were changed in the intervening years. If the 1948 rules had been in place in 1936 she would have won gold; likewise if the 1936 rules had been in place in 1948.

Steve Till
Bishop's Sutton, Hampshire

July 14

So, Caroline Oulton (Letters, July 12) thinks Peter Bradshaw's "attack" on Mamma Mia! almost absurdly vitriolic. After seeing the film last night, my husband thinks Bradshaw's single star was generous – and he is an Abba fan.

Barbara Hibbert
Harrogate, North Yorkshire

July 15
Don't kick Raff when he is trying to get up (Letters, July 12). Presently three of the symphonies are in the CD catalogue and the romantic piano revival has restored the Op 185 concerto. I bet Joe Queenan (Admit it, you're as bored as I am, G2, July 9) likes it.

Edward Veitch
Westhill, Aberdeenshire

July 16
I well remember the days when "You tube!" was a term of abuse (Show and tell, G2, July 14). It was used to identify people who were ignorant, egotistical, overblown, thoughtless or just plain stupid. No change there then!

Willie Macfadyen
Stirling

as are almost all snails – just go to a market in much of southern Europe and you will find numerous different kinds for sale. The "true" escargots are known in England as Roman snails, in France as escargots de Bourgogne (Burgundy snails) and scientifically as Helix pomatia. English garden snails are known in France as petits gris (little grey snails) and scientifically as Helix aspersa (or other names, the rationale for which is too arcane to go into here). As long as English garden snails are cleaned appropriately, as are Roman snails, to clear their guts, they are perfectly edible, though should be cooked thoroughly. Whether they taste different is debatable – the preference for the Roman snail is simply, I suspect, because it is bigger, in fact the biggest kind of European snail.

Professor Robert Cowie
Honolulu, Hawaii

July 14
Well done, Salman

I was at once dismayed and amused to read that Salman Rushdie believes I "take a swipe" at Midnight's Children almost every week ('Everybody needs to get thicker skins', G2, July 11). Amused because the description turns me into a fictional character from James Thurber, lonely and obsessed; dismayed because I actually like his novel very much. I may not be an unequivocal worshipper at the shrine; I've only reviewed him once, a mildly critical piece on Shalimar the Clown; but I do think Midnight's Children, with Haroun and the Sea of Stories, is his best book, and one of the most amazing novels to have emerged from India in the last 30 years. What I've been arguing against for some time is the conflation of that novel, in a certain kind of discourse, with an idea of Indian writing in English, or even Indian writing itself: a conflation that reduces, rather than enlarges, the field. I'm delighted, though, that it's received the Booker of Bookers. The only justification for having someone else win it this time would be to have the pleasurable possibility of a Booker of Booker of Bookers some time in the future.

Amit Chaudhuri
Kolkata, India

July 15

State funeral would be an insult

When Margaret Thatcher was minister for education, she took free milk away from schoolchildren (State funeral planned for Lady Thatcher, July 14). I created the slogan "Margaret Thatcher, Milk Snatcher" and put it on a wanted poster with her picture. My slogan became part of her history. When she became prime minister, we wrote to her from the Chiswick Women's Aid refuge and asked her what she would do for victims of domestic violence. A minion replied on her behalf and said that she was "not interested in women's issues". A state funeral would be an insult to this nation.

Erin Pizzey
London

July 16

Thatcher's legacy is nothing to be celebrated

I cannot believe that I am alone in feeling total disgust that there are plans to honour Margaret

July 17

I would advise Rowan Williams to do something with his eyebrows (Archbishop prepares to face his tormentors, July 15). They have started to look distinctly like a pair of horns and his appearance is increasingly reminiscent of another entity.

Roger Marsh
Morecambe, Lancashire

July 17

Every year, just before Christmas, 10 of us gather to play wind dectets. We always begin with Raff's sinfonietta for two flutes, two oboes, two clarinets, two bassoons and two horns (Letters, July 15). Listen to it — it's wonderful!

Gillian Gadsby
London

July 18

Regarding the film director Manoel de Oliveira, who is still working in his 100th year (Report, July 17), tonight sees the first night of the Proms with music by the American composer Elliott Carter, who is the same age as Oliveira. In fact exactly the same age, as they were both born on December 11 1908.

Cliff Challenger
Bradford

July 21
Ian Jack is mistaken in thinking that Eric Blair's parents' choice of Southwold as a holiday venue may have led to him adopting the nom de plume Orwell (Fashionable paddling — or why the Browns chose Southwold, July 19). Prior to the 1980s, the river crossing at Ipswich en route between London and Southwold would have been over the Gipping. The current Orwell bridge which offers such splendid

Thatcher with a state funeral (Report, July 14). I would also take issue with the view that she "reversed the decline in Britain's postwar fortunes". Leaving aside the well-known arguments about the devastation to Britain's manufacturing capacity, much of which was done not for economic reasons, but simply to emasculate the large trade unions, there are strong arguments to suggest that much that is wrong with 21st-century Britain in social terms can be traced back to the innate selfishness strongly promoted during her time as prime minister.

The breakdown in families and communities, the notion of "no such thing as society", the every-man-for-themselves culture, the "loads of money" ideal, the vast unemployment that directly led to the growth of the disaffected millions, the savage cuts to the public sector — all can be attributed directly to her terms in office. While accepting that my view could be put in the "controversial" element alluded to in the article, surely that controversy, which still splits the country quite markedly, should preclude such a decision. The fact that No 10 appears to have condoned the plans sums up how bankrupt this government has become.

Dr Terry Allcott
Walton by Kimcote, Leicestershire

• Thatcher should only be allowed a state funeral if the contract is put out to compulsory competitive tender and awarded to the lowest bidder. Any offers?

Rob Watling
Nottingham

July 16

Getting to the root of knife-carrying

There is nothing more harrowing than a mother's high-pitched cry echoing down a hospital corridor on discovering her child has been stabbed to death. It resonates further knowing all heroic attempts by medical staff are futile after such extensive irreparable damage has been done. And after two years of research (Tactics against gangs fatally flawed — report, July 14), our understanding of the root causes of knife crime and the motivation among perpetrators is still cloudy.

Having grown up in a rough London school, I know that this culture has been long evolving. Little has changed — only the age of those carrying knives. Young people feel they have to keep up with the ethos of invoking fear because that is what it means to enter adulthood, or be an authority — as daily evidenced by their parents, schoolteachers, police and even country leaders. With the skill-less act of carrying or using a knife, young people earn street credit by invoking fear among their peers and flaunting misplaced bravery.

With complex social problems in London, pressures on families translate into young people feeling demoralised and lacking control. Why don't we give them back that feeling of control, not through fear but through understanding, coping strategies and conflict resolution skills? Many of us had to learn these the hard way, but at least we're here to tell the tale.

Dr Heba Al-Naseri
Northwick Park hospital, Harrow

estuarine views didn't open until the 1980s. George Gipping doesn't sound so good, though.

R Cooper
Woodbridge, Suffolk

July 22

Eric Blair would have seen the Orwell river travelling to and from his parents' house in Southwold (Letters, July 21) — there are fine views from the train just south of Ipswich. And he could have crossed it by road: two of the three river crossings in the town are over the tidal Orwell, not the non-tidal Gipping.

Paul Anderson
Ipswich

July 22

I thought sandwich-board men were long ago redundant (Pining for the boards, July 21). We've brought it on ourselves by proudly displaying brand names on our backs, fronts, heads and feet, thus saving the manufacturers time, trouble and considerable expense.

Neville Denson
St Bees, Cumbria

July 22
So golfer Greg Norman (Same old story for Norman, Sport, July 21) has a new wife "to take care of". Would that wife be three-times-married multimillionaire Chris Evert, winner of 18 tennis singles grand slam titles (to his two majors) and once described by John McEnroe as "an assassin"? Her mum must be so relieved.

Sally Morris
London

July 23
Duke Ellington had the best compliment for a lady (Ask Hadley, G2, July 21): "You make that dress look

July 17

Thatcher's courage should be honoured

It is my duty to reply to some of the strident, spiteful letters about Mrs Thatcher (July 16). I have never had any party affiliations, though I was a trade unionist and a socialist until the late 1970s. Mrs Thatcher had the courage, which neither Wilson or Callaghan possessed, to take on the politically motivated unions, the leaders of whom seemed on a permanent ego trip – down almost to convener level, I would add. Mrs Thatcher also played a vital role in the overthrowing of one of the nastiest fascist governments of the 20th century (the Argentina junta). In my opinion, other than Attlee, who himself was despised by the left wing of his party, she is by far the best of the postwar PMs. The puerile letters from some of your readers do little credit to either of you.

Peter Bolt
Redditch, Worcestershire

July 17

Sign of the times

Salman Rushdie clings to many illusions (Interview, G2, July 11), but possibly the most brazen relates to his remark "In Nashville I signed 1,000 copies [of his latest novel] in an hour, which I think is a record." I suspect Sir Salman only scribbled his signature in the form of his initials, as it is impossible to write a full name 1,000 times in 1,000 books in one hour unless you have the help of three practised henchpersons, one to plonk the virgin title page in front of you, another to whisk each book away, a third to pass it on. As this signing took place in a bookshop, notoriously understaffed, I doubt whether he had such help and, in any event, the appending of mere initials does not count as "signing". I once held the UK record for signing books; some 10 years ago now, at the warehouse of the Superplonk distributor, I signed 1,001 copies of the book, with the help of three staff, in 59 minutes — with my full name.

Malcolm Gluck
London

July 19
Paying for the BBC

Your report on the licence fee (Ofcom hits back at BBC over licence-fee sharing dispute, July 18) misses a crucial point and one on which David Currie and I agree: it is for the government and parliament to decide the level of the fee. But it is not safe to assume that, in five years' time, MPs will decide that the current level, which includes £800m over six years to cover the cost of digital switchover, should continue beyond 2013. That is why I have questioned presumptive language about an excess or surplus. David Currie is right that, in 2013, parliament will face three options: maintain the current fee level and apply the proceeds in full to the BBC; apply the money for another purpose; or reduce the amount the public should pay. What I have argued is that there should be a national debate, involving the public, on the future of public service broadcasting. After all, the licence fee belongs to those who pay it.

Michael Lyons
Chairman, BBC Trust

beautiful." Worked every time.

Peter Caswell
Chairman, Duke Ellington
Society UK

July 24
With reference to the Audit Commission's report on an ageing population, one has to ask what they expect local authorities to provide for us active elders (Report, July 17). Instead of bowling greens, might we be provided with models of the American embassy and broken paving slabs? Sir Michael Jagger might even pop along occasionally to provide moral support. How serious were these people?

Andrew Krokou
London

July 25
Richard Smith (Oh, I'll do it tomorrow, July 22) should relocate, along with his dilatory

family, to Italy, where *dolce far niente* — the joy of idleness — is a treasured lifestyle, not a disease.

John Doherty
Vienna, Austria

July 25

It's a slippery slope: you start with genocide and before you know it you're practising alternative medicine (Karadzic arrest: details emerge of captured warlord's life as a New Age therapist while on run, July 23). It shows the importance of catching these people early.

Tom Sheldon
London

July 26

It's the News of the World that was sleazy (Why Mosley won in the high court, July 25). It's time people stood up against tabloid tyranny. What gives the NoW's editor the right to video the

July 22

I fear the winter and hope for nothing

Up until three years ago I was a member of the working class (Benefits clampdown, July 21). I have no qualifications and I raised my family by working hard and earning little. As such I was never able to have either a pension, a mortgage or insurance. Three years ago, within six days of each other, I had a heart attack and my wife had heart failure (totally unconnected). We as a small family were destroyed.

My wife was in intensive care for a month and my daughter took an overdose believing us both dead. What happened to us as a family can happen to any family. We rallied and my son put himself through university by working in a pub and looking after himself — without a single penny from us because we had nothing.

My point is real poverty grows on you and as the things you have become obsolete or break, the poverty deepens. We are now three adults living on £23 a day. Admittedly we have our rent and rates paid. As heart patients we have been instructed to stay warm in the winter as the cold thickens the blood. To this end I contacted my gas and electric supplier in a bid to have the prepayment meters taken out of my home as the tariff was too high and my income was so low. I was told it would cost £200.

I told the supplier that the meters were in place from a former tenant and I had no credit issues with them. They told me it was not their problem. I went to the ombudsman and now I can have the meters taken out if I pay for the energy by direct debit, the rub being that I have to pay in advance, costing me 79% of my income in one month for this to happen. So it can't and they know it.

Every day I shop for the house. I am conscious of the need to eat healthily but I cannot afford to. Every day I walk past the grapes and look at the price of strawberries. We eat greens and pulses, and we eat pork, but cannot afford chicken. We do not drink, smoke, go out nor entertain and life is hard and getting harder, not just for us but for many.

The television is our only window on a life we once led. We sit destroyed by poverty and watch the world go by as if we were dead but have yet to fall over. While watching the TV we see MPs and MEPs who spend more on taxis than we get to live on and they are telling the country they are going to get tough on us and people like us because we live on benefits.

In relative terms we are poor and getting poorer, but those who represent us are completely oblivious to our needs.

I can speak, but have no voice, and those claiming to represent me have failed me. As the gas and electric prices rise for all, they may also become out of reach for many. Now I fear the winter and hope for nothing.

The BBC news now tells me my benefits will be scrapped and I will be tested (I have been tested twice already). I will have to bare all my privacy in the hope of retaining the right to survive the winter. So I ask myself, why can people demand the destruction of the poor? The answer is simple. There are 600-odd vacancies in Westminster every four years. The job, if you can get it, pays a king's ransom and all that is required is that you follow whatever is in vogue. At the moment, acting Dickensian is all the rage.

Name and address supplied

lives of private citizens in their bedrooms? Since when is the News of the World the arbiter of public morality? I for one am glad to see the screwer screwed.

Tony Robinson
Brussels

July 26
Does this mean sado-masochists will now get a fair crack of the whip?

Brian Carr
St Helens, Merseyside

July 26
How can someone who can't even look after their bicycle be entrusted with looking after the country (Bicycle thief leaves Cameron standing, July 25)?

Peter Halsey
Radlett, Hertfordshire

July 26
While I have every sympathy for David

Cameron on his shopping trip, he is probably one of the last people around to use the word "supper".

Sam Webber
Bickley, Kent

July 26
Re your leader (In praise of... drummers, July 23): you are just encouraging them. Have you any idea what it is like to stand on a stage trying to play a musical instrument while behind you someone is building a shed? Incidentally, the best drummer – if you must have them – is Bernard "Pretty" Purdey. Yours (on four),

Spike Walton
(Bass player), Cardiff

July 28
I must beg to differ with Sam Webber (Letters, July 26). An alarming number of my middle-class friends refer to the

July 23

Meters will fuel poverty this winter

Rarely has a letter touched my heart as much as this (I fear the winter and hope for nothing, July 22). I would like to say this is an isolated case, but the National Consumer Council has looked into this area and found prepayment meters are a problem facing many, particularly the most vulnerable in our society.

People using them have to pay more and generally do so with a sense of unfairness, knowing better-off consumers are benefiting from being able to pay energy bills in other ways. We are calling on energy companies to bring down the cost of prepayment meters, so they are more in line with other types of payment.

We are also calling on energy companies to do more to shield vulnerable people from the worst effects of rapidly rising energy bills. We would like to see energy companies offering low-cost "social" tariffs to less well-off households, such as low-income families and elderly people. Some energy companies are doing well in this area, but others are offering schemes that are inadequate. The government needs to do more to make sure that companies deliver these initiatives. It may be sunny outside now, but winter will soon be here and action is needed now so effective measures are in place to help the 40% of us facing fuel poverty later this year.

Cassie Higgs
Senior policy advocate, National Consumer Council

July 23

Eating sunlight

Hugh Fearnley-Whittingstall praises the way in which jams "elegantly and in an entirely positive manner" defy the seasons (Perfectly preserved, G2, July 21). Yet they have power over space as well as time. Jam's place in the larder became possible thanks to imported sugar made in tropical cane plantations. The sheer calorific boost refined sugar provided, along with its preservative powers, was one of the first fruits of globalisation, allowing workers in factories in Manchester to be fed with calories from the Caribbean. At the same time, the reduction in food-preparation time represented by jam on bread was a factor in moving more women into paid employment. Since this economic shift depended on slavery it was clearly not entirely positive; to some minds, though, the use of sunlight harvested in one part of the world to fuel human activity in another does have a certain elegance.

Oliver Morton
London

July 26

The options for Labour after Glasgow East

Labour's travails (Catastrophe for Labour as SNP triumphs in Glasgow East, July 25) are intrinsic to the New Labour project: a shift to the right based on the assumption that Labour supporters had nowhere else to go. As a not particularly leftwing Labour supporter, it seems so simple. The more cynical Labour has become, the more people have deserted the party.

There are a number of quick, sensible policy

evening meal as "supper" — and are invariably surprised when I turn up in my pyjamas.

Nick Gilbert
London

July 29

I recall the reply given by either Ronnie Scott or Humphrey Lyttelton to the small boy who said, "when I grow up I am going to be a drummer" (Letters, July 26). "You can do one or the other, son, not both."

Ian Benson
Ashford, Kent

July 29

Why are all drummer jokes one-liners? So the bass player can get them.

Jack Houston
London

July 30

Depictions of Radovan Karadzic as a poet and conversationalist

(Reports, July 23)
bring to mind Auden's
lines: Perfection, of a
kind, was what he was
after, / And the poetry
he invented was easy to
understand; / He knew
human folly like the
back of his hand, / And
was greatly interested
in armies and fleets; /
When he laughed,
respectable senators
burst with laughter, /
And when he cried the
little children died in
the streets.

Michael Hayes
Canterbury, Kent

July 30
Re modern usage
(Open door, July 28):
I try to accept most
modern variations, but
where has the chirpy
"Good!" come from in
answer to (the usually
uninterested question)
"How are you?"?

Rowena Rowlands
Wigan, Lancashire

options Brown could announce today and his
ratings would go through the roof: 1) Ditch ID
cards; 2) Tax the very rich who have gained most
from the past decade a bit more; 3) Cancel the
Trident upgrade and announce that the £75bn
saved will be spent on NHS dentists for all, and
reducing class sizes; 4) Announce a timetable for
withdrawal from Iraq; 5) Stop bribing the City,
particularly groups such as non-doms, and make
the case for fair taxes and regulation; 6) Make
the case for the referendum on voting reform
promised in 1997.

Policies like these would be instantly popular,
brave, progressive, yet not particularly radical from
a supposedly centre-left government. Moreover,
they are the kind of policies that energised people
to vote in huge numbers for Labour in 1997. The
alternative is a Tory government by default.

Matthew Bishop
Politics department, Sheffield University

• Having joined the Labour party in 1946, it grieves
me to say this, but if a Scottish prime minister
cannot hold a very safe Scottish seat, it shows
beyond any doubt the complete loss of confidence
in Gordon Brown across the whole of the UK. If
his ministers, advisers etc, will not say it, then let
the members do so. For the good of the country,
government, parliament and the party, go now,
Gordon. It would at least give us a fighting chance
at the next election.

J Blackman
Margate, Kent

July 28

More fallout from Labour's byelection defeat

Patrick Wintour reports that (at last) anxiety is being expressed at senior cabinet level that the party has been neglected (Senior ministers urged: tell battered PM it's time to go, July 26). The SNP had far more volunteers campaigning on the ground in Glasgow East than Labour. I received a desperate email urging me to go to Glasgow and work in the campaign, even though I live 200 miles away. The membership of the Labour party plummeted to 158,868 last month – a 60% fall from the 400,000-plus membership in 1997. That's what New Labour top-down control has done to us.

More of the same will cut the membership further before an election, with even fewer left to campaign. Members must be re-empowered and given a real say in policymaking through a reformed party conference. The national policy forum that met on Friday is not truly representative of members' views because, unlike the constituency section of the national executive committee, it is not directly elected by the members.

Above all, if we are to have a change of party leader, the decision must be taken in the interests of the party as a whole and not just of those MPs who fear losing their marginal seats. There must be a proper election in which there are several viable candidates of different shades of opinion. Now is the time for the cabinet and the NEC to save the Labour party by listening to it.

Gaye Johnston
Vice-chair, Save the Labour Party

• Glasgow East was bad enough for Labour UK nationally, but commentary in London exagger-

July 30

Dinner is the posh meal with candles and the best silver, and supper (Letters, July 28) is the informal family meal to which one's close friends are sometimes invited at the last minute and are welcome to come in pyjamas.

Belinda King
Sudbury, Suffolk

July 30

Essence of a Guardian day: sitting in a traditional local – the John Bull Inn at Alnwick – drinking real ale, knitting from The Rebel Knitter's Guide (July 26), doing the Quick Crossword with my bearded, sandal-wearing husband, after a wild swim in the North Sea.

Clare Addison
Oxford

July 31

Richard Branson attempts to assert that "my green credentials are better than yours" in his long-running game of ping-pong with British Airways (Letters, July 23). Yesterday, however, we read that Branson is to introduce a service which will allow those with the necessary reserves of cash to burn to undertake a tourist flight into space at God knows what cost in terms of fossil fuel consumption (Report, July 30). Never trust a man with a beard.

Rob Jacques
Freiburg, Germany

July 31

How do you know when you are living with a singer (Letters, July 29)? They take the wrong key and never come in on time.

Stuart Hannay
Banyuls-sur-Mer, France

ates how much it was anti-Brown. Many hitherto Labour voters were not so much protest voters as people believing – with good cause – that the SNP's policies and actions at Holyrood have been much what they once expected from Labour. People were not voting for independence, nor necessarily against Brown, but for Alex Salmond's domestic policies. Unhappily for Labour in Scotland, Salmond's social democratic beliefs are not tactical but long-held and genuine. The Labour party in Scotland will only survive if it can become a federally autonomous Scottish Labour party.

Bernard Crick
Edinburgh

July 31

Miliband's sink or swim challenge to Labour

David Miliband's article (Against the odds we can still win, on a platform of change, July 30) was the most clearly expressed and concise political commentary I have ever read. In the space of a few column inches he managed to explain what the Labour party stands for, what it has achieved and what it needs to do now to meet current challenges. The article also gave a convincing argument why the Labour party can succeed where the Conservatives will not. Why has it taken a potential leadership challenge before the Labour party clearly expresses its vision?

Gordon Brown
Farnham, Surrey

August 2008

Events both positive and negative intimated changes ahead in the international order. The spectacular opening and closing of the Beijing Olympics, and the success of China in topping the medals table, pushed aside human rights concerns and announced a new superpower taking its place on the world stage with a confident display of soft power. Meanwhile an old superpower, Russia, showed that its hard power still could not be ignored, by batting aside the Georgians after they had invaded the contested enclave of South Ossetia. Global north-south divisions, as well as east-west, nudged into the news agenda. The impact of global food prices on Haiti and the attempts by Bolivia's president, Evo Morales, to give a greater share of the country's oil and gas wealth to the country's dispossessed warned of deepening conflict between the world's rich and poor. North-south divisions were pointed up in Britain too, when a Tory thinktank said it might be better to let struggling northern cities like Sunderland simply decline and encourage their populations to head south. Climate change was back on the domestic agenda as protesters camped near the site of a proposed new coal-fired power station in Kent. England's cricket captain resigned in tears after his team lost the Test series to South Africa, readers swapped recipes for snails and placentas, and the revelation by one letter writer of the great frozen broad bean shortage led to a high-powered investigation on BBC2's Newsnight.

August 1

On Sunday I attempted to buy some frozen broad beans in my local Waitrose, only to be told that they no longer sell them. Somewhat miffed, I then went to my local Sainsbury's, only to receive the same answer. By now I was intrigued, so I tried Tesco, and again I was rebuffed, customer services saying that probably there was no demand. A quick Google shows I'm not the only person commenting on this phenomenon. Is it a nationwide conspiracy or is there a more mundane answer?

David Scott
Wythall, Worcestershire

August 1

Your letter writer (July 31) questioned my green credentials due to us owning Virgin Galactic. As a matter of interest Virgin Galactic will be able to

August 2

Purl one, drop one against the bomb

Monday morning. Aldermaston Atomic Weapons Establishment. Women of a certain age put up their camp chairs on the verge of the road opposite the gate to Britain's nuclear bomb factory and place a banner saying they are opposed to nuclear weapons. They open their bags and take out their knitting (The Rebel Knitter's Guide, July 26). Fresh-faced police officers look on indulgently, but a trifle anxiously. Occasionally a ball of wool happens, innocently, to roll into the road and a woman gets up awkwardly from her chair and slowly walks to pick it up. The traffic slows and the police officer moves to hurry her up: people on their way to work in such an important place should not be inconvenienced by some crazy old women. The women continue to sit there, wishing into their knitting a dream of a world without the bomb.

Ailsa Johnson
Penzance, Cornwall

August 2

We'll breach bail to go to climate camp

We are five people deeply concerned about climate change who had intended to take time off work to spend next week at the Camp for Climate Action near Kingsnorth in Kent. In the past few days, however, we have been made the subject of pernicious legal restrictions that prevent us from legally attending the protest at Kingsnorth. Yorkshire police have banned a number of people, including us, who recently took part in a peaceful protest on a coal train outside Drax power station from attending the camp in Kent. Originally the restrictions went so far as to confine us to our homes for the duration of the camp. Those severe restrictions were challenged and eventually dropped, but we are still barred from setting foot in the area of northern Kent where the camp is taking place.

The movement to stop E.ON being given the green light to build a new coal-fired power station at Kingsnorth is of vital importance. But the climate camp is designed to challenge not just the expansion of coal but the idea that progress can only be attained through growth and the extension of "free" market ideologies.

On Monday at 3pm we intend to breach our bail conditions and join hundreds, maybe thousands of others at the climate camp. The thought of going to prison even for a short period is daunting, but we cannot accept the logic of bail conditions that stop us attending a legal event at which Royal Society professors mix with families. Scientists tell us that from this week we have just 100 months to solve climate change.

Ellen Potts, Oli Rodker, Johnathan Stevensen, Paul Morozzo, Mel Evans
Penzance, Cornwall

August 2

Sick of the Sats treadmill

The excellent critique by Jenni Russell (Balls' test answer? More of the futile, top-down plans that Labour loves, July 28) on the increasingly restrictive standard assessment tests reflects exactly what many of us in education have been feeling and saying for a very long time. As a teacher

put satellites into space for a tiny fraction of the carbon cost it takes Nasa and a person at less than the carbon cost of someone flying business class to New York and back.

Richard Branson
Chairman, Virgin Group

August 2
Are the Israelis who demand an attack on Iran (Leaders, August 1), which — repulsive though its government undoubtedly is — has never invaded another country and possesses no nuclear weapons, the same Israelis who have launched successive invasions of Lebanon, with much slaughter and huge damage, and possess 200 nuclear warheads?

Gerald Kaufman MP
Lab, Manchester Gorton

August 2
We are two drummers currently at the Edinburgh Fringe,

presenting a topical show trying to redress the negative image of the drummer. It's hard enough remembering the show we rehearsed without your daily supplies of material to our producers on your letters page. Could you please stop?

**Mathew Priest and
Maurice Bacon**
2 Drummers Drumming

August 2
We enjoyed David Jenkins' piece (Literary doubles, G2, July 31) about writers with the same name.

Nicholas Royle
Manchester

Nicholas Royle
Seaford, East Sussex

August 2
In the 1986 World Cup Gary Stevens of Tottenham and Gary Stevens of Everton were both selected for England. At one point the crowd struck up: "Two Gary Stevens,

and headteacher who has spent over 35 years working in state schools, with an increasingly heavy heart, my concerns were compounded this summer when my youngest, summer-born, granddaughter was sick every day during the key stage 1 assessment period. In a discussion with her about how she was feeling, she suddenly said: "I had a number test today. I knew I could do them but it all went too fast. The only thing I got right was my name – even then, I got one of my letters the wrong way round!"

Nothing I could say – and I wanted to weep – could compensate for the way she is beginning to regard herself a someone who cannot learn successfully (this bright, interested and lively child). There are many young children like her who learn differently and often at a slower pace than their peers or older siblings. They start school when they are slightly over four years old. They then enter the treadmill of Sats anxiety, which starts to build up their negative view towards learning, if they do not match the school view of a successful learner.

Worse still, they begin to see it as their fault rather than that of the system that pressures their teachers and schools, not to mention parents, who are equally unhappy about it. I despair of the constant rubbishing of the evidence, the next initiative that never has adequate time to settle down, and then the blame that it is somehow schools/teachers who have misinterpreted it if it doesn't "work". The psychology of how children learn is being completely ignored. And then society wonders why we have such a large number of disaffected young people.

Name and address supplied

August 2

Games in perspective

Have the Beijing Olympics helped to spur China to improve its human rights record? Jonathan Fenby thinks not (China is a law unto itself, July 29). Amnesty's report certainly raises some causes for concern, not least the treatment of dissidents. But if the Chinese government is to be held to account for its human rights record, a wider perspective is needed. The remarkable reductions in poverty are continuing, cut by over one-third since 2001, according to the World Bank. A rural cooperative medical insurance system has been widely introduced and the abolition of school fees in rural areas is under way. A labour contract law has also been initiated to protect the rights of migrant workers. Hopefully when journalists report from the Olympics they will introduce us to the wide range of opinions and not just focus on dissidents as the one true voice of the Chinese people.

Jenny Clegg
Manchester

August 5

Labour, leaders and enduring elites

For someone who can write with pinpoint accuracy about the government's failure to reduce inequality, Polly Toynbee's comments on David Miliband's article (This week, Miliband made winning look possible again, August 2) were a mixture of unsubstantiated optimism and overexcitement.

She attributes anti-Blairite policies to this polite, young man, who has an extremely conformist

there's only two Gary Stevens."

Andy Stobbie
Stockport, Cheshire

August 4

Gary McKinnon to be extradited to America (Report, July 31)? I thought we didn't extradite to countries that torture.

John Lodge
Lancaster

August 6

I was appalled at the tearful exhibition by Michael Vaughan in his press confer-ence yesterday to announce his exit from the Test captaincy (Report, August 4). A comment by the great Australian all-rounder Keith Miller is worth pondering. When asked by a reporter if he was feeling stress during a Test match, Miller – who was a fighter pilot during the war – replied, "Listen, mate, a Messerschmitt up your arse is stress, this is just a fucking game." (Source: Richie Benaud – The Appeal of Cricket)

Steve Moss
Sutton Coldfield,
West Midlands

August 6
Re literary doubles (Letters, August 5), I don't know what the rest of you are complaining about.

Dr Anne Summers
Honorary research fellow,
Birkbeck College

August 7
With all the debate about ecohouses (Put away your prejudices – ecohomes are not ugly, August 5), would it be pedantic to note that the word itself is a rather ugly etymological tautology? Eco is from the Greek oikos, meaning house.

Tim Chapman
Halifax, West Yorkshire

track record, that were not spelt out in any clear way to the average reader. For instance, where did he say that "he would step in and regulate the risk-taking City"? Where did he say that he "chooses equality over the old Blair 'choice' agenda"? He rose swiftly through ranks precisely because of his unswerving commitment to his previous boss.

I recall that Toynbee awaited the arrival of the present prime minister with great enthusiasm. A serious man, a thinker, in comparison to the shallow and flashy incumbent. Now he is her nominee for swift defenestration. As a Labour party member, I also want to look on the bright side, but New Labour was always a flower with no roots, either in principle or practice.

Tim Webb
London

• In the Winter 1958 issue of Universities and New Left Review, Ralph Miliband, in a lucid review of a symposium entitled Who Governs Britain?, notes with approval Philip Toynbee's focus on a power elite in Britain. Nice to see the daughter of the latter supporting the son of the former.

John Lynham
Sheffield

August 5
Haiti's food crisis

Your incisive article (Mud cakes become staple diet as cost of food soars beyond a family's reach, July 29) is a timely reminder of the critical situation faced by millions of Haitians, which is so often ignored by the rest of the world.

As Haiti's neighbour, and thus severely affected

by its fate, the Dominican Republic tirelessly calls for attention to the situation at international forums. Although political progress has and continues to be made and security has improved, the economic infrastructure of the country is still far from sufficiently adequate to enable even a basic quality of life for most Haitians.

The developed nations that have promised aid are far from fulfilling their pledges. With food prices rising, it is even more crucial that the world takes heed of the need to take action before the country is destabilised by the dire conditions which are deepened by the current crisis.

Anibal De Castro
Dominican Republic ambassador to the UK, London

August 7

Faith, hope and carbon capture

George Monbiot's article on coal and energy (The stakes could not be higher. Everything hinges on stopping coal, August 5) is misleading.

Monbiot is right that energy policy must be shaped to reduce carbon dioxide emissions. It must also respond to growing energy needs (although these growing needs must also be checked through greater energy efficiency). Over the next 25 to 50 years, because of cost and availability, coal is expected to meet much of the rising global demand for energy. If unabated, the carbon dioxide emissions would pose unacceptable climate risks.

Carbon capture and storage (CCS) is an unproven technology on the scale required for coal-fired power plants, but the various elements of the technology have been proven to work on a smaller scale. What is required is a concerted effort by all

August 7
There may well be only two Gary Stevenses (Letters, August 2), but when the three Wallace brothers – Danny, Rodney and Ray – all played together in the same Southampton team, the Saints fans chanted "there's only one Mrs Wallace".

Jeff Scott
Brighton

August 8
Jackie Ashley describes Gordon Brown as a principled, decent man (Comment, August 4). Am I missing something? Every journalist in the land seems to be clear that he was totally disloyal to Tony Blair almost throughout the time that he was prime minister and not only betrayed him by endlessly by briefing against him, but always disappeared without trace whenever the going got tough. In my book, loyalty to your

own team is one of the fundamental attributes of a principled and decent man. Isn't this total lack of loyalty one of the reasons that he now cannot command loyalty himself? I have rarely seen a stronger example of someone reaping what they sow.

Clive Gillinson
Executive & artistic director,
Carnegie Hall, New York

August 8
Dr Anne Summers thinks that others have more to complain about (Letters, August 5). I agree.

Joe Cocker
Leominster, Herefordshire

August 8
Anyone for tennis?

Andrew Murray
Kinghorn, Fife

August 9
Simon Barker's letter (August 4) concerning overzealous security operations struck a

major nations to translate this into commercial operation. It seems ridiculous to have to remind people that all technologies are unproven until they are proven. People said electricity could not work on a commercial scale.

Coal can play a part in the energy mix for the UK, but consent must be given to new coal-fired power stations only on condition that operating permits are withdrawn if they fail to capture 90% of their carbon dioxide emissions by 2020. This will send a clear signal to develop a technology that can play a major part in helping to meet UK and global energy needs without risking dangerous climate change.

Martin Rees
President, Royal Society

August 7
Just like Thucydides

David McKie's excellent suggestion that historical writers use "was, like" as a way of presenting invented speech (I've been, like, won over, August 4) was already being adopted in the fifth century BC. The Greek historian Thucydides helped to set the precedent McKie refers to of including "the words that, in his judgment, the protagonists ought to have used" – he even states in his introduction that he has made his speakers say "what seemed to [Thucydides] appropriate in each situation, while keeping as close as possible to the general gist of what was actually said".

Two and a half millennia later, and still no one is quite sure what Thucydides meant by this. But one important piece of evidence is the Greek word with which he scrupulously introduces every direct speech in his work: he does not write *elege tade* (said this), but *elege toiade* (said things like this).

Gail Trimble
Corpus Christi College, Oxford

August 8
Views on the borderlands of Pakistan

Peter Preston's astute analysis of borderland Pakistan (Where writs don't run, August 4) omits to mention the high premium which the Pashtuns who live there place on education. Students at the university college where I work, 40 minutes from the Khyber Pass, are fluent in three languages, and the highest achievers opt for science, especially in medicine and engineering. One student, justifiably nicknamed Einstein by his classmates, learned his basic science at one of those allegedly dangerous madrasas along the Afghan border which the Americans believe to be fomenting terrorism.

The "truth" about these tribal "badlands" between Pakistan and Afghanistan is about as far from the imagination of Washington (including Barack Obama) as were the exploits of John Wayne and his gun-toting friends from the reality of what once happened to America's indigenous population.

David L Gosling
Principal, Edwardes College, University of Peshawar, Pakistan

August 9
Let's celebrate musical treasures

Geoffrey Wheatcroft's criticisms of West Side Story (Comment, August 5) reminded me of a conversation I had in the early 1960s with the

chord. After taking a couple of photographs inside Liverpool's Lime Street station recently, I was approached by a policeman who said that under some terrorist act he had the right to question me. I explained my interest in trains and that the last time I was in this station they were all steam-powered. I showed him my driving licence, bus pass and pension card. However, this was not enough to stop him writing down all my details and checking them over his radio.

Graham Thompson
Stratford-upon-Avon,
Warwickshire

August 11
Regardless of what goes on in the Guardian's offices and surrounding watering holes (A moment on the lips, G2, August 5), out here in the real world kissing and hugging your work colleagues

and clients is certainly not normal.

Paul Dixon
Didcot, Oxfordshire

August 12

So David Tennant is dismissed by Jonathan Miller as "that man from Doctor Who" (G2, August 2). A bit rich coming from that bloke from Beyond the Fringe.

Clive Merrison
Sibton, Suffolk

August 12

It is surprising to see beanburgers advocated as a means of reducing gas emissions (Leaders, August 11).

Copland Smith
Manchester

August 13

What is the harm in granting a 90-year-old woman the thrill of being served fish and chips by a young man in a thong (Care home apology after

doyen of modern dance critics, John Martin, who objected to a show that was not a straight drama, an opera nor a dance but nevertheless set out to be all three. Surely it is vital to point out that West Side Story, warts and all, was a musical famed for its unprecedented (and to date unequalled) integration of every theatrical medium including dance. Nobody who saw those performances in London in January 1958 (I was a young teenager in the front row) could have failed to have been blown away by the warring Jets and Sharks as they powered their way through the opening scene. We were blasted out of our seats by Bernstein's gritty, percussive music and the gangs of sneaker-clad dancers tearing up the stage in high-octane movement.

What lifted West Side Story into a class of its own was the way it urbanised dance, created a seminal jazz-ballet idiom and theatricalised Latin American dance in the "dance in the gym" and "America" scenes. How fortunate that this American production is touring the world and that new generations of theatregoers in London and elsewhere can experience the thrill I felt 50 years ago.

Dr Henrietta Bannerman
London Contemporary Dance School

August 11

Speaking up in defence of Georgia

Let's call things as they are. Russia has invaded Georgia. My government has repeatedly and correctly claimed that Russia supports separatists in Georgia and cannot claim the role of impartial peacekeeper. That is why a resolution to this dispute has not occurred. That is why any responsible government would have plans to control their own territory should all avenues of reasonable diplomacy and negotiation be exhausted. Too many governments have refused to listen to the implications of our warnings. The events of the last two days have sadly proven Georgia correct. As I write, the Russian Federation is bombing targets throughout my country. Your leader (August 9) suggests that a great power's whimsical destruction of a small neighbour should be appeased. We expected more from the great tradition of the Guardian.

Giorgi Badridze
Acting head of mission, Embassy of Georgia, London

August 13

Morales reforms are common sense

You paint an image of Bolivia in which the project of radical reform that brought President Evo Morales to power in December 2005 is struggling (Morales awaits verdict on his revolution, August 8), or as divided between a liberal, free-wheeling capitalism and a centralised, pro-indigenous, income-redistributing socialism (Morales heads for Bolivian poll win but reforms remain at risk, August 11). Neither is entirely true. With President Morales ratified in his mandate with over 60% of the vote, he can regain the political momentum to continue a process of change that has, in two years, substantially decreased rates of extreme poverty and illiteracy, and made strides to improve the lot of pensioners and schoolchildren with targeted benefits.

Indeed, he will be able to put to the test with the Bolivian people a new constitution that guarantees

employee dresses to thrill, August 9)?

Emma Mason
Brighton

August 14
I was interested in Laura Barton's discourse on the horti-cultural applications of placentas (Why plant a placenta? It makes a great lasagne, G2, August 12), but disappointed she was unable or unwilling to confirm the long-held view that midwives have always grown the best roses.

Eric Ogden
Cheadle, Cheshire

August 15
Old-fashioned names aren't dying out (In praise of old-fashioned names, G2, August 14), they've gone to the dogs. In my local park we have various Stanleys, Archies, Harrys, a Dennis and a Doris. Whatever happened to Fido and

Rover? (My dog is Barny because he was in a barn when we bought him.)

Yvonne Canning
Sunderland

August 15

Lucy Cavendish reminds parents to give children names they can call out in the street "without sounding prattish". Thanks, Lucy.

Bernard Pratt
Cheadle, Cheshire

August 15

Peter Bradshaw seems to be forgetting about Sigourney Weaver (Who needs a male lead when you can have Angelina Jolie?, G2, August 14). She played the character of Ripley in Alien, which had been written for a man, with no change in dialogue, bar the odd pronoun.

Deborah Fantini
Brightlingsea, Essex

citizenship rights to all, significantly increases the autonomy of the regions, and includes a national development plan driven by a state-managed capitalism geared to serve the needs and increase the wellbeing of the Bolivian people. Some might call this radical. Others might call it just common sense.

Kepa Artaraz
La Paz, Bolivia

August 14

Top-up fees can only entrench inequality

It is true that top-up fees have not dented the numbers starting university (Fees see rise in numbers of poorer students stall, August 12). After all, higher education is seen as the route to a decent lifetime income. However, for Bill Rammell to call the system "fairer and more progressive" is a travesty. Pay-later course fees within a market system will perpetuate and accentuate inequality within the university system and a skewed graduate labour market. Perhaps 20% of students, likely to be children of the better-off, favoured by the school system, will graduate from select universities targeted by employers, offering top salaries, golden hellos, generous annual increments and bonuses. Helped by parents in many cases, they will probably repay their debts in a few years; these repayments will be a small proportion of their lifetime earnings.

The rest, many from less privileged backgrounds, having attended less prestigious universities, will start on significantly lower salaries, and can expect modest salary growth. They will be penalised for decades, paying effectively 40% tax on lower earnings. For a typical public sector worker such as a teacher, this will take about 15 years. For a graduate in the voluntary sector or a depressed region of the country, probably 25 years. It will hit hardest when, aged around 30, they cannot buy a house, afford family life, or save for retirement, while being heavily taxed to finance health and pensions for burgeoning numbers of senior citizens.

This is regressive, unfair taxation, taking a higher proportion of lifetime earnings from lower-paid graduates. The amount that graduates contribute to financing higher education should depend not on their course fees but on how much they subsequently earn. Let us reconsider the alternative originally favoured, we are told, by the former chancellor, now prime minister: de-couple student tuition from personal debt, and introduce a progressive graduate tax instead.

Lawrence Lockhart
Bath

August 15

A clash of northern soul and southern arrogance

How nice of Cameron's goons at Policy Exchange to remind us what the Tories are really like (Tory party's favourite thinktank brands northern cities failures, August 13). Move "darn sarf"? Most of them talk with that horrible estuary accent.

Without the north we wouldn't have the vote: the Peterloo protesters, the Chartists and the suffragettes were all from the north. The trade unions were born in Manchester and the north gave this country the industrial revolution, which projected a small island to be a world power. The joule unit of energy, Whitworth engineering

August 16

An exhibition of wood engravings about collective nouns for birds (Letters, August 13) by Colin See-Paynton, called Of a Feather – An Avian Alphabet, can be seen at Shandy Hall (home of Laurence Sterne) until August 17 and will be published as a book by the Gregynog Press in November.

Patrick Wildgust
Curator, Shandy Hall,
Coxwold, North Yorkshire

August 18

Mobile phones identify people, within limits; they locate people and they identify their associates ('Snooper's charter' to check texts and emails, August 13). Mobile phones are, in short, 21st-century ID cards. They are far more powerful than the 1940s-style ID cards the Home Office plans to issue us with, which would not locate people or identify their associates. We pay for them voluntarily and we live with the trade-off between utility and loss of privacy that their use represents. There is no point introducing the Home Office's old-fashioned and pedestrian retro cards. No point at all.

David Moss
dematerialisedID.com

August 18

With so many people claiming that A-levels have become easier over the years, it is surprising that no one seems to have noticed how much easier the Olympics seem to have become. World records that were once earned with huge effort are now broken with ease. When Michael Phelps can casually pick up eight gold medals, the whole system is discredited.

Celeste Smith
Prenton, Wirral

standards and Peel's police force — all northern. Manchester didn't have a seaport, so it built a canal to get to one; 5,000 Lancaster bombers which helped defeat Hitler were built at Chadderton. And the world's first modern computer was pioneered at Umist. As the late, great Tony Wilson summed it up, the only thing the south ever gave us was Chas and Dave.

And what would music be without the north? The world-famous Hallé, the Beatles, Hollies, Smiths, Buzzcocks, New Order, Stone Roses, Oasis, Happy Mondays, Arctic Monkeys. In 2012 the cockneys will invite us down to have a good old knees-up at the Olympics. Sorry my old china, but you wouldn't be in a position to hold the games without Manchester's Commonwealth success in 2002, after London messed up a bid for the world athletics championships. Our thanks for this? We can have a football semi-final at Old Trafford. Between United and the scousers we have 31 league titles and eight European Cups — someone should tell Roman Abramovich that you can't buy class.

So thanks, but no thanks. I'll stay up here, where people are friendly, still have the time of day for each other and don't rush to work staring at the floor. We still make proper fish and chips and we can have a pint of Joey Holt's beer for under two quid. The cockneys can be left to wallow in jellied eels and pie and mash, drinking flat beer at £5 a pint.

Alan Quinn
Manchester

• I believe Steve Bell is the most gifted political cartoonist since Gillray. But his on-your-bike drawing (August 14) suggests, by depicting the Gateshead Angel, that it was not a Conservative prime minister's national lottery (John Major), administered by a Conservative chairman of the Arts Council (me), who helped a Labour council bring that miraculous work into being. The next Tory government will cooperate with Labour and Liberal Democrat councils even more closely, I suspect.

Grey Gowrie
London

August 15

Politics is no picnic

As any veteran of the Inter Party Rounders competition knows, it is not the rounders per se which is the highlight of the political year, but the picnic (Diary, August 14). Sadly the weather let us down and we found ourselves with £100 of food on our hands (not the £600 suggested). Making a virtue of necessity, we held a mini picnic anyway, inviting everyone of any political colour or none (big-tent politics at its best) for £5. We have made back our loss and are all set for the rescheduled competition on August 27. This solid shepherding of our financial resources is perhaps a lesson for Messrs Brown and Clegg.

Marcus Walker
Chairman, Conservative Picnic Committee

August 16

Anti-Russian hysteria over Georgia

Many who write about Georgia these days are doing a disservice to truth and to the chances of a viable solution by whipping up anti-Russian

August 18

Paying £9 for an organic chicken may look like reckless spending (The going gets tough for organic, G2, August 14), but it depends what one does with the chicken. We get two meals each to start with, then I use the remainder of the meat to make a chicken-and-mushroom pie, which again gives us another two meals each, and the bones make a chicken stock for soup. That can't be bad value for £9.

Sylvia Markham
Grantham, Lincolnshire

August 19

Five years ago I moved from the north (Macclesfield) to the south-east and every word of your article (In praise of the north, G2, August 14) is true. Southerners don't know what a real market is, chip shops don't do gravy and the place is full of tourists. However, sitting in my garden with a glass of wine, sun shining, eating fresh figs picked from my own tree, and watching the kiwis growing on the vine outside my greenhouse, I think I'll cope!

Janet Ingle
Peacehaven, East Sussex

August 19
I feel that a health warning should have been attached to the beginning of Lita Roza's obituary (August 18). How many persons of a certain age in this country have now got (How Much Is) That Doggie in the Window on the brain?

Murray Marshall
Salisbury, Wiltshire

August 19
Ladies, be grateful you don't live in rural Bavaria, where the "mutterkuchen", or placenta (Letters,

hysteria. The calm reader might thus like to reflect more on the following facts:

1. It was the Georgian president who began this crisis, seriously misjudging his opponent and weakening his own country. In the Japanese culture this would lead to hara-kiri; we in the west usually expect an honorable resignation.

2. The US attempt in Bucharest last spring to add Georgia to Nato must not be forgotten. It was rightly seen by the Russians as an attempt to continue to destabilise them. Again American planners misjudged the power and character of Vladimir Putin; and both are formidable.

3. The above were not isolated phenomena. For years after the dissolution of the Soviet Union, American politicians have repeatedly been humiliating a nation which, whether we like it or not, is both great and proud. They are now reaping the whirlwind and, alas, so are we.

4. Talk of violation of sovereignty has become meaningless after Iraq and Afghanistan, and the invasion of northern Cyprus, not to mention the repeated bombardments of Syria and Lebanon by Israel and its famous attack on Iraqi installations, which many of us fear it would like to repeat in Iran if given half a chance. State sovereignty is, indeed, sacred unless it is we who violate it!

There is a growing feeling that the Bush administration is one of the worst in US history. Sensible Europeans should try to ensure that in its dying days America does not make matters worse; and if Europe cannot restrain its ally, it should stay clear of new American follies.

Sir Basil Markesinis QC, FBA
Bicester, Oxfordshire

August 20

Don't believe that it couldn't happen here

Hicham Yezza (Britain's terror laws have left me and my family shattered, August 18) raises forcefully the question of why there has been only moderate opposition to the erosion of habeas corpus. I fear that one reason is that detention has so far been used only or mainly against Muslims, perceived by many as a homogeneous, distinct group and one which can be often conveniently identified by their names.

This feeds the dangerous illusion "it couldn't happen to me", always the first step in a slide towards authoritarian rule. A law which allows innocent people to be detained on the flimsiest of evidence not only shames those who passed it, but threatens all of us and risks turning the police from protectors into bullies.

Margaret Dickinson
London

August 20

Desolation row

Dear U-No-Hu of the Media… You came to Beijing full of hope. You intended to ask piercing, intelligent questions, and you came across as a bonehead. You dreamed of being the best, but you made a fool of yourself. You wanted to speak Olympian poetry and you wallowed in cliche. You prophesied gold; you picked up lead. You wanted to be cock of the walk, you looked like a turkey. Tears pouring down your face, you are obviously broken in spirit. Confronting the utter desolation of the last four wasted years of your life, you are

August 14), is traditionally sliced up and cooked in a soup that's fed to the newly delivered mother to restore her strength and vitality following the birth of her baby.

Kirsten Cubitt
Sheffield

August 20
Having died in July 2004, David McKie (Just visiting, August 18) ought to know that RW Burchfield is unlikely still to be policing hung participles in Fowler's Modern English Usage.

Charles Owen
Birmingham

August 20
Sigourney Weaver had no dialogue rewritten to accommodate her character's new gender (Letters, August 15), but a male Ripley in Alien probably wouldn't have had to blast the xenomorph into space

wearing only vest and knickers.

Chris Bond
London

August 20
Thank you, Kirsten Cubitt (Letters, August 19), for your placenta "mutterkuchen" contribution. I was having my breakfast! Sadly, I then found Mutter's Kuchen on YouTube and that finished me off completely.

Jim Ensom
Manningtree, Essex

August 21
Much as I enjoyed the résumé of the Emma/Will/Ed love triangle (A month in Ambridge, G2, August 20), I must point out that Emma is in fact the pigman's daughter. The milk-man's daughter is going out with Tom the sausage king. The pigman's son, mean-while, has attracted

hardly able to speak. Can I just ask you? How do you feel?

Tim Pigott-Smith
London

August 23
Debt we owe to our security service

Your leader (August 21) refers to "the days when MI5 was staffed by muscular public-school academic underachievers". This was a cheap jibe. So cheap as to be unworthy of comment, if it did not refer to retired members of the security service who have every reason to feel proud of themselves, yet have, as you well know, no way to respond. It is therefore perhaps right to remind your readers that our security service has a record to be proud of. During the second world war it prevented any serious espionage on British soil; during the cold war, having learnt from their discovery of the Soviet spies active during the war and its aftermath, the service ensured that after 1970 no serious Soviet espionage took place, apart from the one case of Prime in GCHQ.

Soviet records now available show that Britain was the only target of the KGB and GRU of which this can be said. The nature of the terrorist threat does not, alas, allow such a complete record of success, but it is certain that, during the years to which you apparently refer, both Irish and foreign terrorism would have been far more successful had it not been for the counter-terrorism work of the security service.

I have never been a member of MI5, but I worked alongside them for 40 years. I had and have the highest regard for their unswerving dedication to our democracy and its defence. I hope you will apologise.

Gerald Warner
Former coordinator of intelligence and security, London

August 25

Beijing marks a high for Team GB – on to 2012

The outstanding performance of our sportsmen and women in Beijing provides compelling proof that we do not live in a broken Britain. Team GB's total of 47 medals surpassed the stretch target set after the Athens Olympics, resulting in our best performance in a non-boycotted games for almost 90 years. This did not happen by accident. The individual flair and commitment of the medal winners, combined with the new optimism and ambition evident in UK sport, has been reinforced by well-planned and focused government support that saw funding for elite sport leap from £63m ahead of the Sydney Olympics to £265m in the run-up to Beijing. Under the Tories there had been no direct investment in elite sport and Britain finished a dismal 36th place in the medals table at the Atlanta Olympics in 1996.

In sport, as in so many other aspects of public life, spending works, and yet further success is already threatened by Boris Johnson's stated determination in a BBC interview to bring the 2012 London Olympics in "under budget".

Andy Furlong
Thornton, Leicestershire

the interest of the gentleman farmer's daughter, and the milkman's son is married to the local universal nanny. Meanwhile, the vicar is about to marry the solicitor. Which all makes one wonder how shallow the gene pool in Ambridge can possibly be, and why no one ever looks outside the village for a partner.

Barbara Williams
Sparsholt, Oxfordshire

August 22
Sylvia Markham should try a little harder with her organic chickens (Letters, August 18). With a 2.5kg "happy" chicken from a local butcher, my wife and I manage two roast meals over the weekend, a meal with cold chicken on Monday, nasi goreng on Tuesday and chicken pie on Wednesday. I use the

LETTERS TO THE EDITOR

remainder of the chicken to make soup, rather than stock, which is pureed, then frozen for use as either. We don't manage this on just £9. There are extra costs such as sausage meat and stuffing mix. These push the cost up to about £15, but that still works out at £3 per meal for two.

Dr KJ Vines
Yelverton, Devon

August 22

Yngling (Baffled by Beijing, G2, August 19)? Isn't that what Charles Windsor does with a rod and line?

Doug Lawrence
Keighley, West Yorkshire

August 23

Kevin Rudd, Shane Warne, Kylie Minogue, Nicole Kidman, Ned Kelly, Rolf Harris, Skippy the Kangaroo, your boys and girls took one hell of a beating

August 27

Tory hypocrisy over teenagers' health

I'm no fan of Labour's record on public health or on young people, but Conservative allegations that the government "neglects teenage health" (Report, August 25) reek of hypocrisy and poor judgment.

After all, the Tories opposed the ban on tobacco advertising, failed to support the ban on smoking in public places, voted against increases in alcohol duty and – along with Labour – continue to block improvements in school sex and relationships education. All of these initiatives have been shown to have direct beneficial effects on the health of young people.

The Conservatives bemoan the consequences of drug abuse. But by goading Gordon Brown into the upgrading of cannabis back to class B, despite a fall in use when it was reclassified to C and against the advice of its own expert advisory committee, the Tories are seeking to criminalise a whole new generation of young people.

David Cameron has of course announced a drugs amnesty for himself on the basis of his being "allowed a private life before entering politics", while seeking to punish all those who come after him.

The Tories decry single-parent families and say they oppose teenage motherhood, which clearly does damage life chances. Yet they then attack an alleged increase in teenage abortions when that option might well be in the best interests of the girls' health and welfare.

The rational indicator in this area is teenage maternity rates, or at least overall teenage conceptions, on which the Tories curiously fail to cite any figures. Boris Johnson is understating it when he calls Tory family rhetoric "piffle".

Dr Evan Harris MP
Lib Dem science spokesman

August 28
Naked truths and the suffragette movement

I thought Viv Groskop's article was excellent (Sex and the suffragette, G2, August 26). I, too, found the play Her Naked Skin most disappointing. Not the staging, which was admirable, but the lack of content. In fact, the staging was so slick, and the music so good, that it only served to highlight the play's sterility.

As someone who has written on the subject of the suffrage movement – indeed one of my books is acknowledged in the programme notes – I could see that the play's author had done a modicum of research. The facts, as far as they went, were not incorrect. But what was the point of it? To show risible scenes of lesbian sex and a forced-feeding scene? As Groskop concludes: "Surely the suffragettes deserve better than this?" They certainly did not deserve to be used as an opportunist vehicle on which to load all manner of modern baggage.

I left the theatre annoyed that the suffrage movement should have been travestied in this way. Incidentally, I would welcome an explanation of the play's title. I could find no reason for it, other than its titillating appeal.

Elizabeth Crawford
Author, The Women's Suffrage Movement: A Reference Guide

(Olympic medal table, August 21).

Peter Thornton
Ramsbottom, Lancashire

August 23
Has the Guardian considered ending its Free Our Data campaign? I think the government's freed quite enough now, don't you (Personal data on thousands of prisoners is lost, August 21)?

Mark Whitaker
Manchester

August 25
My wife and I are not impressed by the organic chicken debate (Letters, passim). We recently bought a 1oz locally sourced food-miles-free organic free-range canary that had voluntarily agreed to euthanasia. It provided us and our 14 children with a week of nutritious meals. The children used the bones for educationally

stimulating games and the skin has been converted into an attractive range of winter clothing for all the family, with enough left over for shoe and roof repairs for the next decade.

Dr CI Ragan
London

August 26

Those cursed by sharing their name with the famous (Letters, August 23) might like to consider using shortened forms. This has worked well for my brother, Jim, and my father, Tony.

Mick Blunt
Coll, Isle of Lewis

August 30

Gordon Ramsay has 10 Michelin stars (Former protege who has become Ramsay's real kitchen nightmare, August 28)? Them ain't stars, them's asterisks.

Pam Brown
Lakenheath, Suffolk

August 28

Titan prisons are not the solution

The government's proposals to build three titan prisons (Supersize prisons will not solve jail crisis, watchdog warns Straw, August 27) would cement this country's position as the prison capital of western Europe, while squandering billions of pounds of taxpayers' money. The proposals ignore evidence that smaller, local prisons work better than large ones, raise serious concerns about the wellbeing and safety of prisoners and prison staff, and would put at risk relationships between prisoners and their families.

The government cannot build its way out of the crisis in the prison system, and further expansion would be damaging both socially and economically. The government must shelve its plans for titan prisons and instead focus on addressing the causes of the growing prison population. The evidence is clear; titan prisons are not the solution. We urge Jack Straw, the justice secretary, to abandon these misguided proposals for titan prisons before they become a reality.

Juliet Lyon Prison Reform Trust, **Colin Moses** Prison Officers' Association, **Paul Cavadino** Nacro, **Harry Fletcher** Napo, **Rob Allen** International Centre for Prison Studies, **Joyce Moseley** Rainer Crime Concern, **Veronica Linklater** Rethinking Crime and Punishment, **Christopher Jones** Churches' Criminal Justice Forum, **Gareth Crossman** Liberty, **Lucy Gampell** Action for Prisoners' Families, **Sally Ireland** Justice, **Davlin Brydson** Association of Black Probation Officers, **Angela Clay** Association of Members of Independent Monitoring Boards, **Emma Norton** Bindmans, **Denise Marshall** Birth Companions, **Clive Martin** Director, Clinks, **Dr Katherine Rake** Director, Fawcett Society, **Deb Coles and Helen Shaw** Co-directors, Inquest

September 2008

One year on, there was no answer to the "go now" question. The prospects of a general election sank along with Labour's poll rating, as the Conservatives moved 20 points ahead in the run-up to the conference season. But a good speech in Manchester by Gordon Brown — and the growing global financial crisis — removed any immediate prospect of him resigning for the greater good of the party. At the start of the month it seemed that Brown's successor as chancellor had put his foot in it by describing the economic situation as the worst for 60 years in a Guardian interview; by the end of the month Alistair Darling's honest appraisal no longer seemed to be a gaffe, as leading US financial institutions collapsed or — unbelievably — were taken over by the state. The boost the Republican party received from the appointment of the colourful Sarah Palin as its vice-presidential candidate wore off as her inexperience and the depth of the economic problems facing the US became clear. Back home, exorbitant transfer fees and the takeover of Manchester City by an Abu Dhabi billionaire left many football supporters disillusioned. But one foreign import was popular: England manager Fabio Capello turned the tables on Croatia, who put England out of Euro 2008, with a 4-1 away win in a World Cup qualifier. Some, however, thought the win was not so much due to the Italian's coaching skills as the world being turned upside down by the Large Hadron Collider.

September 1

Sarah Palin's favourite meal (McCain moves to steal Obama's thunder by choosing woman running mate, August 30) changed from "moose stew" in the first column to "mooseburger" in the fifth column. Surely it should be the other way around – mooseburger to moose stew. No one in their right mind would try to make a burger out of a stew.

Charles Jennings
Winchester, Hampshire

September 1

The schoolboy error made by the scientists from Pasadena (Quick-thinking flies are one jump ahead of the swatter, August 29) was to use only one swatter and to drop it from above. Research done some years ago demonstrated that flies perceive downward movement better than sideways movement.

September 1

Hopes of triumph over inexperience

The fact that "a girl from the south side of Chicago and the son of a single mother from Hawaii" could make it this far represents everything that is good and hopeful about the US, says Timothy Garton Ash (Comment, August 28). True, but the US, for all its celebration of free markets and self-reliance, has one of the lowest rates of intergenerational social mobility and one of the highest degrees of income and wealth inequality of all the rich OECD countries. Canada, Germany and the Nordics all have substantially lower inequality and higher social mobility. This is yet another source of the US economy's growing weakness, which the next president should confront – but may not, partly because of the blinding power of the "land of opportunity" story.

Professor Robert H Wade
Development Studies Institute, London School of Economics

September 1

Can things only get worse?

Alistair Darling shows his lack of economic history if he thinks the present credit crunch could turn into the worst recession for 60 years (Economy at 60-year low, says Darling. And it will get worse, August 30). Has he forgotten 1974-75 when, in the aftermath of rising crude oil prices, inflation touched almost 27%, with unemployment exceeding 1.5 million? Or 1979-81 under Thatcher when 3 million were out of work, and inflation topped 20% again? Indeed the recession that helped to derail John Major's government was far worse than anything we'll see over the next year or so, with double-figure interest rates and 3 million on the dole once more. Perhaps Darling is thinking we'll be grateful if things don't turn out quite so badly as his doom-laden vision.

Tim Mickleburgh
Grimsby, Lincolnshire

September 2

New life begins at 80

Katharine Whitehorn says women write to her agony column "saying they've got plenty of women friends, but would so like to meet a man because they're sick of talking about health all the time" (The truth about life after 80, G2, August 29). She goes on to say: "I tell them to stop hoping to bump into a literate widower and join the University of the Third Age, a self-help organisation providing courses and companionship". Well, a couple of years ago I did both. I met my literate widower at U3A and, yes – reader, I married him! We celebrate our first wedding anniversary in a few weeks. He is almost 80 but I am not. He taught me to read the Guardian. Great success story all round.

Caryl Heley
Lee-on-the-Solent, Hampshire

September 4

Thoughts on our not so beautiful game

With record sums having been paid for transfers of foreign players to English clubs and the takeover of Manchester City by another foreigner, the news that Michel Platini, the president of Uefa, is to hold an inquiry into the disparity between rich and poor

If you use two sources of movement, you confuse them sufficiently to slow their reaction time considerably. Also, the fly's default taking-off motion is upwards and slightly backwards. So the most effective way to swat a fly is to position your hands about six inches apart and a couple of inches above it, and then clap. You get messy hands, but it does impress your friends.

Professor Jonathan Long
Durham

September 1

Will anyone stand up for those of us who are not "hard-working"? Gordon Brown is forever banging on about his plans to help "hard-working families"; Jackie Ashley implored us to work until our 70s and beyond (Comment, August 25); and now Cllr Prestidge (Letters, August 29) wants a windfall tax to benefit only "hard-working people". As someone who has never worked hard in his life, my vote goes to any party promising to champion the inactive, the lethargic and the indolent.

Dr Howard Mason
Manchester

September 2

I was surprised to hear that Alistair Darling had used such inappropriate language as "pissed off" (Storm warning, Weekend, August 30). Surely he meant "browned off"!

Pauline Dodwell
London

September 4

In the same fashion as President Monroe declared South America to be in the US's "sphere of influence", history has declared Georgia to be in Russia's. Small countries that fall

clubs is to be warmly welcomed (Platini launches inquiry into level of club debts, August 29; You're bought! Abu Dhabi's answer to Sir Alan Sugar in Manchester City takeover, September 2). For too long, the football authorities have failed to take any effective action against the distortion in competition − in both a sporting and a business sense − of football clubs, which cannot be for the "good of the game" or the fans. Let us hope that this time something meaningful results.

Professor Ian Blackshaw
The International Sports Law Centre, The Hague, Netherlands

September 5

Taking a line on poetical correctness

If you want to change how another person behaves, you have to begin by understanding how that person sees himself and his world (Top exam board asks schools to destroy book containing knife poem, September 4). Carol Ann Duffy's poem Education for Leisure is a brilliant description of how a young man who carries a knife sees himself and his world. Only those people who are frightened of learning about how other people see themselves and their world would try to stop children from reading this poem.

Dorothy Rowe
London

September 6

Alcohol control and unruly behaviour

This letter is necessarily brief as I am currently in a secluded village in rural Greece. Nevertheless I cannot let pass the opportunity to add my support to the view of John Harris on the regulation of the sale and supply of alcohol (Brown must call time on the booze trade's lack of restraint, September 2), and equally to the view of Michael Hann on the importance of the public role in challenging unruly behaviour (Why we should step in to halt bad behaviour, G2, September 3). These are two of the critical challenges facing society in the UK today.

The private sector has shown itself incapable of effective self-regulation in the sale and supply of alcohol. Harris has made an important contribution to the debate on such regulation. The government now has a role to play. With regard to the public role in challenging unruly behaviour, it is worth recalling that, almost 200 years ago, the police service was created on the understanding that the police were the public and the public were the police. Each and every one of us has a responsibility to participate in the maintenance of an orderly society.

This is not always easy and can involve some risk, but in reality the probability of harm remains low. Hann is correct in suggesting that challenging disorder should not be seen as a political matter.

Mike Craik
Chief constable, Northumbria police; Acpo lead on licensing

September 8

The courts are for justice, not profits

So Her Majesty's courts service is "a business" which is in crisis "because of a sharp fall in fee income for the courts" (Leaked letter warns of courts crisis over £90m 'black hole' in budget,

in a great power's "sphere of influence" are free internally – as Finland was during the cold war – but bound to eschew alliances inimical to the great power's security (To Russia with love, September 3). So by encouraging Georgia to join Nato and the EU, the US was endangering the peace. That is why Tories are backing Russia.

Peregrine Worsthorne
Hedgerley, Buckinghamshire

September 4

I liked the Diary item (September 3) about the two Keswick street entertainers who were "putting lighted torches down their thongs and, as a finale, sticking lit sparklers between their buttocks and doing handstands". Does the committee organising the 2012 opening ceremony have their address?

David Brodie
Cambridge

September 5

The Chinese pianist Lang Lang is prominent these days (Review, September 2). Perhaps we may even see him performing arrangements of Nono in Baden-Baden.

Ken Ratcliff
Macclesfield, Cheshire

September 6

In the obituaries of Humphrey Lyttelton (April 26) and Geoffrey Perkins (September 1) reference was made to the origins of Mornington Crescent. Accreditation to one of the cast of I'm Sorry I Haven't a Clue, or Geoffrey Perkins, is erroneous. The game was born in 1970 in a small actors' club on Shaftesbury Avenue called Gerry's. It was cobbled together by John Junkin (actor and writer), David Clime (writer) and myself (club owner and actor). We played the game at the

September 4). This is partly due, apparently, to "HM Revenue & Customs, who were our biggest customer, [having] reduced their use of magistrates courts". In consequence, directors are "reviewing all parts of the business to see where savings can be made"; asking the justice ministry or the Treasury to meet the shortfall "is not an option".

I always thought that one of the fundamental requirements of a civilised society was the provision by the state of a system of courts in which disputes between citizens, or between citizens and the state, could be settled, and in which wrongdoers could be tried and, if guilty, punished. I was taught that this system, which we call justice, was the bedrock of a democratic society, and that access to the courts must be protected at all costs. But now it seems that justice has its price, and the system can only work if it pays for itself. When shall we find the minister of justice in the bankruptcy court, because his fee income is insufficient to pay the bills? That of course assumes that the bankruptcy court has sufficient fee income to remain in business.

Bernard Marder QC
(Former circuit judge and former president of the Lands Tribunal), Richmond, Surrey

September 8

Ken's healing spirit

Bill Evershed's memory (Letters, September 4) of my brother-in-law Ken Campbell giving a "private version of his show" in his college common room has prompted me to remember a similar event. The circumstances were – or should have been – sadder: he was talking to my dying mother and bewildered father in their sitting room. He went into a "Campbell riff" just for them — I don't think he knew there was anyone else in the room. He restored their morale, and had them laughing away at his inspired "nonsense", probably better medicine than our "sense".

As for the "material" Bill hopes someone will collect, there will be no Ken to utter it. But here's an anecdote to cheer him, I hope. Ken was teaching his parrot to be truly original, by dint of teaching it parrot discourse, rather than, say, pidgin or human. It was progressing well: the parrot had mastered "I'm up here and you're down there". On second thoughts, perhaps this was all an exercise for the new post of professor of proleptic ventriloquism we hear Ken has been offered on cloud nine.

Penny McCarthy
London

September 12

Foreign disapproval won't affect US voters

Jonathan Freedland offers a new twist in American presidential politics: blackmail (The world's verdict will be harsh if the US rejects the man it yearns for, September 10). If we don't elect the man he prefers, we will incur the wrath of the world. Worse, they might conclude that we are racists, and then our world would truly collapse around us. Mr Freedland and his friends might subject us to another rant in the Guardian, or — God forbid — denounce us in the UN.

As much as we Americans fear the world's verdict, we insist on this annoying ritual of choosing our own leaders every four years. If the

bar to infuriate and bemuse customers who we found boring or boorish. I seek no reward or approbation, just accreditation.

Bunny May
Richmond, Surrey

September 6
Does anyone else have an outdoor banana tree fruiting?

Linda Page
Lewes, East Sussex

September 8
A fly wallchart (Letters, September 6)? What a good idea. Could we have it rolled up rather than folded, please?

Ian Thompson
Enfield, London

September 10
I first met Max Morris (Obituary, September 9) in Beijing in the 50s when, as a member of the NUT, he was a guest of the Chinese Student Union. He

brought with him a selection of rock'n'roll records as a gift for them – which I, as his interpreter, confiscated, saying it was not appropriate in the then political climate. My friends and I had wonderful parties dancing to Bill Haley & His Comets, until we were reported to the authorities and criticised as imperialist lackeys. But it was worth it, and I shall always remember Max Morris for giving me and others a brief time of happiness during a dark and oppressive period.

Esther Samson
(Cheo Ying)
London

September 10
The Large Hadron Collider (The question: Will the world end on Wednesday?, G2, September 8) is akin to a bunch of curious monkeys levering off the cover of the fuse

"Elect Obama or I'll kill your dog" tactic doesn't work, we may just wake up in November and realise we have "passed up a once-in-a-generation chance for a fresh start". Pity.

To address the sinking feeling in Mr Freedland's stomach, I offer this advice: quit following the presidential race. It's doing you no good. Instead, get a life-size poster of the man you yearn for. Turn on some nice music, perhaps Beethoven's Ode to Joy. The next four years should pass much more pleasantly.

Bill Ireland
Ontario, California, USA

September 13
Democracy is emerging in China

I do feel Ze Xia went over the top with her swingeing condemnation of the Chinese government (Letters, September 11). I hold no special brief for China. In the late 1960s my wife and I and our 11-year-old son were caught up in the cultural revolution and locked up for two years in a small hotel room, never allowed out, and fed on a poor diet.

Even so, it would be churlish to deny the economic and social advances that have been made in China – first in the centrally planned economy from 1949 to 1974 and then in the capitalist-driven economy ever since. I've been back several times since the late 80s when the Chinese government apologised – in a sense it was, in their eyes, a kind of "rehabilitation".

When I lived in China it wasn't difficult to be aware of how life had changed for the better – great new housing projects, schools, hospitals etc. Life for the poor – the vast majority of the population – had been pretty barbaric in the centuries leading up to 1949 – famines, tyrannical rule by landlords and feudal subjugation of women. In the 30s China was among the poorest nations of the world. I can't quite understand what "cultural traditions" Ze Xia feels China has lost under the communist government. Tell that to the painfully hobbling women I used to see whose feet had been bound as little girls before the 1949 revolution.

Rough things go on in China today, but – painfully slowly – democracy is emerging, if only driven by the hundreds of millions who use the internet. A sense of balance and history is required when you start looking at a developing country like China.

Eric Gordon
London

September 13

Science going round in circles

I was struck by the chance juxtaposition on adjacent pages of the gigantic ring of the Large Hadron Collider at Cern and that of Stonehenge (September 11). Both circles are the work of man trying to understand and to some extent control his world. It was no mean scientist who calculated exactly where the summer solstice sun would rise, and a huge enterprise for prehistoric people to organise the building of their monolithic circle. The physicists and engineers who have built Cern can only be their descendants.

Gillian Nelson
Inverness

box and sticking a screwdriver in to see what happens.

Andy Smith
Kingston-upon-Thames

September 10
I'd just like to say what an honour it is to have a letter printed in the final edition of the Guardian.

Phil Thorp
Bury, Lancashire

September 10
We have an outdoor banana tree fruiting, up north (Letters, September 6). Either that or it's engaging in global warming propaganda.

Duncan Blackie
Sheffield

September 12
Wednesday 8.30am: scientists tamper with the fundamental fabric of the universe (Test run success for big bang re-creation, September 10).

Wednesday 10pm:
Croatia 1 England 4.

Anthony Tasgal
London

September 13
My wife had a letter
in the Todmorden
News last week. This
week the paper carries
a response from the
local Tories which
begins: "Ms Steph
Booth (wife of the
actor Tony Booth,
stepmother of Cherie
Blair, stepmother-in-
law of Tony Blair) ... "
Good to see the Tories
hanging on to the
traditional values of
judging women by
their relatives rather
than on any new-
fangled notion of what
is, in my wife's case,
undisputed talent and
intelligence (The new
Tories, September 10).

Tony Booth
Todmorden, West Yorkshire

September 13
I am a bit confused
over the issue of

September 16

Crisis of confidence in the banking system

The collapse of Lehman Brothers, the swallowing
up of Merrill Lynch, the threat to the world's
biggest insurance company, AIG, and the
nationalisation of Freddie Mac and Fannie Mae,
together with Northern Rock, herald the end
of the free-wheeling deregulatory era of finance
capitalism that lasted from the early 1980s to 2007
(Reports, September 15).

Many other pillars of the capitalist establishment
– Halifax Bank of Scotland, Barclays, Royal Bank
of Scotland, UBS, Deutsche Bank and Citibank
– are widely thought to be undercapitalised and
therefore at risk. But are the Asian sovereign funds
now going to fund the gap after the US Treasury's
punitive treatment of investors in Lehman, and
Freddie and Fannie?

We urgently need a radical new architecture
for financial markets – one that puts emphasis
on security and trust, rather than high risk
and greed.

The outline of this is already clear. Investment
banks should be statutorily separated from the
high-street commercial banks (the repeal of the
US Glass-Steagall Act in 1999 was a major mistake).
Securitisation – the trading worldwide of complex
and obscure financial derivatives – should be
prohibited, or at least subject to approval by a
revamped Financial Services Authority. Credit
rating agencies should be made independent of
the institutions whose creditworthiness they
assess (astonishingly, at present they are not).
And the City mega-bonus culture which has
driven the recklessness of toxic lending should
be brought under control by enforceable Bank

of England guidelines and by requiring fancy remuneration packages to be sanctioned by a more interventionist FSA.

Michael Meacher MP
Labour, Oldham West & Royton

• As more financial dominoes tumble, with the demise of Merrill Lynch and Lehman Brothers, it seems that Bush's enduring legacy might well be the collapse of the capitalist system. It's a funny old world.

George Czernuszka
Manchester

September 17

Labour punch-up on the Titanic

Witnessing the faction infighting between Brownites and Blairites has been like watching the crew having a punch-up on the deck of the Titanic (Ministers fuel talk of anti-Brown challenge, September 15). Just to set the record straight, I am not part of this plot and have not asked for leadership nomination papers. I am still up for a leadership election if there is one, but it must be based upon a thoroughgoing, open debate about policies and not personalities. The two New Labour factions currently slugging it out have barely a policy difference between them and have supported every New Labour policy over the last 11 years, which has led us to the brink of a Tory government.

In July I suggested a compromise to hold the party together: a structured and inclusive policy debate about the future for Labour. If this shows support for radical change, as I suspect, it is only

female executive pay (Special report, September 11). Am I supposed to commiserate with women because so few of them occupy the highly paid ranks of the FTSE 100, or congratulate them on not adding to the obscenity that already exists?

Ian Ragan
London

September 13
Is it just a coincidence that in its first set of financial figures since the Commons watchdog's tightening of MPs' expenses, John Lewis reports a massive drop in profits (Report, September 12)?

Clyde Shaw
Norwich

September 16
Damien Hirst's money-making activities do seem to cause concern, not only with Robert Hughes (Report, September 9). Why

shouldn't an energetic young artist find a perfectly legal way of taking large amounts of cash from some very wealthy people? I'd rather Hirst had the dosh than some of his mysterious clients. Do we know where they got it from in the first place?

Jacob Butler
Matlock, Derbyshire

September 16
Well done, and thank you (Fall of the doctor who said his vitamins would cure Aids, September 13).

Nick Partridge
Chief executive,
Terrence Higgins Trust

September 16
We can't take bottles of cosmetics with us on flights, but you can take a highly toxic substance like phenol into the Channel tunnel (Eurostar train services cut by third following fire,

in this context that the party should convene an election for a new leader.

John McDonnell MP
Lab, Hayes and Harlington

September 20

Fed up with being sold short by the City

I resent taxpayers' money being spent to shore up the glorified gambling den of the money markets (Rescue plan relieves last banks standing, September 19). I have a better idea — taxpayers' money could go to the lowest-paid to relieve them of having to pay so much. They would spend it and stimulate the economy. We could call it the New Deal. Even better, deal with the housing crisis as well by spending taxpayers' money on new social housing. We could call it socialism to show we care about people.

Anne Watson
Oxford

• My investments have been unsound, my spending reckless. I find myself embarrassingly overdrawn and in possession of a lot of junk. I wonder if the central banks could forward me some extra liquidity — £35K should cover it.

Peter Dawson
Ilkley, West Yorkshire

September 20

Creationism in the classroom

The forced resignation of Michael Reiss as director of education for the Royal Society is very disturbing

(Professor steps down over creationism row, September 17). Not for the Christian cause, but for what it says about the state of paranoia and defensiveness into which the scientific establishment has declined. What he was saying about how people learn, or don't learn, was common sense. It is unlikely that people who hold creationist views will be prepared to listen to my case for evolution if I refuse to engage with what they say and treat them respectfully. Scientists must be seriously lacking in self-confidence if they not only outlaw the very mention of alternative points of view, but also effectively ostracise one of their number who is sufficiently assured of his own position that he is prepared to give the views of others a hearing.

John Saxbee
Bishop of Lincoln

September 20

Threat to democracy in Latin America

On September 10 President Evo Morales of Bolivia declared the US ambassador persona non grata. On September 11 (the 35th anniversary of the military overthrow of Salvador Allende in Chile) the president of Venezuela asked the US ambassador there to leave the country. President Hugo Chávez believed he was facing the possibility of an imminent coup d'etat in which he said the US administration was involved. President Morales believed that his government was facing serious destabilisation which was also being fomented by the US. A third country, Paraguay, announced 10 days previously that it had detected a conspiracy involving military officers and opposition politicians.

September 15)? I think this is health and safety not gone nearly mad enough.

Kit Jackson
London

September 17
Could it be that the smoke-free rooms of New York bankers are not working as well as the old ones (Nightmare on Wall Street, September 16)? Smoking a cigar or pipe makes me ponder, whereas the replacements can make prudence go out of the window. Just a thought.

David Hockney
London

September 17
Thank you for publishing an advertisement (September 15) from Future Heathrow listing the many companies and organisations supporting the ludicrous proposal for

a third Heathrow runway. Now I and other residents of west London know precisely which companies and goods to boycott.

Laurence Kaye
London

September 18

The best comment I've heard about the Cerne Abbas giant (Report, September 16) came from a boy who asked his mother, "Why is his willy on upside down?"

Mary Cotton
Shoreham-by-Sea

September 18

If Guardian writers have trouble spelling Gandhi's name (Open door, September 15), may I suggest a mnemonic? "Gandhi says hi" works for me.

Cynthia Curran
London

September 19

In the midst of this banking crisis (Crunch

Latin America now faces its most serious crisis since the reintroduction of democracy at the end of the 20th century. The plot against democracy in Venezuela centred on a conspiracy, revealed in telephone conversations between senior military officers broadcast on national television, to assassinate the democratically elected head of state. In Bolivia, the separatist prefects of the five eastern and southern departments have begun a campaign of violence and economic sabotage designed to destabilise the democratic regime.

These events show unequivocally who defends democracy and who threatens it today. We are appalled by the failure of much of the international media to provide accurate and proportionate coverage of these events. All democrats throughout the world should rally to defend democracy in Latin America.

Harold Pinter, John Pilger, Tony Benn, Ken Loach, Jean Lambert MEP, Ian Gibson MP, Kelvin Hopkins MP, Billy Hayes General secretary, CWU, **Bill Greenshields** President, NUT **and 23 others**

September 24

Natural alternatives to GM crops

Ian Pearson needs to get his science straight before considering taking a stance in support of GM (Science minister attempts to reopen the debate on GM crops, September 22). Properties such as innate pest or blight resistance, drought or salt tolerance and yield are sophisticated processes that manifest from the function of multiple genes working in a tightly regulated, coordinated manner. The introduction of such properly functioning complex gene networks in plants by the crude and genetically disruptive GM transformation process is currently not possible. Fortunately, we have better alternatives that can contribute to alleviating the world's food problems now.

First, the biotechnological procedure of marker-assisted selection (MAS), which uses our increasing knowledge of gene maps, can significantly expedite the identification of new crop varieties with complex desirable properties created by natural cross-breeding programmes. Unlike GM, there are no inherent safety concerns with MAS that makes use of the vast gene pool of any given food crop in a manner that retains natural gene order and function.

Second, a 1996 report by the National Research Council in the US highlighted that there already exist many crops − such as fonio, pearl millet and African rice − that are naturally adapted to harsh climates and marginal soils as well as being nutritious and tasty. Unfortunately, outside interference has led to these hardy staples being displaced by maize, wheat and Asian rice. In the face of climate change, the world needs fast solutions to its food problems, which MAS and a return to traditional food varieties can provide and which GM simply cannot deliver.

Dr Michael Antoniou
King's College London

September 25

Cut taxes for the poor, not interest rates

I am grateful to Gordon Brown for his explanation for the economic crisis (Labour in Manchester, September 24): "the world spun on its axis" this

time, G2, September 17), we need calm leadership from an experienced politician with a strong economic grasp. Haven't heard anything from David Cameron, then. But no doubt he will resurface next week with 20/20 hindsight telling us what he would have done this week.

Jonathan Harris
St Austell, Cornwall

September 19
We enjoyed our free coffee vouchers (Reader offer, September 17), but imagine our distress when we sat down in Starbucks and found we'd handed over the crossword as well as the vouchers. We had to actually talk to each other for 20 minutes.

A Gullett & C Laughton
Cheltenham

September 22
A Home Office lawyer says Gurkhas' service

to the crown is not in itself "a sufficient tie" to allow those who retired before 1997 to settle in the UK (Report, September 18). This presumably means that the oath of loyalty they swear is a hollow gesture and that pre-1997 Gurkhas were in effect poorly paid mercenaries.

Bruce Ross-Smith
Oxford

September 22
Global warming bulletin: parakeets have eaten my grapes.
Chris Hardy
London

September 23
Phew! Now the Large Hadron Collider at Cern is shut down, maybe the black hole into which the financial system was disappearing will cease functioning (Giant particle collider may be shut down until next year,

week. Well, of course it did. Precisely seven times this week the sun came up in the morning, as usual, and people went to work expecting to have a job to go to the next morning, as usual. Sadly, for many in the construction industry this didn't happen. Having worked at full pelt for the past eight years building schools, hospitals, housing, public and commercial projects, the axe-wielding is becoming merciless. Just in time for Christmas.

Have we run out of food or building materials? Has everyone sunburned the top half of their buttocks to such an extent that building has come to a halt? For the first time in years I am hearing "capitalism" and "gravedigger" in the same sentence, spoken by people in my local who have far from radical views.

Gavin Paul
Manchester

September 27

Another financial brick in the wall

Robert Reich calls for "new regulations related to disclosure" (The £700bn question, September 26). This suggestion proposes closing the door fully 30 years after the herd of Wall Street bulls has escaped. And it would do no good, for the real point is this: Wall Street and the City – ie the whole of the finance sector – cannot disclose what it does not know. And regulators – central bankers and politicians – cannot regulate the unknown.

We are in this mess because regulators allowed investment banks to use sound financial products – solid bricks-and-mortar mortgages, credit-card loans and loans to the productive sector – to create a tottering tower of artificial products, far removed from the reliable income streams generated by those good people and businesses paying their mortgages, loans and credit-card bills. This tower of financial products, now teetering above a shaky housing market, is known as "unfunded". A straightforward mortgage is funded — at least until default. These fancy liabilities are not — yet our regulators, including the Bank of England, tolerated their creation.

At the end of 2007 the US Federal Reserve estimated financial sector debt at 110% of US GDP, or $15.4tn. It was 63% just 10 years ago. The trouble is, we can't be sure of this number, as much of this debt — or these liabilities — is either fraudulently hidden, or else buried in incomprehensibly complex computer models. That is why there is no trust in this business.

US regulators and politicians are now trying to insert a brick of $700bn into a tottering tower of at least $15.4tn. A Sisyphean task if ever there was one.

Ann Pettifor
Executive director, Advocacy International

September 29
Labour needs a fresh approach

If Labour is to win the next general election it needs to show more confidence in itself and refresh its arguments against the Tories. The party's new general secretary, Ray Collins, should be setting the tone which others can follow. His most recent letter to party members does not inspire much confidence; the opening paragraph states: "Being a Labour member is not always easy … " He goes on make tired and outdated claims arguing for "Labour's investment and reform versus Tory cuts".

September 22). Perhaps the doom merchants were right after all.

Chris Sanders
Dunstable, Befordshire

September 25
So Britain's last known survivor of the western front campaign in the first world war, Harry Patch (Soldiering on at 110, September 23), has been awarded a knighthood by the Belgian government and the Légion d'honneur, France's highest award. But no knighthood by his own country? Surely a more deserving person than political stooges, overpaid captains of industry and ageing pop stars and thespians.

Brendan Martin
London

September 25
The piece on death row by Marcel Berlins (Torture on death row, September 22) was

worthy of Voltaire. Congratulations.

Margaret Drabble
London

September 26

You report (September 24) that "the longest and the most frequent flights were taken by those who were most aware of environmental issues, including the threat posed by climate change". Could we call this the Bono paradox?

Haward Soper
Leicester

September 26

"Did the BBC World Service really need to tell listeners that Mozart was a composer?" asks Marcel Berlins (G2, September 24), before going on to inform us that Zorro was a "do-gooder" who wore a black cape and a mask.

Alaric Dynevor
Huddersfield

David Cameron's Conservatives can be beaten by the Labour party. But this will only happen if the party takes pride in what it has achieved since 1997 and is able to convince the public that the government can deliver services which are not only progressive and fair, but also offer value for money. If Mr Collins is unable to spruce up Labour's campaigning, the party's national executive committee would do well to reappoint his predecessor, Peter Watt, a man who should never have lost his job in the first place.

Benjamin Wegg-Prosser
Moscow

September 29

Conservatives' cultural reflex

This week Birmingham hosts the Tory party conference. I hope it is not too much of a culture shock for Dominic Grieve (Multicultural ideal 'terrible' for UK – Tories, September 27), who chooses this moment to warn of the "terrible legacy" of multiculturalism. He needn't worry. Birmingham is a diverse city – most people think of it as one of our strengths – and we are tolerant enough to survive a temporary influx of Tories.

But if it is odd to warn of the perils of multiculturalism while visiting one of the most multicultural cities in Europe, the timing is all too predictable. The financial system is in chaos, food and fuel prices are escalating, a looming recession leaves many people fearful of their future, and David Cameron's opinion poll lead is halved. What better time than now to raise fears about British identity?

We are threatened by economic insecurity, to which neither Cameron nor Brown offer compelling solutions. We are not threatened by difference, diversity or multiculturalism. Dominic Grieve gives the wrong answer to a question we are not asking.

Cllr Salma Yaqoob
Birmingham

September 30

Lazy, hazy days of a 1940s summer

Could we please call time on the "grey, joyless austerity" cliche as applied to postwar 1940s Britain (Comment, September 29)? For those who have only seen the period in grainy black-and-white newsreels, may I point out that the great beaches were still as yellow; the sea and sky, now free of hostile submarines and aircraft, were still as blue. Huge crowds attended the resumed football matches, the pitches and shirts wonderfully bright in my memory.

Although the winter of 1947 was grim (we moved house on a cart amid the whirling snow; it was wonderful), the summer was gloriously hot, as Compton and Edrich scored close on 4,000 runs each for Middlesex. Don Bradman's unbeatable team were here in 1948. Another fine summer came in 1949, as I lay revising in a flower meadow. I had a wonderful time growing up on Tyneside in a world without media overload, fashion-mania and youth-culture flimflam.

I recall a general sense of relief and achievement – "we had come through", and with a government that was implementing universal education and health provision, there was hope that the iniquities of the 1930s would not return.

Men were coming back from the war and the prison camps; a life-affirming baby boom got

September 27

I like to think I'm pretty far removed from hockey mom politics (Never mind Palin's politics. Just check out the earrings, G2, September 25). But in support of Sarah Palin, let's try grouping her with the male politicians she is competing with, rather than fretting about earrings. At least until the men start wearing them.

Dr Sarah Beck
University of Birmingham

September 27

You don't need a booklet to learn how to write letters to the editor (Letters, September 25). Just keep them short, relevant and contemporary, and avoid the use of green ink.

Keith Flett
London

September 29

Dr Sarah Beck may not have noticed (Letters, September 27), but many men, including this 80-year-old, have been wearing earrings for a very long time.

Chris Birch
London

September 29

Thank you, Keith Flett, for your letter-writing masterclass (Letters September 27). If you are reading this, it worked.

Ian Thompson
Enfield, Middlesex

September 30

Gianfranco Zola is wrong to say that even Diego Maradona could not have won a game "single-handed" (Sport, September 26) because we all know he did.

Charlie Cooper
Hull

under way. Rationing was in force, but it was a life that we were used to, and its acknowledged fairness was reflected in the popular detestation of "spivs". Then came the glorious day when sweets came off the ration. Demand, alas, outstripped supply and the decision was reversed – but I had learned a valuable lesson: I abandoned priggishness and have decorously stuffed my face ever since.

Alan Myers
Hitchin, Hertfordshire

September 30

Newman's magic

I had the great privilege of knowing Paul Newman (Obituaries, September 29). For 20 summers, I worked as a volunteer at his Hole in the Wall Gang Camp in Ashford, Connecticut. I've heard it said the camp was one of Mr Newman's favourite places on earth. I believe it, as the camp is part joy-filled magic, part hideaway for sick children. I didn't know the movie star. But I did have the honour of meeting a man who would patiently bait hooks for squealing campers for hours on a warm summer's day. Or lull a cabin full of homesick children to sleep with a bedtime story. I didn't know the outspoken activist. But I did have the privilege of meeting a man who often visited and would always, always stop and listen to any child's story with warmth and interest. I didn't know the social entrepreneur. But I watched the fruits of one man's dream grow into a network of camps and support programmes for children and families the world over.

Rose DiSanto
London

Illustration by
Gary Kempston,
first published
on May 5 2008
with letters
responding
to an article
by Geoffrey
Wheatcroft
on the student
protests of 1968.

"Of course, many of the gains were
rolled back. The conclusion, surely, is
not that it was wrong to fight, but that
we have to fight again. As the French
activists said, 'Ce n'est qu'un début'
– it was only the beginning."